INVESTMENT AS A DRIVE OF ECONOMIC GROWTH

INVESTMENT AS A DRIVE OF ECONOMIC GROWTH

K.S. Arockiasamy
B. Revathy

KALPAZ

ISBN: 978-93-5128-149-8

Price: ₹ 790

First Published, 2016

Published by

Kalpaz Publications
C-30, Satyawati Nagar,
Delhi-110052
Ph. : 9212142040
E-mail: kalpaz@hotmail.com

Printed at: G. Print Process.

Cataloging in Publication Data—DK
Courtesy: D.K. Agencies (P) Ltd. <docinfo@dkagencies.com>

Arockiasamy, K. S., author.
Investment as a drive of economic growth / K.S. Arockiasamy, B. Revathy.
pages cm
Study conducted in Tirunelveli District of Tamil Nadu, India.
Includes index.
ISBN 9789351281498

1. Saving and investment—India—Tirunelveli (District) 2. Saving and investment—Government policy—India—Tirunelveli (District) 3. Economic development—India—Tirunelveli (District) I. Revathy, B., author. II. Title.

HG5740.T57A76 2015 DDC 339.430954 23

Contents

Chapter-I

Introduction

1.1 Introduction

Investment has different meanings in the context of finance and economics. Finance investment is putting money into something with the expectation of gain and there upon a thorough analysis to have a high degree of security for the principal amount, as well as security of return, within an expected period of time. In contrast, putting money into something with an expectation of gain without making a thorough analysis is speculation or gambling. Thus, Finance Investment involves decision making process in order to ensure security of both the principal amount and the Return on Investment (ROI) within an expected period of time.

Savings form an important part of the economy of any nation. With the savings invested in various options available to the people, the money acts as the driver for growth of the country. Indian financial scene, too, presents a plethora of avenues to the investors. Though certainly not the best or deepest of markets in the world, it has reasonable options for an ordinary man to invest his savings. Banks are considered as the safest of all options, banks have been the roots of the financial systems in India. Promoted as the means to social development, banks in India have indeed played an important role in the rural upliftment. For an ordinary person, banks have acted as the safest investment avenue wherein a person deposits money and earns interest on it. The two main modes of investment in banks, savings accounts and fixed deposits have been effectively used by one and all. However, today the interest rate structure in the country is headed southwards, keeping in line with global trends. With the banks offering a little above nine per cent in their fixed deposits for one year, the yields have come down substantially in recent times. Added to this, is inflationary pressures in the economy and one is in a position to know where the savings are not earning. The inflation is creeping up, to almost eight per cent at times, and this means that the value of money saved goes down instead of going up. Just like banks, post offices in India have a wide network. Spread across the nation, they offer financial assistance as well as serve the basic requirements.

Among all saving options, post office schemes have been offering the highest rates. Added to this, it is the fact that the investments are safe with the department, being a Government of India entity. So, the two basic and most sought after features, such as return safety and quantum of returns was being handsomely taken care of. Though certainly not the most efficient systems in terms of service standards and liquidity, these have still managed to attract the attention of small and retail investors. Recently, the government slightly increases the interest rates in small savings options; this avenue is expected to attract some more new investors.

Public Provident Funds act as options to save for the post-retirement period for most people and have been considered as good option largely due to the fact that returns were higher than most other options and also helped people gain from tax benefits under various sections. This option, too, is likely to lose, on account of reduction in the rates offered. Another often-used route to invest has been the fixed deposit schemes floated by companies. Companies have used fixed deposit schemes as a means of mobilising funds for their operations and have paid interest on them. The safer a company is rated, the lesser the return offered has been the thumb rule. However, there are several potential roadblocks in these. First of all, the danger of financial position of the company not being understood by the investor lurks. The investors rely on intermediaries who more often than not, don't reveal the entire truth. Secondly, liquidity is a major problem with the amount being received months after the due dates. Premature redemption is generally not entertained without cuts in the returns offered and though they present a reasonable option to counter interest rate risk (especially when the economy is headed for a low interest regime), the safety of principal amount has been found lacking. Many cases like the Kuber Group and DCM Group fiascoes have resulted in low confidence in this option. The options discussed above are essentially for the risk-averse people who think of safety and then quantum of return, in that order. For the brave, it is dabbling in the stock market.

Stock markets provide an option to invest in a high risk, high return game. While the potential return is much more than 10-11 per cent any of the options discussed above can generally generate, the risk is undoubtedly of the highest order. But then, the general principle of encountering greater risks and uncertainty when one seeks higher returns holds true. However, as enticing as it might appear, people generally are clueless as to how the stock market functions and in the process can endanger the hard-earned money. For those who are not adept at understanding the stock market, the task of generating superior returns at similar levels of risk is arduous to say the least.

This is where Mutual Funds come into picture. Mutual Funds are essentially investment vehicles where people with similar investment objective come together to pool their money and then invest accordingly. Each unit of any scheme represents the proportion of pool owned by the unit holder (investor). Appreciation or reduction in value of investments is reflected in Net Asset Value (NAV) of the concerned scheme, which is declared by the fund from time to time. Mutual fund schemes are managed by respective Asset Management Companies (AMC). Different business groups/financial institutions/banks have sponsored these AMCs, either alone or in collaboration with reputed international firms. Several international funds like Alliance and Templeton are also operating independently in India. Many more international ` mutual fund giants are expected to come into Indian markets in the near future.

In economics, investment means creation of capital or goods capable of producing other goods or services. The two main classes of investments are: *(i)* Fixed Income Investment such as bonds, fixed deposits, preference shares, and *(ii)* Variable Income Investment such as business ownership (equities) or property ownership.

On the basis of tenure, the investments are classified as: *(i)* Short-term Investment and *(ii)* Long-term Investment.

Investments made for a period of one to three years are termed as short-term investments and that are invested for more than three years are termed as long-term investments. Almost everyone holds some portfolio of investment in the form of financial assets like bank deposits, bonds, stocks and so on; and real assets like motorcycle, house, gold, etc. With reference to individuals, investment decisions should be made very wisely and with proper research and analysis.

1.2 Savings

Savings form an important part of the economy of any nation. With the savings invested in various options available to the people, the money acts as the driver for growth of the country. Indian financial scene, too, presents a plethora of avenues to the investors. Though certainly not the best or deepest of markets in the world, it has reasonable options for an ordinary man to invest his savings.

Investors are savers but all savers cannot be good investors, as investment is a science and an art. Savings are sometimes autonomous and sometimes induced by the incentives like fiscal concessions or income or capital appreciation. The number of investors is estimated at about 50 million out of population of more than one billion in India. Savers come from all classes except in the case of the population who are below the poverty line. The growth of urbanisation and literacy has activated the cult of investment. More recently, it is from the 80s that the investment activity has become more popular with the change in the Govt. policies towards liberalisation and financial deregulation. The process of liberalisation and privatisation was accelerated by the government policy changes towards a market oriented economy, through economic and financial reforms stated in July 1991. Each and every professional is well educated, so they know various schemes of investment which yield more return and bear less risk.

Money begets more money when it is properly managed. At present, an individual has a variety of investment opportunities. As there are different types of investment channels, public get confused when and where they plan to make investment, by selecting the best sort of investment and rejecting the rest is very difficult to the investors. Hence, one must pay much attention as regards to investment decision. An investment decision must be made with definite objectives. Before proceeding, the investor should be very clear as to specific requirements and aspirations. It could be a return or capital appreciation or safety or tax relief or any other peculiar factor that a particular investor desires. Depending upon that and on the basis of the objectives, investors make the investment decision by selection. Such a process offers the silver lining of golden return to investors. People invest to multiply their savings in order to fulfill their aspirations for a bigger house, a higher education for their children or a secured retirement for them. To achieve these objectives, the investor has a wide variety of products and services to choose from. One can deposit savings in a bank account, buy shares or bonds on the stock exchange, or buy a life insurance policy or invest in a retirement plan among other investment alternatives. Investment means an asset or an item that is purchased with the hopes that it will generate income or appreciate in the future. In economic sense, investment is the purchase of goods that are not consumed today but are used in the future to create wealth.

In order to diversify the risk, they will invest money in different investment patterns. There might be some criteria that they follow in selecting or determining the investment pattern. So, this study has been undertaken to identify the preference of the professionals in their investment decisions. Investments have become immensely popular with the public because of the existing possibilities for making enhanced return. Now-a-days, people are interested in making investment, as it offers attractive returns and protects the future of the investor from unexpected happenings.

1.3 Investment

Investment is the employment of funds with the aim of getting return on it. In general terms, investment means the use of money with hopes of making more money. In finance, investment means the purchase of a financial product or other item of value with an expectation of favourable future returns. Investment of hard earned money is a crucial activity of every human being. Investment is the commitment of funds which have been saved from current consumption with the hopes that some benefits will be received in future. Thus, it is a reward for waiting for money. Savings of the people are invested in assets depending on their risk and return demands. Investment refers to the concept of deferred consumption, which involves purchasing an asset, giving a loan or keeping funds in a bank account with the aim of generating future returns. Various investment options are available, offering or differing risk-reward tradeoffs. An understanding of the core concepts and a thorough analysis of the options can help an investor create a portfolio that maximises returns while minimising risk exposure.

The "Investor" can be an individual, a government, a pension fund, or a corporation. Similarly, all types of investments, including investments by corporations in plant and equipments and investments by individuals in stocks, bonds, commodities, or real estate. In all cases, the investor is trading a known rupee amount today for some expected future stream of payments that will be greater than the current outlay. Investing is a widespread practice and many have made their fortunes in the process. The starting point in this process is to determine the characteristics of the various investments and then matching them with the individual's needs and preferences. All personal investments are designed to achieve certain objectives. These objectives may be tangible such as buying a car, house etc. and also may be intangible such as social status, security, etc. Similarly, these objectives may be classified as financial or personal objectives. Financial objectives are safety, profitability, and liquidity.

Personal or individual objectives may be related to personal characteristics of individuals such as family commitments, status, dependents, educational requirements, income, consumption and provision for retirement, etc. Elements of investments are risk and return relationship, time, liquidity, tax savings. diversification of funds is an important principle of investment for earning higher rate of interest. Wide varieties of investment avenues are now available in India. An investor can himself select the best avenue after evaluating the merits and demerits of different avenues. Even financial advertisements, newspaper supplements on financial matters and investment journals offer guidance to investors in the selection of suitable investment avenues.

The income is divided into two components, namely, consumption and investment. The amounts not consumed are saved and invested. But investments are also useful for present and future consumption in the case of consumer durables, cars, gold and silver, etc. But investments generally promote larger consumption in future as they lead to more income and larger capital appreciation in the years to come. Investment avenues are multifold and each has its own risk-return characteristics. Risk less investments in the common parlance are bank deposits, government securities, bonds of government and semi government bodies, post office savings schemes, post office deposits, provident funds and pension fund schemes, insurance for life, endowment, accident, etc.

1.4 Objectives of the Study

1. To highlight the different investment avenues available to the investors.
2. To investigate the reasons behind the investment decisions.
3. To identify the factors influencing the preference of the investors.
4. To analyse the investors' attitudes towards a specific investment pattern.
5. To understand the problems faced by the professionals in the process of building their investment pattern.
6. To examine the level of satisfaction of the investors towards their preferred investment pattern.
7. To summarise the findings based on the analysis and interpretations of the study and to offer suggestions.

1.5 Scope of the Study

The present study is only confined to investment pattern and preferences of Professionals in Tirunelveli District. An attempt is made to assess the preference of different investment avenues of professionals. Professionals (viz., Doctors, Engineers and Advocates) are covered in the study. Doctors who possess MBBS as their basic educational qualification in Allopathic Medicine (General Physician) and have additional higher degrees like MD, MS, etc., if any and also do practice are chosen for the survey. Regarding engineers those who possess BE degree as their basic educational qualification irrespective of their specialisation such as civil, electrical, electronics, marine, aeronautical, communication engineering, etc., and also have additional degrees like ME, MS, etc., but at the same time they are employed or self-employed are chosen for the study. Relating to advocates those who possess the BL degree as their basic education and having additional higher educational degrees like ML, Ph.D. if any and also doing practice are chosen.

1.6 Operational Definitions

1.6.1 Investment

Investment means the use of funds for productive purposes, for securing some objectives like income, appreciation of capital or capital gains or for further production of goods and services with the objective of securing profits.

1.6.2 Investment Pattern

The individual style of investors in preferring and investing in different investment avenues such as postal deposits, bank deposits, life insurance, gold and other precious metals, real estate, shares, bonds, mutual funds and government securities, etc.

1.6.3 Professional

Professional is a term connected with a job that needs special training or skill, especially one that needs a high level of education and also a professional is a person who is paid to undertake a specialised set of tasks and to complete them for a fee. The traditional professions were doctors, engineers, lawyers, architects and commissioned military officers. Today, the term is applied to nurses, accountants, educators, scientists, technology experts, social workers, artists, librarians (information professionals) and many more.

1.6.4 Professional Investors

The investors of the profession are the professional investors. Among the different groups of professionals, three groups of professionals such as doctors, engineers and advocates and their investment patterns and preferences are covered for the survey.

1.6.5 Bank Deposits

Depositing a certain sum in a bank with a fixed rate of interest and for a specified time period is called a Bank Fixed Deposit (FD). At maturity, the investor is entitled to receive the principal amount as well as the interest earned at the pre-specified rate during that period. The rate of interest for Bank Fixed Deposits varies between four and six per cent, depending on the maturity period of the FD and the amount invested. The interest can be calculated monthly, quarterly, half-yearly, or annually, and varies from bank to bank.

1.6.6 Bank Recurring Deposits

The investor invests a specific amount in a bank on a monthly basis for a fixed rate of return. The deposit has a fixed tenure, at the end of which the investor can get the principal sum as well as the interest earned during that period. The rate of interest, calculated quarterly or as specified by the bank, varies between four and six per cent, depending on the maturity period and the amount invested. A Recurring Bank Deposit is a powerful tool for regular savings.

1.6.7 Post Office Monthly Income Scheme

It is a low risk saving instrument, which can be availed through any post office. It provides an interest rate around eight per cent per annum, which is paid monthly. Minimum amount, which can be invested, is Rs 1,000 and additional investment in multiples of 1,000. Maximum amount is Rs 3,00,000 (if Single) or Rs 6,00,000 (if held Jointly) during a year. It has a maturity period of six years. Premature withdrawal is permitted if deposit is more than one year old. A deduction of five per cent is levied from the principal amount if withdrawn prematurely.

1.6.8 Life Insurance

A life insurance policy is a contract between an individual (termed as insured) and an insurance company (insurer) to pay the insured, or his nominated heirs, a specified sum of money on the happening of an event. The event could be the expiry of the insurance policy or the death of the insured before the expiry (date of maturity) of the policy as per the terms of the policy. In a simple example, a person takes an insurance policy and nominates his wife as the beneficiary. On the death of insured, his wife gets the amount of the life insurance policy.

1.6.9 Public Provident Fund

Public Provident Fund is a long term savings instrument with a maturity of 15 years and interest payable at eight per cent per annum compounded annually. A PPF account can be opened through a nationalised bank at anytime during the year and is open all through the year for depositing money. Tax benefits can be availed for the amount invested and interest accrued is tax-free.

1.6.10 Real Assets

There are tangible assets in contrast to financial assets or securities. Real assets include real estate, land, gold, coins, stamps, art, and antiques.

1.6.11 Securities

As per the Securities Contracts Regulation Act (SCRA), 1956, securities include instruments such as shares, bonds, scrips, stocks or other marketable securities of similar nature in or of any incorporate company or body corporate, government securities, derivatives of securities, units of collective investment scheme, interest and rights in securities, security receipt or any other instruments so declared by the Centre Government.

1.6.12 Equity/Share

Equity, also called shares or scrips, is the basic building blocks of a company. Total equity capital of a company is divided into equal units of small denominations, each called a share. For example, in a company the total equity capital of Rs 2,00,00,000 is divided into 20,00,000 units of Rs 10 each. Each such unit of Rs 10 is called a Share. Thus, the company then is said to have 20,00,000 equity shares of Rs 10 each. The holders of such shares are members of the company and have voting rights.

1.6.13 Bond/Debenture

It is a fixed income (debt) instrument issued for a period of more than one year with the purpose of raising capital. The centre or state government, corporations and similar institutions sell bonds. A bond is generally a promise to repay the principal along with a fixed rate of interest on a specified date, called the Maturity Date. In the Indian securities markets, the term 'bond' is used for debt instruments issued by the centre and state governments and public sector organisations and the term 'debenture' is used for instruments issued by private corporate sector.

1.6.14 Mutual Funds

These are funds operated by an investment company which raises money from the public and invests in a group of assets (shares, debentures, etc.), in accordance with a stated set of objectives. It is a substitute for those who are unable to invest directly in equities or debt because of resource, time or knowledge constraints.

1.6.15 BSE Sensex

It is the most popular index that tracks the movements of shares of 30 blue-chip companies on a weighted average basis. The rise and fall in the value of the Sensex, measured in points, broadly indicates the price-movement of the value of shares, of late, technology has played a major role in enhancing the efficiency, safety, and transparency of the markets. The introduction of online trading has made it possible for an investor to trade in equities at the click of a mouse.

1.6.16 Portfolio

A Portfolio is a combination of different investment assets mixed and matched for the purpose of achieving an investor's goals. Items that are considered a part of the portfolio can include any asset one owns from shares, debentures, bonds, mutual fund units to items such as gold, art and even real estate etc. However, for most investors a portfolio has come to signify an investment in financial instruments like shares, debentures, fixed deposits, mutual fund units.

1.6.17 Treasury Bills

These are short-term (up to one year) bearer discount security issued by government as a means of financing their cash requirements.

1.7 Hypotheses

1. There is no significant difference among the professionals in the awareness level of financial assets.
2. There is no significant difference among professionals in the awareness level of physical investment avenues.
3. There is no significant difference among the professionals in the awareness level of marketable investment avenues.
4. There is no significant difference among the professionals regarding the sources of awareness on different investment avenues.
5. There is no significant relationship between family domain variables of the professionals and the investment motivating factors.

6. There is no significant relationship between profile variables of the professionals and the investment motivating factors.

1.8 Methodology of the Study

1. 8.1 Sources of the Study

The study is mainly based on the survey method. Both primary and secondary data are analysed to get appropriate conclusions. Primary data are fresh data which are collected directly from the professionals of various categories. Secondary data which are relevant to the study are collected from various books, magazines, business dailies and from other published materials.

1. 8.2 Sampling Technique

Sample size is 480 respondents chosen from doctors, engineers and advocates by adopting convenience sampling technique, as the exact number of professionals, namely, doctors, engineers and advocates are unknown. 160 respondents are selected among the doctors, 160 respondents among engineers and remaining 160 respondents are selected among the advocates. Thus, equal importance is given based on the nature of the profession.

1.8.3 Collection of Data

The study is mainly based on primary data, which are collected from the above mentioned categories of professionals through questionnaire. However, secondary data are also used in this study to certain extent so as to generate required theoretical framework.

1. 8.4 Tools for Analysis

Various statistical tools are applied to analyse the primary data through Percentage analysis, Mean score analysis, F-test, Factor analysis, Regression analysis. Garrett ranking are used to interpret the data and to arrive at relevant inferences. For effective analysis and easy understanding, the data are tabulated.

1.9 Social Relevance of the Study

The economic performance is reflected in the growth of income or GDP and growth refers to a rise in output and incomes. The rate of growth in income and distribution of income are the factors which influence the savings and are a function of the growth process. As the economy develops, production of goods and services would increase, leading to a rise in their consumption and the standard of living of the people. The growth of the economy is reflected through the rise in incomes of the people, but development is a wider term, which includes both growth and qualitative improvement in the standard of living of the people and a better distribution of incomes. Development thus involves a rise in the level of income and the level of investments leads to better standard of living in general through growth plus socio-economic changes and development.

1.10 Chapter Design

This study has been organised and presented in six chapters.

Chapter I

First chapter deals with the introduction of the study which explains the concept, statement of the problem, significance of the study, objectives, hypotheses, methodology and social relevance of the study and also the chapter design.

Chapter II

The second chapter describes the review of the literature of various researches related to investment.

Chapter III

The third chapter highlights the profile of the relevant study area

Chapter IV

The fourth chapter exhibits the conceptual view about the investment avenues; it includes the meaning of the investment, definition, objectives, and its types etc.

Chapter V

The fifth chapter deals with the analysis and interpretation of data pertaining to investment patterns and preferences of professionals like doctors, engineers and advocates.

Chapter VI

The sixth chapter includes the summary of findings, suggestions, conclusion and an agenda for future research.

Chapter-II

Review of Literature

2.1 Introduction

In today's less income growth and highly increasing cost of living economy, one has to know how to use his/her savings or idle funds to generate higher returns. Availability of too many options and no clear idea about these choices is creating a hostile situation for the investor to choose the best among the available lot. Conducting a literature review is a vital component of the research process. Familiarity with the previous research and theory in the area of the study would help in conceptualising the problem, conducting the study and interpreting the findings. The literature studies that have been conducted reveal the impact of the investment related activities in India as well as other countries.

Investment is a commitment of funds in real assets or financial assets. Investment involves risk and gain. In the present dynamic global environment, exploring investment avenues are of great relevance. Investment skills developed over a period of time are considerably influenced by experience and spadework carried out to arrive at conclusions. The success of an investment activity depends on the knowledge and ability of investors to invest the right amount, in the right type of investment, at the right time.

Investment in equity shares involves high risk due to direct relation between economic conditions and company performance with stock market. Stock markets are volatile in nature. Any drastic negative changes in the financial world leads to heavy losses to the investor, however selecting the right company share at right time with long term investment perspective will give huge profits to the investor. Especially investing in blue-chip company stocks for long term helps to gain good returns. To secure investment from unanticipated turn of market events, investor must update himself with information relating to the company stock in which he/she invested and stock market related news.

Investors who want to earn a fixed rate of return with a view to secure and safeguard the funds for a future event can invest their funds in fixed deposits. It is the best way for saving money for longer periods, but liquidity of investment is a problem. Most of the banks are offering fixed interest rate between nine per cent and 10.50 per cent. The minimum tenure of fixed deposit is seven days and maximum tenure is 10 years.

Savings bank account deposits are another investment option which helps investors to earn good interest for the amount they saved in the savings account of a bank. Due to deregulation of savings account interest rates by RBI (Reserve Bank of India), many banks have increased their interest rates. It is easy for investors to invest or deposit in savings bank account and withdraw money from savings account. Bonds are another investment option for investor who wants to invest for a fixed rate of return.

Public Provident Funds act as options to save for the post retirement period for most people and have been considered good option largely due to the fact that returns are higher than most other options and also have helped people gain from tax benefits under various sections. This option too is likely to lose some of its sheen on account of reduction in the rates offered. Another often-used route to invest has been the fixed deposit schemes floated by companies. Companies have used fixed deposit schemes as a means of mobilising funds for their operations and have paid interest on them.

Success in most things is relative, and not less so in the field of investment. Success to investment means earning the highest possible return with the constraints imposed by the investor's personal circumstances—age, family needs, liquidity requirements, tax position and acceptability of risk. If possible, performance should be measured against alternative investments, or combinations of investments, available to the investor within those constraints. Genuine success also means winning the battle against inflation, against the fall in the real value of savings and capital. For sensible investing, one should be familiar with the characteristics and features of various investment alternatives. Therefore, a large number of research articles and books have been published on them. The following studies are reviewed as a part of this study.

2.2 Studies Relating to Journals and Theses

National Council of Applied Economic Research (1961), in this study "Savings in India", noticed that irrespective of occupation followed and educational level and age attained, households in each group thought that saving for the future was desirable. It was found that desire to make provision for emergencies was a very important motive for saving and importance was next given to 'saving for old age'. Among motives for saving, provision for emergencies, old age, and purchase of a house occur with the same frequencies in all occupational and educational groups. The proportion of households expressing a preference for financial assets Financial assets increases with the level of education. The preference for financial assets, especially bank accounts and small savings, while rising markedly with education, does not seem to increase with income, except at the lowest end of income distribution.

Thus, it would appear that efforts must be taken to popularise financial forms of savings particularly among the less educated members of upper-income group. Profitability seems to be the most important motive for determining saving preference. Safety is another significant consideration for most people and liquidity ranked third.[1]

Tamilkodi (1983), in her study "Small Savings Schemes in Tamil Nadu: A Trend Study (1970-80)", stated that the psychological appeal provides an opportunity for ordinary men, women, and even children to park their savings. It reaches a large number of people and covers a wide range of areas. She also suggested that efforts should be taken to simplify the procedure of small savings schemes to suit the needs of illiterate and socially downtrodden people. Further, she suggested an increase in the rate of interest of small savings schemes to meet the challenges of commercial banks[2].

Jayaraman (1987), in his study on "A Study of Small Savings Schemes in North Arcot District", stated that instead of issuing special bonds for unearthing black money the Government of India can encourage investment of black money in various small savings schemes. He further stressed the need to draft the assistance of voluntary agencies at the school and college level for further mobilisation of savings[3].

Mukhi (1989), in his study on "National Savings Certificates: A Saving Grace" revealed that NSC has been one of the most popular tax savings instruments in this country. He has stated that contractor and others who have to provide security while bidding for contracts finds it extremely convenient to buy NSC and pledge these to the appropriate authorities while earning 12 per cent per annum on the pledged securities. He also stated that the major attraction of NSC is its simplicity. Even the average investor does not have to scratch his head to understand the scheme.[4]

Arangasami (1992), in his study on "A Study of Small Savings Schemes in Tamil Nadu with Special Reference to Madras District during 1981-82 to 1990-91", observed that more and more dependence on mobilisation of resources through small savings will ensure and promote self-reliance. He concluded that the Centre Government should give proper assistance and encouragement to the small savings agencies, which will be useful not only in mobilisation of funds but also for the economic development.[5]

Radha (1995), in her study "A study of Investment Behaviour of Investors of Corporate Securities", found that investors have certain primary objectives and gave importance to them while making investment plans. Capital appreciation was considered as the most important objective. It was seen that the investor's pre investment objectives have differed depending upon their occupation and income.[6]

Kannan (1996), in his study "Investor's Protection: A Study on Legal Aspects" attempted to point out varies legal provisions available for safeguarding the interest of investors in corporate segment. It pointed out that the capital market emerged as a major source of finance for the Indian corporate sector and also helped the investors to invest their savings. The study pointed out that irrespective of laws, the investor's grievance and complaints were increasing. The study listed major Acts and sections available for investor protection.[7]

Muhlesen M. (1997), in his article "Improving India's Saving Performance", said that India's saving rate is relatively high, compared to other countries. He concludes that with a view to increase the efficiency of savings, allocation and financing the heavy infrastructure needs of the Indian economy, particular attention should be paid to long-term saving instruments.[8]

Somasundaram, (1998), in his study on "A Study on Savings and Investment Pattern of Salaried Class in Coimbatore District", found that the bank deposits and chit funds were the best known modes of savings among investors and the least known modes were Unit Trust of India (UTI) schemes and plantation schemes. Attitudes of investors were highly positive and showed their intention to save for better future. Nearly two-thirds of the investors were satisfied with their savings. Both income and expenses of a family influenced the level of satisfaction over savings. A large proportion of investors were concerned about their children's well-being. Among the dissatisfied investors, majority were of the opinion that cost of living was too high. The most common mode of investment was bank deposits. However, a shift was noticed from bank deposits to other forms of investment. Almost all the investors had invested in gold and silver. Among several parameters in investing, safety of money was considered to be the most important element. Next, the investors expected regular return from their investments[9].

Augustine, L., Gavini and Prashanth Athma (1999), have conducted study among the post office scheme investors about their perception towards the scheme, motives for saving, their awareness and satisfaction with the service. About 10 per cent of the investor's income was saved in urban areas and 10 to 20 per cent of income was saved in rural areas, indicating higher level of consumption in urban areas. Television played a major role in creating awareness about the post office schemes both in urban and rural areas, followed by newspapers in urban and radio in rural areas. More than 90 per cent of the sample investors were not aware of the loan facility or encashment before maturity available on postal saving schemes. Lower income group (below Rs 8,00,00) preferred postal schemes to higher income group. Around 37 per cent of investors felt that the bank deposits were better than postal schemes. However, 73 per cent of sample investors were satisfied with the post office schemes[10].

D.L. Narayana (1999), in his thesis titled, "Income, Savings and Investment of Household Sector in Chittoor District", attempted to review the economy. The study examined the asset structure of the household, classifying the entire range of assets into physical and financial assets. The study stated that the average investment of a self-employed farmer household was greater than that of business people. The investment in farm assets decreased when the education level increased, at the same time the investment in consumer durables increased. Rural households gave importance to precious metals, followed by bank deposits and chit funds and currency. He pointed out that more than three and a half per cent of the rural households were practicing dis-saving and 65 per cent were doing positive saving.[11]

Org Marg (1999), in his study titled "Investors Choices over the Investment Advances", revealed that investor's preferred fixed deposit in bank, post office and insurance scheme followed by government bonds and equity shares". The survey took seven parameters which influenced one to choose an investment avenue, i.e., capital appreciation, safety, liquidity, and rate of return, guaranteed return, manageability and tax shelter. Guaranteed return coupled with capital appreciation was the expectation of the most of the investors.[12]

V. K. Somasundaram (1999), in his dissertation titled, "A study on Saving and Investment Pattern of Salaried Class in Coimbatore District", focussed that on understanding the behaviour of the salaried class investor and examining the awareness level to understand the attitude of the investor towards savings and investment practice. The study established that savings can be augmented from salaried class if the financial system is more attractive. The major findings of this research work are that a majority of the investing population is in the age group of 21 to 40 years. The age and education of the investor's are the major influencing factors of investment selection. With respect to the stock market, the peer group is the major influencing factor. About 82 per cent of the investors preferred bank deposits, followed by provident fund and then by investment in gold and silver. Majority of the salaried class preferred safety for the investment made followed by regular return and capital appreciation. The study also suggested a model for investment decision making.[13]

Gavini and Athma (1999), in their study on "Small Saving Schemes of Post Office Need to Be Known More", found that social considerations, tax benefits, and provision for old age were the reasons cited for savings in urban areas, whereas to provide for old age was the main reason in rural areas. Among the post office schemes, Indira Vikas Patra (IVP), KVP and Post Office Recurring Deposit Account (PORD) were the most popular, in both urban and rural areas.[14]

Brad M. Barber (2000), in his study on "The Behaviour of Mutual Fund Investors", argued that the representative heuristic leads investors to buy past winners, the disposition effect renders investors reluctant to sell their losers, and framing effects cause investors to react differently to various forms of fund expenses. Given extant evidence on the persistence of mutual fund performance, one can reasonably argue that the purchase of last year's winning funds is rational. However, we argue that selling and winning fund investments and neglecting a fund's operating expense ratio when purchasing a fund is clearly counterproductive.[15]

Kar Pratip, Natarajan I. and Singh J.P. (2000), in their research paper "Survey of Indian Investors", concluded that the households investment in shares, debentures and mutual funds was below 10 per cent and the equity investor households portfolio was of relatively small value and undiversified. Further, they found that one set of households, in spite of their lower income and lower penetration level of consumer durables, were in the securities market, while another set of household with higher income and higher penetration level of consumer durables did not have investment in securities market.[16]

Securities and Exchange Board (2000), in this study "Survey of Indian Investor", reported that safety and liquidity were the primary considerations which determined the choice of an asset. Ranked by an ascending order of risk perception fixed deposit accounts in bank were considered very safe, followed by gold, units of UTI-US64, fixed deposits of non-government companies, mutual funds, equity shares, and debentures. Households' preference for instruments in which they commonly invested matched the risk perception. Bank deposits, which had an appeal across all income classes and tax-saving schemes were preferred by middle-income and higher-income groups. There was a correlation between the income levels and investments of households in market-related securities.[17]

Zathik Ali (2000), stated that it is the duty of the government to safeguard the interest of the small investors who have no spokesmen to expose their problems. Most of the small savers depend upon the interest accruing from their small investments for their livelihood. The budget proposals such as hike in income tax surcharge reduction in the interest rate on GPF, higher level budget-deficit, increase in the prices of urea and ration rice and the doubling of the tax on dividends will have adverse effect on the savings of the people.[18]

Kevin James (2000), in his research article "The Price of Retail Investing in the UK", evaluates the financial wealth services provided by investment funds in UK. The study identifies that the retail investors largely delegate the management of their wealth to investment funds. These funds in turn charge retail investors for the portfolio and risk management services they provide, sparing retail investors the burdensome task of performing these various services themselves. So in order to choose a sensible fund (a fund that meets his or her requirements), a retail investor must be able to ascertain the services provided and the price charged by each of the funds he or she may consider.[19]

Datar (2001), in his study on "Interest Rates on Small Savings and Provident Fund Scheme", has argued for linking interest rates on Small Saving (SS) schemes to market rates and rationalising the tax benefits available to them. As a result SS schemes become relatively unattractive; alternatively the government would need to borrow from other alternative sources.[20]

Karthikeyan (2001), in his study on "Small Investors' Perception on Post Office Small Savings Schemes", found that there was significant difference among the four age group in the level of awareness for Kisan Vikas Patra (KVP), National Savings Schemes (NSS), and Deposit Scheme for Retired Employees (DSRE), and the overall score confirmed that the level of awareness among investors in the old age group was higher than in those of the young age group. No difference was observed between male and female investors except for the NSS and KVP. Out of the factors analysed, necessity of life and tax benefits were the two major ones that influence the investors both in semi-urban and urban areas. Majority (73.3 per cent) of investors of both semi-urban and urban areas were very much willing to invest in small savings schemes in future provided they have more for savings.[21]

S. Venkatraman (2003), in his study on "Investor's Choice—A Survey", pointed out that the financial scene in India has changed over the last seven years. The avenues for investment, which were there before are still there; but investors are keeping a distance from many of them. Investment in equity was a craze in the eighties and the early nineties. After the first security scam, many retail investors had run away from them, never to return. Then, many investors made fortunes at the height of the stock market boom in the early 1990s. Many others lost a lot of money during that time. Though the interest in the stock market revived after 1995, it proved short-lived. Particularly after the second security scam, small investors deserted the equity market. Equity investment was no longer the favourite of several investors. Investment in mutual funds was quite popular since the launch of US-64 by the UTI in 1964. After the monopoly of UTI ended in 1989 with the entry of many new players, investment in units of mutual fund with several schemes became attractive—only so long as the stock market was buoyant. The income schemes of mutual funds, where the corpus was used for investment in fixed income securities were found relatively safe to growth schemes. Investors, depending on their individual perceptions, chose from among the several schemes offered by mutual funds. NBFC deposits, once the first preference of several investors, are no longer so. The failure of many NBFCs pauperised many investors. The strength of the surviving NBFCs are based on their financial muscle and professional management. They are able to retain their existing customers and attract new customers. No longer are they offering high rates of interest and better yields as interest rates in general. Bank deposits, the traditional medium of savings for many, seemed to be surging. Not because of superior quality service or technological improvement. Safety considerations have overtaken return considerations and banks are getting more and more 'walk-in' deposits. Interest rates are sliding and there are several investors grumbling loudly as they depend only on the interest income for their livelihood. Banks seem to be the unintended beneficiaries of NBFC failures. Postal deposits and schemes had their middle income low and income patrons. Marginally better interest rates and tax benefits were the financial attractions. Indigenous institutions like chit funds and benefit funds have their own loyal patrons. The failure of a few nidhis/benefit funds has not dampened the interest of investors in the surviving ones. What emerges from our Survey is that there are several investment avenues available in the country. But investors who had tasted better returns from many investment media find that they are no longer so and are keeping away from them. Investment in equity is generally for the risk takers. The risk averters can still invest in them, retain the shares to get dividend and some shares. It is the risk takers who trade in equity and make gains.[22]

Akiko Kamesakaa et al. (2003), in their study on "Investment Patterns and Performance of Investor Groups in Japan", found that the foreign investor trading is associated with positive feedback market timing and that this trading earns high returns. Alternatively, individual investors use positive feedback trading in their market timing but earn low returns. Consequently, documented evidence are consistent with information-based models (foreign investors) and behavioural based models (individual investors). It is a particularly new and interesting finding that evidence of both information-based trading and behavioural-based trading occurs in the same market and show that foreign investors, banks, and securities firms are the clear market-timing winners of TSE. The market-timing performance of insurance firms, companies, and investment trusts is not notable. Japanese individual investors are the clear losers.[23]

Dr G.V. Chalam (2003), in his article "Investors Behavioural Pattern of Investment and their Preferences of Mutual Funds", published in

Southern Economist, February 1, 2003, concluded that off all the sections of the society, the household group contributes much of the capital, forming the lifeblood for the economy. According to his analysis, the mutual fund business in India is still in its embryonic form as they currently account for only 15 per cent of the market capitalisation. The success of mutual funds business largely depends on the product innovation, marketing, customer service, fund management and committed manpower. The investment pattern of the investors reveals that a majority of the investors prefer real estate investments followed by mutual fund schemes, gold and other precious metals.[24]

Dr K. Santi Swarup (2003), in her research article "Measures for Improving Common Investor Confidence in Indian Primary Market — A Survey" concentrates on the decisions taken by the investors while investing in primary markets. The study indicates that the sample investors give importance to their own analysis as compared to brokers' advice. They also consider market price as a better indicator than analyst recommendations. The study also identifies factors that are affecting primary market situation in India. Issue price, information availability, market price after listing and liquidity emerge as important factors. This study suggests that investors need to be assured of some return and current level of risk associated with investment in the market is very high. They have had bad experience in terms of lower market price after listing and high issue price. Accordingly number of measures in terms of regulatory, policy level and market oriented were suggested to improve the investor confidence in equity primary markets. However, this paper does not highlight the measures for improving investors' confidence in secondary market.[25]

Brian M. Lucey and Michael Dowling (2005), in their study "The Role of Feelings in Investor Decision-making", provided that a synthesis of the emerging research on the influence of feelings on investor decision-making and equity pricing. Section 4 described how investors appear to allow their mood the time of making an investment decision to influence their judgments. While this is an efficient decision-making tool and is consistent with our knowledge of how people generally make decisions, it can result in errors if the investor allows irrelevant mood states to influence their judgments. Section 5 described another manner in which investors allow their feelings to influence their investment decisions. It was shown that investors can sometimes invest in an equity based on whether they like or dislike a company. While this is consistent with what we know about how people make decisions, it is not usually consistent with efficient equity pricing. Given the strength of the theoretical support for investors investing in a manner consistent with their feelings, this research area deserves further investigation. Especially, as many of the findings in the area are inconsistent with existing theories of how investors should make investment decisions.[26]

C.S. Shylajan and Sushama Marathe (2006), in their research article "A Study of Attitudes and Trading Behaviour of Stock Market Investors", identify the major factors responsible for determining the attitudes and trading behaviour of stock market investors. Based on their shared investing attitude and behaviour, the stock market investors are classified into two categories, i.e., aggressive investors and non-aggressive investors.[27]

Ranganathan K. (2006), in his article "A Study of Fund Selection Behaviour of Individual Investors Towards Mutual Funds: With Reference to Mumbai City", noted that financial markets are affected by the financial behaviour of investors. He observed that consumer behaviour from the marketing world and financial economics had brought together a need to study an exciting area of 'behavioural finance'. This study was an attempt to examine the related aspects of the fund selection behaviour of individual investors towards mutual funds in the city of Mumbai.[28]

John Graham and Alok Kumar (2006), in their study "Do Dividend Clienteles Exist? Evidence on Dividend Preferences of Retail Investors", evaluates portfolio holdings of retail investors of older and low income category. This study suggests that these investors prefer dividend paying stocks. The study also highlights the trading behaviour of retail investors and indicates that the investor trades around dividend events are consistent with clientele behaviour. Further, it also points out that old and low income investor exhibits abnormal buying behaviour following dividend announcements.[29]

Alistair Byrne, C.F.A. (2007), in his study on "Employee Saving and Investment Decisions in Defined Contribution Pension Plans: Survey Evidence from the U.K.", surveyed the members of a UK defined contribution pension plan to explore the attitudes and knowledge of employees faced with pension saving and investment decisions. The results are consistent with behavioural economics in that many employees show limited interest in their pension arrangements. Not all members have received advice about their pension, but those who have are more likely to have calculated their savings needs, to have higher levels of investment knowledge, and to actively review their investments than those who have not. The members' investment preferences appear broadly consistent with traditional finance theory, although the popularity of property may reflect familiarity bias.[30]

Dr K. Ravichandran (2007), in his study on "A Study on Investors Preferences Towards Various Investment Avenues in Capital Market with Special Reference to Derivatives", viewed that in the current scenario, investing in stock markets is a major challenge ever for professionals. Derivatives act as a major tool for reducing the risk involved in investing in stock markets for getting the best results out of it. The investors should be aware of the various hedging and speculation strategies, which can be used for reducing their risk. Awareness about the various uses of derivatives can help investors to reduce risk and increase profits. Though the stock market is subjected to high risk, by using derivatives the loss can be minimised to an extent.[31]

Mittal Manish and Vyas R.K. **(2007),** in their research paper "Demographics and Investment Choice among Indian Investors", investigated how investment choice gets affected by the demographics of the investor. Their study was based on responses obtained from the respondents belonging to a wide cross section. Non-probabilistic sampling method was employed to select the respondents. They found that investors of different age groups do wary significantly with regard to mutual funds and debentures/bonds as their choice of Investment Avenue. As far as occupation is concerned, they found that service class people would like to invest their money in equities and mutual funds, while business class showed an inclination to invest their money in debentures/bonds and real estate/bullions. Housewives prefer safe investments like real estate/bullions, while professionals invest their money in post office deposits and derivatives. Students prefer high risk investments like derivatives and equities[32].

Chris Veld and Yulia V. Veld-Merkoulova (2007), in their study "The Risk Perceptions of Individual Investors", mentioned that the results can be potentially useful for the financial institutions in finding out which risks are most important for their clients. Another area where the results of this study can be useful is on the topic of benchmarking. It finds an interesting discrepancy between investor responses and the results of an experimental questionnaire study on risk measures. In general, individual investors claim that they find the initial investment to be the most important benchmark. However, the experimental questionnaire study shows that for a large amount the market return and the initial investment are virtually equally popular benchmarks. For a small investment the market return is considered to be the most important benchmark. In either case, the investors seem to make different choices from their stated preferences.[33]

K. Balanaga Gurunathan (2007), in his study "Investors' Requirements in Indian Securities Market", stated that the securities market development is expressing the economic development of the country. The object of economic activity in any country is to promote the well-being and standard of living of the people, it depends upon the distribution of income in terms of goods and services in the economy. Trading in money and monetary assets constitute the activity in the securities markets and are referred to as the capital market activities, the capital market activities are based upon the investors' confidence based upon their return on investment and anticipating the capital appreciation from their investment. The revival of investors' protection in the corporate securities market is necessary to make market more efficient by means of converting savings to investment. If the investors have not been protected properly by means of rate of return and capital, the corporates will not be able to collect the funds from the market with cheap rate and effectively in future days. This can be done by a series of systematic measures which would build their confidence in the systems and processes and protect the interest of investors.[34]

Dr Bhagaban Das and Ms Sangeeta Mohanty (2008), in their study "Mutual Fund vs. Life Insurance: Behavioural Analysis of Retail Investors", found that the different investment pattern do not provide the same level of services with respect to age of the retail investors in India. Although the investment patterns provide more or less the same service, there exist differences depending on the education level of the investors. It is observed that investors with the graduate and postgraduate level of academic qualification are investing more in life insurance and the professionals are investing more in mutual fund. The investors have a wide difference with respect to their profession and also the different investment patterns vary widely. The government servants invest more in life insurance and the private sector employees in Mutual funds.[35]

Prof V.E. Rama Moorthy and Ms T.R. Rajeswari (2008), in their study "An Empirical Study on Factors Influencing the Mutual Fund/ Scheme Selection by Retail Investors", made an attempt to understand the financial behaviour of Mutual Fund investors in connection with the scheme preference and selection. The post survey developments are likely to have an influence on the findings. Behavioural trends usually take time to stabilise and they get disturbed even by a slight change in any of the influencing variables. Hence, surveys similar to the present one need to be conducted at intervals to develop useful models. Nevertheless, it is hoped that the survey findings will have some useful managerial implication for the AMCs in their product designing and marketing.[36]

Lalitha and M. Surekha (2008), in their article "Retail Investor in Indian Capital Market Profile, Pattern of Investment and Profitability", The Indian Journal of Commerce, concluded that the retail investor is here to stay and the capital markets may well emerge as strong contenders for traditional investment avenues like bank/post office deposits. They also focused on investor's education and investment decision of retail investors[37].

Baskaran (2008), in his study on "A Study on Savings and Investment Habits in Tamil Nadu", cleared that perception of investors has an impact on their risk bearing capacity and range of investment. It is also stated that perception is influenced by age, experience, and tax payment and it has an association with saving motives and behaviour of individuals. Discriminant analysis shows that experience is the discriminating factor and it is also to be remembered that if people get good service and good return during their investment tenure, they will have positive perception, otherwise negative perception will persist.[38]

Pradeep Gupta (2008), in his study on "Investment Decisions in Equity or in Mutual Fund", stated that the Indian stock market is semi-efficient by nature and, is considered as one of the most respected stock markets, where information is quickly and widely disseminated, thereby allowing each security's price to adjust rapidly in an unbiased manner to new information so that, it reflects the nearest investment value. Some investors liked to keep a certain percentage of their portfolio into mutual funds and the rest they wanted to manage by themselves. It can also be seen from findings that an investor has made higher returns in a long run by investing into direct equities, but if one wants to make a higher returns in the short run and midterm horizon, and then definitely mutual funds are the best buy.[39]

Pallavi Seth et al. (2008), in their study on "Financial Literacy and Investment Decisions of Indian Investors"—A Case of Delhi and NCR", indicated that the financial literacy of investors in Delhi and NCR was different for different financial instruments. Around 96 per cent of them have savings account in the banks, but the mere acquaintance with banks is not adequate, as only around 30 per cent had knowledge about National Savings Certificate and Public Provident Fund. While 98 per cent of the investors knew about Life Insurance, only about 45 per cent preferred Life Insurance as the most effective financial instrument, which would be helpful at the time of contingencies. Around 92 per cent of the investors knew about Mutual Funds but only 24 per cent preferred them. Financial literacy is found to be affected by age, income and educational level of the individuals. High-income respondents had high financial literacy than lower income people. The study also revealed that people consider Life Insurance as the most effective financial instrument followed by Fixed Deposits in banks. It has also been found that most of the people relied on telecast in the TV channels or advertisements put out in the newspapers and magazines to learn about financial products followed by 'advice' from friends. But, while investing in share market, around 21 per cent people relied on brokers.[40]

Ning Zhu (2008), in his study on "Individual Investor Trading", mentioned that the Individual behavioural patterns seem to provide more probable explanations to many findings of individual investor trading. Although many of individuals' trading patterns seem to jeopardise their financial well-being and the overall welfare loss from individuals' behavioural biases may indeed be limited. Although whether individuals suffer considerably from their trading an activity remains an open question, more studies seem to confirm that their trading activities carry important weight to asset price formation. Therefore, unlike the traditional wisdom that assumes individual investors to be insignificant noise traders, future studies in finance and economics have to take individual investors more seriously and devote more attention to individual investors' trading activities.[41]

Dr Joseph Anbarasu and Clifford Paul. S. (2008), in their study "Savings Pattern of People and the Impact of Insurance on Savings with Special Reference to Tiruchirappalli", examined that the determinants of private saving in the process of development. Various factors are involved in the saving rate with both the level and the rate of growth of disposable income. The returns and the reason for saving have a significant impact, but the magnitude of the impact is modest. Public saving seems to crowd out private saving, but less than proportionately. Furthermore, the spread of saving avenues and reason have an impact and changes in the external environment have an impact on private saving.[42]

Arwinder Singh and H.S. Sandhu (2008), in their study "Investors' Adoption of Internet Stock Trading: A Study", indicated that attitude dimensions and demographic variables contributed significantly in classifying investors as adopters or non-adopters of Internet stock trading. As regards attitude dimensions, 'variety of financial products and safety' contributed significantly in discriminating between adopters and non-adopters of net trading followed by the factor such as 'convenience and transparency'. As far as the demographics were concerned, the mature/older, experienced, and businessmen investors were less likely to use Internet-based trading as compared to young, inexperienced, and non-businessmen investors.[43]

Mittal M. and R.K. Vyas (2008), in their article "Personality Type and Investment Choice: An Empirical Study", observed that investors have certain cognitive and emotional weaknesses which come in the way of their investment decisions. According to them, over the past few years, behavioural finance researchers have scientifically shown that investors do not always act rationally. They have behavioural biases that lead to systematic errors in the way they process information for investment decision. Many researchers have tried to classify the investors on the basis of their relative risk taking capacity and the type of investment they make. Empirical evidence also suggests that factors such as age, income, education and marital status affect an individual's investment decision.[44]

Kathirvel, N. (2009), in his article "Investment Option with Reference to Insurance Products", concluded that the insurance plays a very important role in the financial sector of our country. The IRDA Act, 1999 is a landmark in the Indian insurance industry which opened up the insurance sector to the private sector participants in 2000. Keen element in the reform process was the participation of overseas insurance companies though restricted to 26 per cent of the capital. The act protects, promotes and ensures orderly development at the life and own life industry. The insurance companies are required to use the vast network of banks and post offices to market the micro-insurance products and unit linked product for the low income group and rural poor of the society.[45]

R. Kasilingam and G. Jayabal (2009), in their article "Alternative Investment Options to Small Investors", concluded that if the savings of the individuals are not channelised in a proper manner, then it may find its way into unproductive channels such as investment in gold or it may lead to unscrupulous rise in the consumption pattern, both of which are not good for the economy.[46]

Ritadhi Chakravarti (2009), in his study "An Empirical Analysis of Investment Determinants in Indian States: 1998-2006", pointed out that the India's economic reforms in 1991 permitted investors to freely choose their preferred investment locations across the various states in the Indian union, leading to competition between states to attract investment projects through a bettering of their investment climates. The performance of states over the past 17 years in terms of attracting investments has widely varied: two states, Maharashtra and Gujarat have together accounted for over 30 per cent of India's investments projects while other states have been much less successful. Some states, after a period of considerable neglect, have seen steady upswings in investment inflows while some others have fallen from their past images as good investment destinations. Investors select states as investment destinations predominantly on the basis of their contemporary socio-economic performance as opposed to their past images as investment destinations.[47]

BBS Parihar, Rajeev Sharma, and Deepika Singh parihar (2009), in their article "Analysing Investors Attitude Towards Mutual Funds as an Investment Option", concluded that the factors responsible for investment in mutual funds are, 'return potential' which has got first rank, 'liquidity' the second rank and 'flexibility', 'affordability' and 'transparency' have been ranked third, fourth and fifth, respectively. Majority of investors have still not formed any attitude towards mutual fund investments. The main reason behind this has been observed to be lack of awareness of investors about the concept and working of the mutual funds.[48]

G. Prabakaran and G. Jayabal (2009), in their article "Investors Risk Tolerance Towards Mutual Fund Investments", concluded that empirically it has been proved that the mutual fund investors are from low and moderate risk tolerant groups and the socio-economic variables do alter the risk tolerance of individual investors. The mutual fund organisations must consider these socioeconomic variables of the investors that have an important influence on investment decision making.[49]

Krishnamoorthi, C. (2009), in his research paper "Changing Pattern of Indian Households: Savings in Financial Assets", concluded that irrespective of the developments in the capital market/economic conditions, investors like to invest regularly and this investment behaviour is highly related to educational background.[50]

Jagannath Mallick (2009), in his study "Trends and Patterns of Private Investment in India", stated that the economic structure and structural changes in private investment in the Indian economy. The analysis revealed that the rate of capital formation had increased in the private sector and decreased in the public sector after economic reforms. Further, the industrial sector had been ranked one in terms of its contribution to the growth of private investment followed by the service and agricultural sectors in India in the short term as well as long term. However, the growth of private investment in the service sector was considerably higher in the post reform period than the pre-reform period. Further, the annual average growth of private investment in the service sector was almost equal to the industrial sector in the post-reform period. Therefore service sector played a very important role in attracting private investment during the economic reforms period. The service sector comprises, among others, consumer and producer services. Further, it was found that the contribution of producer services, which includes real estate, ownership of dwellings and business services, and others, contributed to the growth of private investment in the service sector in India. In this context it is very important to study whether or not identifiable structural transformations in terms of private investment occurred in India.[51]

Hayat M. Awan et al. (2009), in their study on "A Study on Investment Behaviour of Individual Investors", examined that the determinants of investment behaviour of individual investors and their relative importance in shaping overall investment behaviour. The impact of investment behaviour on investment decisions is also studied. Data were collected by obtaining direct responses from 246 individual investors and also by obtaining responses from 28 brokers. It developed two separate research instruments administered at individual investors and brokers selected using random sampling technique from four cities: Lahore, Islamabad, Karachi and Multan. It categorised individual investors on the basis of demographics, level of investment and investment objectives and conducted analysis of variance among responses. Responses obtained from individual investors based on structured questionnaire were analysed quantitatively while responses of brokers based on open ended questions are analysed qualitatively. Different statistical tools, e.g., AHP, ANOVA, Means, Cross-tabulation, Frequencies and Regression are used to obtain the results of the study. Findings suggest that behavioural dimensions of investor involvement and overconfidence are significantly related to market sentiments. Findings reveal that the behavioural trait of involvement is most significantly related to technical analysis and also found that behavioural dimensions of risk attitude and overconfidence are significantly associated with fundamental analysis.[52]

Inderst, G. (2009), in his study "Pension Fund Investment in Infrastructure", stated that the need for investment in infrastructure continues to grow, private sector financing for infrastructure projects has developed around the world. Given the long-term growth and (potentially) low correlation aspects of infrastructure investments, pension funds have also shown interest in increasing their exposure to this area, along with their move into alternative assets. Such investments cover a wide spectrum of projects from economic infrastructure such as transport, to social projects such as hospitals and involve different forms of financing (primary *vs.* secondary, debt *vs.* equity, private *vs.* listed, direct *vs.* indirect). Data explaining the size, risk, return and correlations of this diverse asset class is therefore limited, which may be making pension fund investors cautious. Given investing in such assets also involves new types of investment vehicles and risk for pension funds to manage such as exposure to leverage, legal and ownership issues, environmental risks as well as regulatory and political challenges such caution may well be justified.[53]

Vandna Singh and Komal (2009), in their study "Prospects and Problems of Real Estate in India", pointed out that the factors of the real estate. The study concluded that the real estate is a very wide concept and it is highly affected by the macro-economic factors like GDP, FDI, per capital income, interest rates and employment in the nation. The most important factor in the case of real estate is location which affects the value and returns from the real estate. India needs a stronger capital market base for property financing. The international investors will give in particular a familiar investment vehicle. Private investors could also enter into indirect investment in real estate. Although interest in new projects is most likely to come primarily from institutional investors, the rising middle class is likely to seek new instruments aside from direct property investments in the medium term. So, the investment in real e state in India is a very good investment opportunity. But one should be very careful while taking decision in this direction due to rising inflation and interest rates. Legal issues should also be kept in mind while choosing a property.[54]

Manish Agarwal et al. (2009), in their study on "A Study of Investors' Expected Rate of Return on their Investment", concerned that the capital market plays an important role in the era of financial liberalisation. To study the behaviour of the investor, and the relationship between the clients and the financial advisor, is the sole attempt of present study. In particular, this study aims at understanding and interpreting the behaviour of working employees of private and public sector on their investment decisions. Such knowledge will be highly useful for financial advisors as it will help them to advise their clients regarding investments that will maximise their expected rate of return. The study shows that how an investment is chosen on the basis of expected rate of return which gets affected by demographic variables, which in turn helps to advise the clients better. The clients on the other hand, are being advised to make investment that suits their profile. The present study expects to improve the mutual trust between the advisor and his clients.[55]

Anand Patil Digambar et al. (2010), in their study "Residential Location Choice: A Study of Household Preferences for the City of Nagpur", found that the sensitivity of various parameters on residential location, type and ownership preferences of the housing demand in Nagpur city. These findings can have immense bearing on policy and regulatory frameworks for future residential development anticipated in the Master Plan of the city. The proposed Master Plan has indicated future residential zones along with non-residential activities taking into consideration parameters for collective and comprehensive improvement of the city. However, it has often been found that with the present housing preferences exhibited, the proposed residential zones do not appear to attract future residential demand unless some policy level interventions are made. Some of the groups are very sensitive to geographical parameters, whereas others are more responsive to economic and social parameters. Changing the geographic, social and economic parameter values through various policies, actions and strategies can alter the attractive potential of these zones for target groups and help residential demand allocation along the lines of anticipated plan. However, limited sample size used for this study restricts it only for exploration of parameter responsiveness with limited predictive capacity. Large sample sizes drawn from an urban area following the same methodology will help not only to explore the significant variables but also allow predicting the demand responsiveness with certain changes in control variables.[56]

Lalit Mohan Kathuria and Kanika Singhania (2010), in their research paper "Investor Knowledge and Investment Practices of Private Sector Bank Employees", published in The Indian journal of commerce, July-September 2010 concluded that the marketers of investment avenues should keep advertising in the print as well as electronic media. Another highlighting finding of the study was that even the bank employees considered insurance as an investment tool rather than risk coverage instrument. Also, another significant finding was that only four per cent of the respondents made their investment decisions with the help of investment planner. There is an immense need to raise the level of awareness about the various investment avenues among the bank employees.[57]

Syed Tabassum Sultana (2010), in her study "An Empirical Study of Indian Individual Investors' Behaviour", discussed that the characteristics of the Indian individual investors along made an attempt to discover the relationship between a dependent variable, i.e., risk tolerance level and independent variables such as age, gender of an individual investor on the basis of the survey. Indian investors with high income, education, salary are independent in making investment decisions and are conservative investors. From the empirical study it was found that irrespective of gender, most of the investors (41 per cent) are found to have low risk tolerance level and many others (34 per cent) have high risk tolerance level rather than moderate risk tolerance level. It is also found that there is a strong negative correlation between age and risk tolerance level of the investor. Television is the media that is largely influencing the investor's decisions. Hence, this study can facilitate the investment product designers to design products which can cater to the investors who are low risk tolerant.[58]

S. Joseph Anbarasu et al. (2010), in their study on "Study on Socio-Economic Status and Awareness of Indian Investors of Insurance", mentioned that the opening of insurance to private players, there has been a great growth in insurance in India. But India is far behind world averages in terms of insurance penetration, and insurance density. This research determines the socio-economic status and awareness of 1655 investors of insurance from Trichy, Tamilnadu. The study reveals that awareness is low and needs to be improved among the uneducated, lower age group and daily wage class. The study also shows that real growth in life insurance will occur when customers realise the true value of life insurance beyond tax saving.[59]

James E. Corter (2010), in his report "Investor Attitudes towards Risk and Uncertainty and Reactions to Market Turmoil", confirmed that investment risk tolerance predicts a measure of actual risk of the investor's portfolio; portfolio risk in turn predicted whether or not the investor had suffered significant losses in portfolio value as a result of the recent market disruptions. Self-reported actual portfolio losses correlated positively with negative emotional reactions. Finally, both risk tolerance and negative emotional reactions to losses predicted self-reported changes in investment strategy. Investment Risk Tolerance (IRT) did not directly influence emotional reactions, nor was it proven to buffer the negative emotional effects of large portfolio losses, though a trend in that direction was observed. This may be due to a double effect of risk tolerance: on the one hand, investors' emotional reactions to losses may be mitigated by higher levels of risk tolerance, but on the other hand higher levels of risk tolerance are associated with riskier portfolios, and thus to higher exposure to actual losses in a market downturn.[60]

Gaurav Kabra et al. (2010), in their study on "Factors Influencing Investment Decision of Generations in India: An Econometric Study", concluded that the modern investor is a mature and adequately groomed person. In spite of the phenomenal growth in the security market and quality Initial Public Offerings (IPOs) in the market, the individual investors prefer investments according to their risk preference. For e.g., risk averse people choose life insurance policies, fixed deposits with banks and post office, PPF and NSC. Occasions of blind investments are scarce, as a majority of investors are found to be using some source and reference groups for taking decisions. Though they are in the trap of some kind of cognitive illusions such as overconfidence and narrow framing, they consider multiple factors and seek diversified information before executing some kind of investment transaction. The purpose of this study was to determine whether the variables such as demographic characteristics (age, gender) and investment patterns could be used individually or in combination to both differentiate among levels of men and women investment decisions and risk tolerance and develop some guidelines to the investment managers to design their investment schemes by considering these views of individuals.[61]

Syed Tabassum Sultana (2010), in his study on "An Empirical Study of Indian Individual Investors' Behaviour", pointed out that the Indian investor today have to endure a sluggish economy, the steep market declines prompted by deteriorating revenues, alarming reports of scandals ranging from illegal corporate accounting practices like that of Satyam to insider trading to make investment decisions. From the empirical study it was found that irrespective of gender, most of the investors (41 per cent) are found to have low risk tolerance level and many others (34 per cent) have high risk tolerance level rather than moderate risk tolerance level. It is also found that there is a strong negative correlation between age and risk tolerance level of the investor. Television is the media that is largely influencing the investor's decisions. Hence, this study can facilitate the investment product designers to design products which can cater to the investors who are low risk tolerant.[62]

Saravana Kumar, S. (2010), in his article "An Analysis of Investors' Preference towards Equity and Derivatives", published in The Indian journal of commerce, July-September 2010 concluded that the most of the investors are aware of high risk involved in the derivative market. To reduce the risk in the market, the investors should strictly follow the stop loss method. The study reveals that most of the investors prefer cash market where the script can be held for long term and the risk is less and is transferable to others with minimal time period. Even though risk is higher, some investors prefer derivative market where return is also higher. The investors are highly satisfied with equity shares because of many reasons, i.e., liquidity, low investment, capital appreciation, etc.[63]

Giridhari Mohanta et al. (2011), in their article "A Study on Investment Preferences among Urban Investors in Orissa", revealed that investors invest in different investment avenues for fulfilling financial, social and psychological need. While selecting any financial avenue they also expect other type of benefits like, safety and security, getting periodic return or dividends, high capital gain, secured future, liquidity, easy purchase, tax benefit, meeting future contingency, etc. They also make a good portfolio for them and think for their future with an objective of getting high capital gain from a particular avenue. It is seen that there is significant relationship between income and occupation on investment avenues in order to satisfy safety, periodic return, liquidity, better future and future contingency needs, etc. Risks bearing capacity and educational level of investors are also the two main factors which affect investment avenues selection. Male urban investors are more participative in nature with regard to investment avenues selection as against their female counterparts, as they are more exposed with the environment and market knowledge.[64]

Vidushi Handa et al. (2011), in his study on "Comparative Study of Investors Preference and their Satisfaction between Mutual Funds and Direct Investment in Equity Market", pointed out that simple forms of savings in the form of deposits or administered savings are no longer sufficient to meet the ever-increasing requirements of the household. Thus, the time has come to save intelligently through the various avenues of investment. The time has come to look at investment avenues, which can beat inflation and help our money to grow further in order to meet our future requirements. Investments in various forms will enable us to meet inflation and protect our purchasing power along with aiding us to generate a sustained income during post retirement. One of the available investment avenues is investment in stock market. It has been statistically proven in many markets, including ours, that over time, equity outperform most asset classes. It helps to think of risk as an opportunity. "Nothing ventured, nothing gained" applies just as much to the stock market as to other aspects of life. Both stock market and mutual fund is yet to reach its peak level. There is still a lack of knowledge about mutual fund and stock market amongst the majority of market players. High degree of volatility in the recent times in the Indian market has led to development of mutual fund. Today, investors prefer more mutual funds to enter into stock market rather to invest directly in stock market. The study concluded that there would be good future prospects for mutual fund and stock market.[65]

Alex Wang (2011), in his article "Younger Generations' Investing Behaviours in Mutual Funds: *Does Gender Matter?"*, concluded that knowledge, experience, and income are important factors that influence younger generations' investing behaviours in mutual funds. Moreover, gender emerges as the most important factor that differentiates younger generations' investing behaviours in mutual funds. Wealth advisors are also urged to consider helping their clients manage their wealth by being aware of gender-predicted differences in client situations.[66]

Joseph Anbarasu D., Clifford Paul S. and Annette B. (2011), in their article "An Empirical Study on Some Demographic Characteristics of Investors and its Impact on Pattern of their Savings and Risk Coverage Through Insurance Schemes", concluded that the saving pattern of the people is crucial to the government in designing policies to promote savings and investment. Their study reveals that the people are aware about the importance of saving, but the awareness about investment opportunities is low. Steps have to be taken by the government and private companies to increase the awareness by advertising campaigns. Investment companies need to offer schemes that are affordable by the low income, uneducated, unsalaried and families with children. Investment companies should make the provision and increase benefits, for their schemes, to allow people to invest in the monthly mode, which is preferred by most investors. If people invest in long term saving schemes and infrastructure, the national saving rate will increase, which in turn will lead to a more prosperous India.[67]

Mohammad Reza et al. (2011), in their study on "A Study on Small Investors' Behaviour in Choosing Stock Kuala-Lumpur Stock Market", investigated that the small investors' behaviour in choosing stock in Kuala-Lumpur stock market. Small investors usually capture the numerous factors to purchase a definite share within the security market. These factors dramatically influence investors' behaviour and change their decisions to purchase a particular stock. According to this description, the main purpose of this study is to identify the key determinants of choosing stock by small investors. A purposive sampling technique is employed to recruit 12 small investors based on desired range of demographic characteristics (for example, sex and age), experience levels in purchasing stock and value of purchasing per time in ringgit (Malaysian unit of currency). The research evidence reveals 13 effective factors in choosing stock which can influence small investors' decisions for stock selection. These factors are in order of importance involving financial statements of companies, accounting instruments, past stock price (return), firms' public information, profitability variables, consult with experts, financial ratios, past trading volume of stocks, second-hand information resources, discounted cash-flow tools, government policies, calculation of risk and economic variable.[68]

Dr Arifur Rehman Shaikh, Dr Anil and B. Kalkundarikar (2011), in their study on "Analysis of Retail Investor's Behaviour in Belgaum District, Karnataka State", explained that the economic liberalisation has resulted in an increase in number of investment avenues available for retail investors, depending upon their risk appetite they can choose between bank deposits, government/private bonds, shares and stocks, Exchange Traded Funds (ETF), mutual funds, insurance, derivatives, gold, silver, currencies, real estate, etc. This has been identified on the basis of cross analysis by applying correlation analysis. The research makes a pertinent revelation that the level of investment knowledge significantly leverages the returns on the investments. From the calculated correlation analysis data it can be observed that 0.096 point change in knowledge boosts investors return expectation byone point. Investors having extensive investment knowledge has the return expectation of multifold when compared to other knowledge categories and the correlation analysis between the occupation of investor and the level of risk assumption shows that there is a negative correlation between these two variables, analysis shows that a one point change in occupation will lead to negative change of 0.053 in the level of risk taken by the investors.[69]

Dr M. Selvam et al. (2011), in their study on "Investors' Attitude on Stock Selection Decision", found the fact that the average value of the five factors, namely, return on equity, quality of management, return on investment, price to earnings ratio and various ratios of the company influenced the decision makers. Further, other five factors, namely, recommendation by analyst, broker and research report, recommended by friend, family and peer, geographical location of the company and social responsibility were given the lowest priority or which had low influence on the stock selection decision by the retail investors.[70]

Dr Prashanta Athma et al. (2011), in their study "Gold ETFS: An Emerging Investment Option", analysed the knowledge of gold ETFs. Hence, the study is undertaken to fill the research gap with the objectives to focus the Gold ETF as a strong asset class; to stress upon the inclusion of Gold ETF in a portfolio for risk diversification; to assist the investor in the selection of best Gold ETF option and to analyse the tax implications of Gold ETF. The investment in the Gold ETF is low due to the low awareness among the investors and the sentimental attachment of the investors towards holding gold in physical form. If the uncertainty over the global economies and volatility in the equity markets are to continue for some more time, Gold ETFs are bound to find not only more number of investors, but also more number of Mutual Fund Players to launch them in the coming future. However, initiatives are to be taken by the mutual funds offering Gold ETFs, Government SEBI and members of the stock exchanges for creating awareness among the investors[71].

Dr Sarang S. Bhola and Ms Priyanka S. Zanvar (2011) in "A study on Investment Pattern of Socio-Economic Class 'A1'", segmentation of an investor group requires a complete understanding of the peculiarities of the financial service industry and also the psyche of the investors. This study has made an attempt to understand the investment pattern of respondents in socio-economic class A1 with connection to the preferences and selection of investment avenues. The study shows that behavioural trends usually take time to stabilise and they get disturbed even by a slight change in any of the influencing variables. Therefore, the study of demographic characteristics of the investor is very necessary to segment the investment industry. Hence, studies similar to the present one need to be conducted at regular intervals to develop useful models. Nevertheless, it is hoped that the study findings will have some useful managerial implication for the financial services industry in their segmentation and product designing.[72]

P.K. Mishra et al. (2011), in their study on "The Dynamics of Savings and Investment Relationship in India", stated that the study of the empirical relation between savings and investment in developed as well as developing countries has received considerable attention in recent years. Economists often claim that higher savings contribute to increased investment and GDP growth in a country. Thus, the purpose of this paper is to investigate the dynamics of the relation between savings and investment in India for the period from 1950-51 to 2008-09. Using annual data, the study reveals the co-integration between savings and investment and suggests the feedback causality between them. And, the most interesting part of the result is that while cointegration provides the evidence of long-run equilibrium relationship between savings and investment, the time series plotting of both the variables over the study period infers the fact that investment remained greater than the savings in India.[73]

Iqbal Mahmood et al. (2011), in their study on "Behavioural Implications of Investors for Investments in the Stock Market", stated that the irrational behaviours of investors in the investment market. It has conceptualised and then developed a risk perception centered model in this study. Different socio-economic and attitudinal variables have been incorporated in the model. Impact of these variables on the dependent variables of reinvestment intentions and return expectations can be tested. It has been recommended in the study that there should be stability and consistency in policies relating to various risk sources, transparent and timely spread of information about listed companies for all the investors at the symmetric level and development of mechanism for the training of new investors. The investment professionals should take these factors into account while designing portfolio of their clients.[74]

K. Lakshmana Rao (2011), in his study on "Analysis of Individual Investors' Behaviour Towards Mutual Fund Schemes (A Study on

Awareness and Adoption of Educational Levels)", presented the mutual fund investors awareness and adoption of different mutual fund schemes with educational levels. Educational level is the important factor that influences the behaviour of investment decisions. Increasing educational level attainment is associated with decreased levels of risk tolerance. An investor's level of formal education has found to influence risk tolerance. 350 respondents have been selected for this study, for three districts and five schemes in the Andhra Pradesh. The chi-square test has adopted to examine the association between the formal and technical education factors with the awareness and adoption of the mutual fund schemes.[75]

Sanjay Kanti Das (2011), in his study on "An Empirical Analysis on Preferred Investment Avenues among Rural and Semi-Urban Households", highlighted that the certain factors like education level, awareness about the financial system, age of investors etc make significant impact while deciding on the avenues for investment. The study is based on personal interviews of household heads, using a structured questionnaire. Actually, the present study identifies the preferred investment avenues among the individual investors using self assessment test. The present study is based on primary sources of data which are collected by distribution of a close ended questionnaire. The data has been analysed using percentage and chi-square test with the help of statistical software. Further, it is observed that the level of income also influences the investment decisions. Higher income group shows relatively high preference towards investment in share market, conversely lower and average income group shows keen preference towards insurance and banks as the most preferred investment avenues.[76]

Limei Che (2011), in his study on "Investors' Performance and Trading Behaviour on the Norwegian Stock Market", noted that the timing ability of individual investors at the investor level. With the availability of a unique monthly holding data set on stocks, mutual funds and bonds in the Norwegian stock market from December 1992 to June 2003, were well positioned to use both new timing technique and existing methods to investigate investors' timing ability. The researcher first checked the correlation between investors' equity portfolio weight and future stock market excess returns to investigate whether investors were able to time the stock market by shifting their assets between equity and bonds. This research has found out the sizable individual investors had the ability to successfully time the stock market over one month, three months and six months forecasting horizons. The timing ability is strongest over the three month forecasting horizon. If some individual investors timing ability is not spurious, then the portfolio performance of these investors should be higher than other investors who have no or even negative timing ability. The performance analysis shows that individual investors who can successfully time the stock market do have higher portfolio performance, which supports the results that these investors can successfully time the stock market.[77]

N. Geetha and Dr M. Ramesh (2011) in "A Study on People's Preferences in Investment Behaviour", examined on people's choice in investment avenues of Kurumbalur of Perambalur distirct. Data were collected using structured questionnaires. The sample size of area is analysed by tools selected for this study was two hundred and ten respondents were randomly selected from the town. Data were analysed using descriptive statistics and chi-square technique. After analysis and interpretation of data it is conducted by taking a limited number of sample sizes which is stated earlier. And this study reflects the perceptions of those respondents who are residing in Kurumbalur. There might be a chance that the perceptions of the respondents of different are varied due to diversity in social life, living pattern, income level, etc. All the age groups give importance to invest in Insurance, NSC, PPF and bank deposit. Income level of a respondent is an important factor which affects portfolio of the respondent. Middle age group, lower income level group respondents preferred to invest in insurance, NSC, PPF and bank deposit rather than any other investment avenues. Kurumbalur respondents are aware of various investment avenues like insurance, PPF, bank deposits, small savings like post office savings, etc. Awareness programme has to be conducted by Stock Brokering firms because most of the respondents are not aware of this new service about stock market.[78]

Dr D. Muraleedharan (2012), in his study on "A Study on the Level of Perception and Usefulness of Audited Financial Statement and Annual Reports among Investors in India", conducted that an experiment in which subjects performed analytical procedures and answered the questions. This study analyses the decision effectiveness of audit reports in Mysore city. The sample respondents were selected from this city to enquire into the perceptions of respondents towards the effectiveness auditing information in their investment decisions in view of the city having heterogeneous, economic, social and cultural environment, which represents the country adequately. The empirical results have been presented under Universal findings. The major findings were evidenced with regard to the effectiveness of audit report[79].

Dr Binod Kumar Singh and Dr Binod Kumar Singh (2012), in their study on "A Study on Investors' Attitude Towards Mutual Funds as an Investment Option" covered the operations of mutual fund, comparison between investment in mutual fund and bank and calculation of NAV, etc. In this paper, the impacts of various demographic factors on investors' attitude towards mutual fund have been studied. For measuring various phenomena and analysing the collected data effectively and efficiently for drawing sound conclusions, Chi-square test has been used and for analysing the various factors responsible for investment in mutual funds, ranking was done on the basis of weighted scores and scoring was also done on the basis of scale.[80]

Smita Srivastava and Gunjan Saxena (2012), in their study on "Investment Trend Now and Then: A Survey Based Study of Moradabad (U.P.)", mentioned that the investment is the best way to multiply money. Getting into the investment without having the complete knowledge of all the available options and understanding own financial goal is like going for treasure hunt without any map and clues. However, the financial needs and goals keep changing throughout the different phases of one's life time. The paper attempts to know the awareness level of the investment alternatives available amongst the investors and compares the investment trend now from 20 years back. The area of the study is Moradabad, a city in Uttar Pradesh and the sample size is 150. The data used in the study comprises of both primary and secondary data. It is found in the survey that the investment decisions vary as per investor's age, experience, profession, financial circumstances, family structure and other factors. Most of the investors are risk averse and thus ignore risky investments like derivatives, equities and prefer safe heaven like bank deposits, post office deposits, gold, etc. There is very little enhancement in the awareness level for newer financial instruments amongst investors over the years.[81]

Dr Aparna Samudra and Dr M.A. Burghate (2012), in their study on "A Study on Investment Behaviour of Middle Class House Holds in Nagpur", examined that the rationale behind choosing this research topic is the premise that the middle class in India has gained attention of the economists, policy makers and the marketers, as still there remains a considerable untapped potential in this income class of India. The majority of the respondents of the selected middle class households take investment decision on their own. The government initiatives in this direction would help the investors to take more sound investment decisions which would in turn improve the degree of sophistication that households bring to bear in their saving and investment decisions. The government should also design policy to make people invest in various instruments rather than stashing cash at home.[82]

Dr S. Radhika and Mr K. Srinivasan (2012), in their study on "A Study on Investment Pattern in Mutual Funds and Preference of Retail Investors in Chennai City for Karvy Consultants Limited, Chennai", viewed that the various factors identified in the study provide some valuable input regarding the investor's pattern, their preference and priorities. This will guide the organisation in designing financial products for the various segments of investors. The buying intent of mutual fund product by a small investor can be due to multiple reasons depending upon the risk return trade off. Due to the reduction in the bank interest rates and high degree of volatility in Indian Stock market, investors are looking at an alternative for their investments, which will provide them higher, returns and also safety to their investments.[83]

Dr G. Santhiyavalli and M. Usharani (2012), in their study on "A Study on Investment Avenues with Particular Reference to Mutual Fund", stated that the Indian financial system fosters savings among the public and channels them to their most efficient use through financial institutions or intermediaries operating in the money and capital markets segments. One such financial intermediary which has played a significant role in the development and growth of capital markets is mutual fund. Like most developed countries the mutual fund cult has been catching on in India. There are various reasons for this. Mutual fund makes it easy and less costly for investors to satisfy their need for capital growth and income generation. In addition to this, a mutual fund brings the benefit of diversification and money management to the individual investors, providing an opportunity for financial success that was once available only to a select few. This paper will focus on saving pattern of investors, investment avenues, awareness about various investments and preference towards mutual funds and their different types. Customers believe that the mutual fund industry falls short of expectations in meeting their needs at the time of economic uncertainty and market volatility. The investors always prefer to invest in financial products which give risk free returns. This confirms that the investors prefer to play safe in the market. Thus the mutual fund industry has to bring many innovative concepts and should frame distinct marketing strategies to satisfy the need of investors.[84]

Dr Bernadette D'silva et al. (2012), in their study on "A Study on Factors Influencing Mutual Fund Investment in India", explored that the factors that are responsible in increasing the Mutual Fund investment in India. The study also helps to understand the role of demographics in mutual funds in India. This enables the fund managers to understand the investment pattern and preferences of investor's investing in mutual funds. Further, analysis of the study reveals that financial literacy of respondents is very important for making investment in mutual funds. Therefore, mutual fund companies should promote financial awareness amongst the respondents so as to channelise their income and savings towards mutual funds. Finally, the study also analyses that the purpose of an investor, behind investing in mutual fund definitely influence in the selection of the mutual fund scheme for investment. Thus, the need of the hour for all the domestic mutual fund companies is to expand their investor base which can be possible, only when the companies are determined to understand the value drivers and thus lure retail investors to invest in mutual funds.[85]

Dr C. Anbalagan and Pujitha B. (2012), in their study on "A study on Investor's Preferences on Investment of Capital Market in India", mentioned that the securities market operations promote the economic growth of the country. More efficient is the securities market, the greater is the promotion effect on economic growth. In the current scenario, investing in stock markets is a major challenge ever for professionals. The investors should be aware of the various hedging and speculation strategies, which can be used for reducing their risk. Awareness about the various uses of derivatives can help investors to reduce risk and increase profits. Though the stock market is subjected to high risk, by using derivatives the loss can be minimised to an extent. Indian markets are amongst the best regulated markets in the world. There is need for greater integration with international markets in terms of capital flows, products and processes and also there is need to introduce new age financial products to encourage participation of new age investors.[86]

Pandey Jatin (2012), in his study on "A Study on Factors Influencing Consumer Understanding on Retirement Investment Funds", analysed that the main part of the retirement planning is to calculate how much wealth has to be created and it is needed to consider all the risks and needs of the future. There are many risks which occur at the post-retirement such as longevity risk, inflation risk, interest rate risk, stock market risk; unexpected healthcare needs need costs which should be manageable. Considering all these, the retirement planning should be made. The study aims to understand how consumers of retirement related investments choose among the various available alternatives and to know what factors are considered and traded while choosing a particular retirement fund. Primary data were collected through survey method through questionnaire. This study revealed the bi-dimensionality of risk perception. The two factors that seem to influence investor decision on retirement investment funds are lack of perceived control and lack of assuredness. This means that for customers of retirement funds control and assurance are the major reasons that contributes to the perception of risk and need of being assured of the returns and having control over their investment specific to retirement is an important attitudinal requirement.[87]

Vennila and R. Nandhagopal (2012), in their study on "Investors' Preference Towards Mutual Funds in Coimbatore City", stated that a good majority of the remaining respondents were distributed in the Degree qualifications. Eight per cent and 8.80 per cent of the investors have Diploma/ ITI and up to HSC qualifications respectively. One should take a look at the portfolio of the funds for the purpose. Excessive exposure to any specific sector should be avoided, as it will only add to the risk of the entire portfolio. Most of the investors rely on investment consultants to choose the right fund for them. They monitor their investments periodically. They find a need to increase the public awareness of mutual funds.[88]

Dhiraj Jains and Nakul Dashora (2012), in their study on "A Study on Impact of Market Movements on Investment Decision—An Empirical Analysis with Respect to Investors in Udaipur, Rajasthan", stated that the investment markets are becoming more risky and each and every passing day makes investors behave differently upon different market dynamics. The basic methods of market analysis (fundamental, technical and quantitative) though are playing an important role in investment decisions, the behaviour of the investors has become more important and hence the 'Behavioural Finance', is emerging and becoming the topic of various researches and studies. The study analyses the rationality of the investors of Udaipur during different market expectations, dividend and bonus announcements, the impact of age, income levels and other market related information on investment decisions of investors from Udaipur. The research brings out certain characteristics of investors living in

Udaipur. The ability to understand the judgment criteria like rationality and irrationality in investment pattern and behaviour which enables the investor to be cautious as its consequences affect the lifestyle, asset value and relationship with others. The present study has shown that investors prefer investing in both primary and secondary market instruments. Most of the decisions are rational and influenced by the various information available in market. It was also found that investors prefer the wait and watch policy for taking their decision, and are very cautious and their decisions are influenced by various psychological factors and behavioural dimensions[89].

Jatin Pandey (2012), in her study on "A Study on Factors Influencing Consumer Understanding on Retirement Investment Funds", revealed the bi-dimensionality of risk perception. The two factors that seem to influence investor decision on retirement investment funds are lack of perceived control and lack of assuredness. This means that for customers of retirement funds control and assurance are the major reasons that contribute to the perception of risk and need of being assured of the returns and having control over their investment specific to retirement is an important attitudinal requirement[90].

Sanjay Kanti Das (2012), in his study on "Investment Habits among the Households: An Empirical Analysis", revealed in most cases investors across all categories found them to be safer with taking up the insurance policies. A significant portion of respondents also shows keen preference towards unit linked insurance policies so as to get short term gains. It is also observed that most of the respondents show their keen interest towards the insurance products so as to get tax benefits, life protection and average profitable investment avenues. This is perhaps the most striking features of general investors and the most important factor that influences the investment decisions. Further, it is observed that the level of income also influences the investment decisions. Higher income group shows relatively high preference towards investment in share market, conversely lower and average income group shows keen preference towards insurance and banks as the most preferred investment avenues[91].

2.3 Summary

Review of past literature on investment avenues and their preference helped in the generation of ideas, formulation of hypotheses, and selection of various tools for analysis and to arrive at meaningful conclusions. There are many studies available on investments. No doubt, all these studies have stimulated and encouraged to chalk out a design for this study, which encompasses a wider field than any of the studies referred to. This topic "Investment Pattern and Preferences of Professionals" is a new attempt.

References

1. National Council of Applied Economic Research (1961), *Savings in India*, New Delhi.
2. Tamilkodi, A.P.P., (1983), *Small Savings Schemes in Tamil Nadu: A Trend Study* (1970-80), unpublished thesis, University of Madras, Tamilnadu.
3. Jayaraman, R., (1987), *A Study of Small Savings Schemes in North Arcot District*, 1976-86, unpublished thesis, University of Madras, Tamilnadu, India.
4. Mukhi, M.D., (1989), "National Savings Certificates: A Saving Grace, *Business World*, 6-19, December 1989, pp. 107-120.
5. Arangasami, A., (1992), *A Study of Small Savings Schemes in Tamil Nadu with Special Reference to Madras District during 1981-82 to 1990-91"*, unpublished thesis, University of Madras, Tamilnadu, India.
6. Radha, V., (1995), *A Study of Investment Behaviour of Investors of Corporate Securities*, Doctoral Dissertation, Alagappa University, Karaikudi, India.
7. Kannan (1996), *Investors Protection – A Study on Legal Aspects*, Ph.D. thesis submitted to Alapappa University, Karaikudi.
8. Muhlesen M. (1997), "Improving India's Saving Performance", *Finance and Development.*
9. Somasundaram, V.K., (1998), *A Study on Savings and Investment Pattern of Salaried Class in Coimbatore District,* unpublished thesis, Bharathiyar University, Coimbatore, Tamilnadu.
10. Augustine, L., Gavini and Prashanth Athma, (1999), "Small Saving Schemes of Post Office Need to be Known More", *Southern Economist,* 37(20), pp. 13-14.
11. Narayana D.L. (1997), *Income, Savings and Investment of Household Sector in Chittoor District,* Ph.D. thesis submitted to Srivenkateswara University, Tirupathi.
12. Org Marg (1999), *Investors choices over the Investment Advances,* Survey Report.

13. Soma Sundaram V.K. (1999), *A Study on Savings and Investment Pattern of Salaried Class in Coimbatore District*, Ph.D. thesis submitted to Bharathiyar University.
14. Gavini, Augustine, L., and Prashanth Athma, (1999), "Small Saving Schemes of Post Office Need to be Known More", *Southern Economist*, 37(20), February 15, pp. 13-14.
15. Brad M. Barber (2000), *The Behaviour of Mutual Fund Investors*, School of Business Administration, University of Michigan, Ann Arbor, MI 48109-1234.
16. Kar Pratip, Natarajan I. and Singh J.P. (2000), *Survey of Indian Investors*, published in *SEBI-NCAER*.
17. Securities and Exchange Board of India (2000), *Survey of Indian Investor*, Mumbai.
18. Zathik Ali, M. (2000), "Impact of the Budget on the Savings of the Small Investors", *Southern Economist*, 39(4), pp. 9-10.
19. Kevin James (2000), "The Price of Retail Investing in the UK", Social Science Research Network, Available from http://papers.ssrn.com/sol3/papers.cfm?abstract_id=428041.
20. Datar, M.K., (2001), "Interest Rates on Small Savings and Provident Fund Scheme", *Economic Political Weekly*, 36(48), pp. 4450-4451.
21. Karthikeyan, B., (2001), *Small Investors' Perception on Post Office Small Savings Schemes*, unpublished thesis, Madras University, Tamil Nadu, India.
22. S.Venkatraman (2003), *Investor's Choice - A Survey*, Indian Liberal Group, Chennai.
23. Akiko Kamesakaa et al (2003), "Investment Patterns and Performance of Investor Groups in Japan", *Pacific-Basin Finance Journal*, 11, pp. 1 –22.
24. Dr G.V. Chalam (2003), "Investors Behavioural Pattern of Investment and Their Preferences of Mutual Funds", *Southern Economist*.
25. Dr K. Santi Swarup, (2003), "Measures for Improving Common Investor Confidence in Indian Primary Market: A Survey", National Stock Exchange India Limited, Available from http://www.nseindia.com/content/research/Paper64.pdf.
26. Brian M. Lucey and Michael Dowling (2005), "The Role of Feelings in Investor Decision-Making", *Journal of Economic Surveys*, Vol. 19, No. 2, Blackwell Publishing Ltd. 2005, 9600 Garsington Road, Oxford OX4 2DQ, UK and 350 Main St., Malden, MA 02148, USA.

27. Shylajan C.S. and Marathe Sushama, (2006), "A Study of Attitudes and Trading Behaviour of Stock Market Investors", *The ICFAI Journal of Financial Economics,* Vol. 4, No. 3, pp. 54-68.

28. Ranganathan K. (2006), "A Study of Fund Selection Behaviour of Individual Investors Towards Mutual Funds: With Reference to Mumbai City", *ICFAI Journal of Behavioural Finance*, 3(2), pp. 63-88.

29. John Graham and Alok Kumar, (2006), "Do Dividend Clienteles Exist? Evidence on Dividend Preferences of Retail Investors", Social Science Research Network, Available from http://papers.ssrn.com/sol3/papers.cfm?abstract_id=482563.

30. Alistair Byrne, C.F.A. (2007), "Employee Saving and Investment Decisions in Defined Contribution Pension Plans: Survey Evidence from the U.K.", *Financial Services Review,* 16, pp. 19–40.

31. Dr K. Ravichandran (2007), *A Study on Investors Preferences Towards Various Investment Avenues in Capital Market with Special Reference to Derivatives*, Bharathidasan Institute of Management, Tiruchirapalli.

32. Mittal Manish and Vyas R.K. (2007), "Demographics and Investment Choice among Indian Investors", ICFAI University, *Journal of Behavioural Finance.*

33. Chris Veld and Yulia V. Veld-Merkoulova (2007), "*The Risk Perceptions of Individual Investors*", Department of Accounting and Finance, University of Stirling, United Kingdom.

34. K. Balanaga Gurunathan (2007), "Investors' Requirements in Indian Securities Market" *Delhi Business Review,* X, Vol. 8, No. 1.

35. Dr. Bhagaban Das and Ms. Sangeeta Mohanty (2008), "Mutual Fund vs. Life Insurance: Behavioural Analysis of Retail Investors", *Journal of Business and Management*, Vol. 3, No. 10.

36. Prof V.E. Rama Moorthy and Ms T.R. Rajeswari (2008), "*An Empirical Study on Factors Influencing the Mutual Fund/Scheme Selection by Retail Investors*" School of Business Management, Accounting and Finance, Sri Sathya Sai Institute of Higher Learning, Prasanthi Nilayam, Puttaparthi, Andhra Pradesh – 515 134.

37. Lalitha and M. Surekha (2008), "Retail Investor in Indian Capital Market Profile, Pattern of Investment and Profitability", *The Indian Journal of Commerce.*

38. Baskaran (2008) "*A Study on Savings and Investment Habits in Tamil Nadu*" Alagappa Institute of Management, Karaikudi.

39. Pradeep Gupta (2008), "*Investment Decisions in Equity or in Mutual Fund*", Research Report, M.P. Birla Institute of Management, Associate Bharatiya Vidya Bhavan, Bangalore-560001.

40. Pallavi Seth et al. (2008), *Financial Literacy and Investment Decisions of Indian Investors, — A Case of Delhi and NCR*, Birla Institute of Management Technology, Greater Noida.
41. Ning Zhu (2008), *Individual Investor Trading*, University of California, Davis and Nomura International.
42. Dr Joseph Anbarasu and Clifford Paul. S. (2008), "Saving Pattern of People and the Impact of Insurance on Savings with Special Reference to Tiruchirappalli", *College Science in India,* 2:1, June 2008, Tiruchirappalli, Tamil Nadu, India.
43. Arwinder Singh and H.S. Sandhu (2008), *Investors' Adoption of Internet Stock Trading: A Study*", Professor, Department of Commerce and Business Management, Guru Nanak Dev University, Amritsar-143005, Punjab (India).
44. Mittal M. and R.K. Vyas (2008), "Personality Type and Investment Choice: An Empirical Study", ICFAI University, *Journal of Behavioural Finance*, 5(3), pp. 6-22.
45. Kathirvel, N. (2009), "Investment Option with Reference to Insurance Products", *Southern Economist.*
46. R. Kasilingam and G. Jayabal (2009), "Alternative Investment Option to Small Investors", *Southern Economist.*
47. Ritadhi Chakravarti (2009), *Michigan Journal of Business.*
48. BBS Parihar, Rajeev Sharma, and Deepika Singh parihar (2009), "Analysing Investors Attitude Towards Mutual Funds as a Investment Option", *The ICFAI Journal of Management Research.*
49. G. Prabakaran and G. Jayabal (2009), "Investors Risk Tolerance Towards Mutual Fund Investments", *Southern Economist.*
50. Krishnamoorthi, C. (2009), "Changing Pattern of Indian Households: Savings in Financial Assets", *RVS Journal of Management.*
51. Jagannath Mallick (2009), "Trends and Patterns of Private Investment in India", Institute for Social and Economic Change, Rao Road, Nagarabhavi, P.O., Bangalore - 560 072.
52. Hayat, M. Awan et al. (2009), *A Study on Investment Behaviour of Individual Investors*, Institute of Management Sciences, Bahauddin Zakariya University, Multan.
53. Inderst, G. (2009), *Pension Fund Investment in Infrastructure*, Financial Affairs Division, Directorate for Financial and Enterprise Affairs, Organisation for Economic Co-operation and Development, 2 Rue André Pascal, Paris 75116, France, www.oecd.org/daf/fin/wp.

54. Vandna Singh and Komal (2009), "Prospects and Problems of Real Estate in India", *International Research Journal of Finance and Economics*, ISSN 1450-2887, Issue 24, Euro Journals Publishing, http://www.eurojournals.com/finance.htm.

55. Manish Agarwal et al. (2009), *A Study of Investors' Expected Rate of Return on their Investment,* International School of Informatics and Management, Sector-12, Mansarovar, Jaipur -302 020, Rajasthan.

56. Anand Patil Digambar et al. (2010), "Residential Location Choice: A Study of Household Preferences for the City of Nagpur" Institute of Town Planners, *India Journal*, 7 - 3, pp. 01–19.

57. Lalit Mohan Kathuria and Kanika Singhania (2010), "Investor Knowledge and Investment Practices of Private Sector Bank Employees", The Indian Journal of Commerce.

58. Syed Tabassum Sultana (2010), An Empirical Study of Indian Individual Investors' Behaviour, *Global Journal of Finance and Management*, ISSN: 0975 - 6477, Vol. 2, No. 1, pp. 19-33.

59. S. Joseph Anbarasu et al. (2010), "Study on Socio Economic Status and Awareness of Indian Investors of Insurance", *E-Journal of Business and Economic Issues,* Vol. V, Issue: III.

60. James E. Corter (2010), *Investor Attitudes towards Risk and Uncertainty and Reactions to Market Turmoil,* Teacher's College, University of Columbia.

61. Gaurav Kabra et al. (2010), "Factors Influencing Investment Decision of Generations in India: An Econometric Study", *Asian Journal of Management Research*, ISSN: 2229–3795.

62. Syed Tabassum Sultana (2010), "An Empirical Study of Indian Individual Investors' Behaviour", *Global Journal of Finance and Management*, ISSN: 0975 - 6477, Vol. 2, No. 1, pp. 19-33.

63. Saravana Kumar, S. (2010), "An Analysis of Investor Preference towards Equity and Derivatives", *The Indian Journal of Commerce.*

64. Giridhari Mohanta et.al. (2011), "A Study on Investment Preferences among Urban Investors in Orissa", *Prerana, Journal of Management Thought and Practice*, ISSN: 0974-908X, Vol. 3, Issue: 1.

65. Vidushi Handa et al. (2011), "Comparative Study of Investors Preference and their Satisfaction between Mutual Funds and Direct Investment in Equity Market", *International Journal of Marketing and Management Research*, Vol. 2, Issue-7, ISSN: 2229-6883.

66. Alex Wang (2011), "Younger Generations' Investing Behaviours in Mutual Funds: Does Gender Matter?" *The Journal of Wealth Management,* Spring.

67. Joseph Anbarasu D., Clifford Paul S and Annette B. (2011), "An Empirical Study on Some Demographic Characteristics of Investors and its Impact on Pattern of their Savings and Risk Coverage Through Insurance Schemes", *The IUP Journal of Risk and Insurance.*

68. Mohammad Reza et al (2011), "A Study on Small Investors' Behaviour in choosing Stock case study: Kuala-Lumpur Stock Market", *African Journal of Business Management* Vol. 5(27), pp. 11082-11092.

69. Dr Arifur Rehman Shaikh, Dr. Anil B. Kalkundarikar (2011), "Analysis of Retail Investor's Behaviour in Belgaum District, Karnataka State", *International Journal for Management Research*, Vol. 1, No. 2, pp. 22-39.

70. Dr M. Selvam et al. (2011), "Investors' Attitude on Stock Selection Decision", *International Journal of Management and Business Studies,* Vol. 1, Issue: 2, ISSN: 2231-2463 (Print).

71. Dr Prashanta Athma et al. (2011), "Gold ETFS: An Emerging Investment Option", *International Research and Educational Consortium,* Vol. 2, Issue: 1, ISSN: 2229-4104.

72. Dr Sarang S. Bhola and Ms. Priyanka S. Zanvar (2011), "A Study on Investment Pattern of Socio-Economic Class A1", *Vishwakarma Business Review*, Vol. I, ISSN: 2229-6514.

73. P.K. Mishra et al. (2011), "The Dynamics of Savings and Investment Relationship in India", *European Journal of Economics, Finance and Administrative Sciences*, ISSN 1450-2275, Issue: 18.

74. Iqbal Mahmood et al (2011), "Behavioural Implications of Investors for Investments in the Stock Market", *European Journal of Social Sciences,* Vol. 20.

75. K. Lakshmana Rao (2011), "Analysis of Individual Investors' Behaviour towards Mutual Fund Schemes (A Study on Awareness and Adoption of Educational Levels)", *Journal on Banking Financial Services and Insurance Research*, Vol. 1, Issue: 7, ISSN: 2231-4288.

76. Sanjay Kanti Das (2011), "An Empirical Analysis on Preferred Investment Avenues among Rural and Semi-Urban Households", *Journal of Frontline Research in Arts and Science,* Vol. 01, pp. 26-36.

77. Limei Che (2011), "Investors' Performance and Trading Behaviour on the Norwegian Stock Market", dissertation report BI Norwegian Business School, ISSN: 1502-2099.

78. N. Geetha and Dr M. Ramesh (2011), "A Study on People's Preferences in Investment Behaviour", *International Journal of Management Reviews*, Vol. 1, Issue: 6, Online, ISSN: 2249 – 2585.

79. Dr D. Muraleedharan (2012), "A Study on the Level of Perception and Usefulness of Audited Financial Statement and Annual Reports among Investors in India Hamid Reza Gholamniaroshan, *Asia Pacific Journal of Research in Business Management,* Vol. 3, Issue: 3, ISSN: 2229-4104.

80. Dr Binod Kumar Singh and Dr Binod Kumar Singh (2012), "A study on Investors' Attitude Towards Mutual Funds as an Investment Option", *International Journal of Research in Management,* ISSN; 2249-5908 Issue: 2, Vol. 2, p. 61.

81. Smita Srivastava and Gunjan Saxena (2012), "Investment Trend Now and Then: A Survey Based Study of Moradabad (U.P.)", *Asia Pacific Journal of Research in Business Management,* Vol. 3, Issue: 1, ISSN: 2229-4104.

82. Dr Aparna Samudra and Dr M.A. Burghate (2012), "A Study on Investment Behaviour of Middle Class House Holds in Nagpur", *International Journal of Social Science and Interdisciplinary Research,* Vol.1, No. 5, ISSN: 22 27 3630.

83. Dr S. Radhika and Mr K. Srinivasan (2012), "A Study on Investment Pattern in Mutual Funds and Preference of Retail Investors in Chennai City for Karvy Consultants Limited, Chennai", *International Journal of Multidisciplinary Management Studies,* Vol. 2, Issue: 2, ISSN: 2249-8834.

84. Dr G. Santhiyavalli and M. Usharani (2012), "A Study on Investment Avenues with Particular Reference to Mutual Fund", *International Journal of Multidisciplinary Management Studies,* Vol. 2, Issue: 1, ISSN 2249-8834.

85. Dr Bernadette D'silva et al. (2012), "A Study on Factors Influencing Mutual Fund Investment in India", *Research Journal of Commerce and Behavioural Science*: Vol. 1, No. 05, March 2012.

86. Dr C. Anbalagan and Pujitha B.V.T.S. (2012), "A study on Investor's Preferences on Investment of Capital Market in India", *International Journal of Research in Finance and Accounting,* Vol. 1, No. 2, Dec-Feb. 2011-2012, ISSN: 2277-1204.

87. Pandey Jatin (2012), "A Study on Factors Influencing Consumer Understanding on Retirement Investment Funds", *Asian Journal of Research in Banking and Finance,* Vol. 2, Issue: 5, ISSN: 2249-7323.

88. Vennila and R. Nandhagopal (2012), "Investors' Preference Towards Mutual Funds in Coimbatore City", *European Journal of Social Sciences,* ISSN: 1450-2267, Vol. 29, No. 1, pp. 115-125.

89. Dhiraj Jains and Nakul Dashora (2012), "A Study on Impact of Market Movements on Investment Decision an Empirical Analysis with Respect to Investors in Udaipur, Rajasthan", *Journal of Arts, Science and Commerce,* E-ISSN 2229-4686, ISSN 2231-4172, Vol. III, Issue: 2(2), [88].

90. Jatin Pandey (2012), "A Study on Factors Influencing Consumer Understanding on Retirement Investment Funds", *Asian Journal of Research in Banking and Finance*, Vol. 2, Issue: 5, ISSN: 2249-7323.

91. Sanjay Kanti Das (2012), "Investment Habits among the Households: An Empirical Analysis", *Asian Journal of Research in Banking and Finance*", Vol. 2, Issue: 6, ISSN: 2249-7323.

Chapter-III

Profile of the Study Area

3.1 Introduction

Tirunelveli is a historically popular southern district of Tamil Nadu. This district is popular educationally, socially, economically, literally and culturally in Tamil Nadu. The leaders and people of this district have played a remarkable role in the freedom struggle. The darkness of British rule was dispelled by the selfless sacrifice of many patriots. Among them, Veerapandia Kattabomman was a warrior who fought till the end against the British rule. Subramania Bharathi inspired the mass through his poems of patriotism. V.O. Chithambaranar floated the first swadeshi (native) shipping business against the British and Vanchinathan, went to the extent of assassinating the local British collector for the sake of upholding the reputation of the country. Their contribution is cherished even today. Many administrators, academicians, industrialists and agricultural experts have come from Tirunelveli district. This soil is rich in cultural heritage also.

3.2 Puranic Association

The *Tirunelveli Sthalapurana* prescribes a tradition for the origin of the name Tirunelveli. The puranic version goes that one Vedasarma, a staunch devotee of Shiva, on his pilgrimage from the north to the south was invited by Lord Shiva in his dream to his abode on the banks of the sacred river Tamiraparani. The delighted devotee came to 'Sindupoondhurai', which is on the banks of the river and stayed there with his family. Once there was a famine which forced Vedasarma to collect paddy by way of begging and continuing his daily prayers. One day he spread out the paddy to dry under the sun before the Lord, and went for his ablutions in Tamiraparani. He prayed to the Lord for rain which he thought could be a remedy for the famine. His prayer was answered and when he was bathing, a thunder storm broke-out and it rained heavily. Vedasarma rushed to the place where he had spread the paddy. He witnessed a miracle. Despite rain around the area, the paddy that he had spread did not get even a single drop of rain and did not get soaked. Since then, according to the *purana* the town is called as "Tiru-nel-veli" (Sacred hedged paddy).

3.3 Ancient Origin of the District

On acquisition from the Nawab of Arcot in1801, the British named it as Tinnevelly district, though their headquarters was first located in Palayamkottai the adjacent town, where they had their military headquarters during their operations against the Palayakars. Two reasons may be attributed for naming it after Tirunelveli. One is because, it was and is the chief town of the district and the other is that it was already called as Tirunelveli Seemai under the Nayaks and Nawabs. Both Tirunelveli and Palayamkottai grew as the twin towns of the district.

3.4 District Formation

Tirunelveli District was formed in the year 1790 by the East India Company, later came under the direct control of the British Crown Queen Victoria. The name Tirunelveli has been composed from the three Tamil words, i.e., 'Thiru-Nel-Veli' meaning Sacred Paddy Hedge, with effect from 20.10.1986 the district was bifurcated and new Tuticorin district was formed.

3.5 District Administration

The district administration is headed by the District Collector with his office at the district collectorate. The responsibilities of the District Collector include maintenance of law and order, coordinating various development and welfare activities in the district, etc. The Collector is assisted by the District Revenue Officer in matters of land revenue, land matters, public distribution system, etc and by the Project Officer, District Rural Development Agency for various development schemes. Other officers who assist the Collector in his work are Personal Assistant (General), Personal Assistant (Development), Additional Personal Assistant (Land), Personal Assistant (Agriculture), Personal Assistant (Survey and Land Records), Personal Assistant (Noon Meal Programme), Personal Assistant (Small Savings), Special Deputy Collector (PGRC), Personal

Assistant (Accounts), Assistant Director (Panchayats), Assistant Director (Audit), Assistant Director (Mines), Special Deputy Collector (Stamps), Assistant Director (Town Panchayats), District Adi-Dravidar and Tribal Welfare Officer, District Backward Class Welfare Officer, Public Relations Officer, District Supply Officer, Assistant Commissioner (Excise) and Inspection Cell Officer.

Table 3.1: Details of Other Administrative Setup in Tirunelveli District

No. of Firkas	60
No. of Villages	559
No. of Village Panchayats	425
No. of Town Panchayats	38
No. of Municipalities	7
No. of Municipal corporation	1

Source: *Tirunelveli District Handbook, 2011-2012.*

3.6 Geographical Data and Boundaries

Tirunelveli District having geographical area of 6759 sq kms, in the Southeastern portion of Tamil Nadu is triangular in shape. It lies between 8°.05' and 9°.30' of the Northern latitude and 77°.05' and 78°.25' of Eastern longitude. The district is located in the southern part of Tamil Nadu and surrounded by Virudhunagar District on the north, Western Ghats on the West, Kanniyakumari District on the south, Tuticorin District on the East. The lifeline of the district is Tamiraparani River, which feeds the district and quenches the thirst of residents.

Table 3.2: Land Classification

Land Category	*Area in Hectares*
Wet	79,668
Dry	3,58,151
Assessed Waste	39,274
Unassessed Waste Dry	57,696
Poramboke	25,456
Forest lands	1,22,055
Total	**6,82,300**

Source: *Tirunelveli District Handbook 2011-2012.*

3.7 Mineral Resources

3.7.1 Limestone

It is available at several places in the district. The major part comes from the crystalline limestone deposit occurring near Ramayanpatti, Talaiyuthu and Padmaneri. A total reserve of 4.06 million tonnes limestone up to a depth of 15.2 meter in Ramayanpatti band and 5.08 million tonnes up to a depth of 15.25 meter in Talaiyuthu band has been estimated. The limestone available here contains Calcium Oxide (CaO) from 34.97 to 55.49 per cent, Magnesium Oxide (MgO) from 0.31 to 7.24 per cent.

The Padmaneri band consists of six limestone lenses with an aggregate strike length of about 800 meter. The average width is 4.75 meter 0.199 million tonnes of cement grade limestone is estimated from this band. The Singikulam band extends over a strike length of 17 km. It contains seven limestone lenses with an aggregate strike length of about 6.4 km. and average width of 13 meter. About 3.160 million tonnes of cement grade limestone is estimated from this band.

Six bands of good quality limestone occur near Pandapuli and 4,34,000 tonnes of limestone suitable for the manufacture of cement and chemical industries have been estimated.

3.7.2 Sulphides

Light traces of sulphides occur in and around Pattankadu and Munradaippu. This mineral is of no economic importance.

3.7.3 Ilmenite - Garnet Sands

Occurrence of red garnet sands in the beds of the river Nambiar and Uvari has been recorded. The proportion of garnet is 75 per cent in the rich deposits and 45 per cent in the surface sands. Local concentration of limenite sands are noticed near Vijayapatti and Kuttankuli.

3.8 Forest

The total area of the forest of the district is 1,22,055 ha, of which 81,700 ha. is set apart for Tiger reserve of Mundanthurai and Kalakadu. The entire forest of the district stretches along the Western ghats.

Various types of forests from luxuriant tropical wet evergreen forests to southern thorn scrub forests occur in the district. Owing to its diverse geographical factors, the forests in the district are technically classified as Southern hill top tropical evergreen forests, West Coast tropical evergreen

13. No. of Polling Stations	:		2,532		
14. Voter as on 01.01.2013	:	*Male*	*Female*	*Others*	*Total*
		1,09,926	11,11,293	11	22,21,230

Source: *Tirunelveli District Handbook, 2011-2012.*

3.15 Administrative Setup

This district is having three revenue divisions comprising of 11 taluks, 60 firkas, 19 Development Blocks, 616 revenue villages and 425 village panchayats.

3.16 Demographic Details

The population of this district was 27,23,988 as per 2001 census and 30,72,880 as per 2011 census. The density of population per sq km was 399 as per 2001 census and 455 persons as per 2011 census. Tirunelveli, Tenkasi and Ambasamudram are the most densely populated taluks in the district.

The Sex ratio is 1024 females for every 1,000 males in the district as per 2011census. The literacy rate is 76.09 per cent in the district as per 2011 census.

Out of the total population, males are 13,33,939and females13,90,049 as per 2001census. Out of the total population, males are 15,18,595 and females 15,54,285 as per 2011census. The district having schedule caste population of 4,81,052 which represents 17.66 per cent to total population as per 2011 census. Schedule tribes are found to be very small in numbers 8,358 which is 0.31 per cent of the total population. 4.36 per cent of state population lives in Tirunelveli district.

3.17 Irrigation

The district is blessed with the western ghats from which all the perennial rivers follow and drain towards the east. The surface water of the district is drained into major river basin, viz, Thamiraparani, Vaippar, Nambiar and Hanumanathi. Thamiraparani is the major river basin in the district. The other streams which are seasonal in nature are Servallar, Manimuthar, Ramanathi, Pachayar, Chittar and Uppodai rivers which drain into the Tamiraparani basin. The sources of irrigation are canal, tank and well, which covers 1,33,106 hectares. Among the total area irrigated, well irrigation covers 50,096 hectares, tanks 55,382 hectares and canal 27,128 hectares.

3.18 Tourist Spots

Courtallam is situated at the western ghats in Tenkasi taluk. The famous waterfalls on rocks and tiny droplets are sprinkled in the air. The water falls of Courtalam have medicinal value as they run through forest and herbs before their decent. Pappanasam Agasthiar falls also attracts tourist and pilgrims.There is a wild life sanctuary at Mundanthurai and Kalakadu. Spotted deers, liontailed monkeys, elephants and tigers are plenty.

3.19 Religious Significance

The Nellaiappar temple at Tirunelveli, Sankaranainar temple at Sankarankoil, Kasiviswanathar temple at Tenkasi and Vanamamalai Temple at Nanguneri are the land marks of the district signifying the Hindu culture. Palayamkottai has many Christian missions and Athankaraipallivasal and Pottalpudur Darga have considered to be important sacred places for Muslims.

3.20 Saral Festival - Courtallam

It is popularly said monsoon, happiness, waterfalls and Courtallam go hand in hand. The waterfalls on rocks and tiny droplets are sprinkled into the air, giving a fog-like appearance. The breeze carries this fog far. The phenomenon is called Saral in Tamil. This is the only spa of its kind in the south. During this festival, tourists come in droves from all over the country to participate in the ritualistic bathing. The falls are known for its therapeutic value. The Saral Festival is replete with cultural programmes, competitions, fun and frolic. A pleasant climate during the peak season sets the right mood for festivities.

3.21 Destinations of Scenic Beauty, Forests and Sanctuaries

3.21.1 Kalakkadu Wildlife Sanctuary

Kalakkadu Wildlife Sanctuary is situated in an area of 223 km^2 in the Tirunelveli district, including the foothills of western ghats and the adjoining area. The flora ranges from forests of tropical wet evergreen green to tropical dry deciduous and thorn forest at down hills. Liontailed Macaque, nilgiri langur, bonnet macaque and common langur, nilgiri tahr, sambar, sloth bear, gaur, elephant, tiger, flying squirrel, panther, wild dog, pangoline are some of the wild life seen in the sanctuary. Besides, a wide range of birds and reptiles could be seen. Trekking can be done with prior permission from the forest (wildlife) department. The place receives an annual rainfall of 1,000-4,000 mm annually. It enjoys the south-west and north-east monsoon. The best season is from September to March. The nearest airports are at Madurai, 200 km away, and at Trivandrum, 140 km away. The nearest railway station is Cheranmadevi, 20 km from here. The Kalakkadu Wildlife Sanctuary and the Mundanthurai Wildlife Sanctuary are situated in an extensive preserve declared as a Project Tiger Reserve.

3.21.2 Mundanthurai Wildlife Sancturay

There is nothing to differentiate this sanctuary from that of Kalakkadu, except the absence of the elephant and the gaur. Located in the Tirunelveli district, this 567 km^2 sanctuary of dry deciduous to tropical wet evergreen forests patches of pure reeds. Animal wealth includes tiger, bonnet macaque, langurs, slender loris, sloth bear, sambar, chital and wild dog. Sancturay is excellent for various species of avi-fauna and varieties of reptiles and insects. Trekking with prior permission from the forest (wildlife) department, along trekking trails can be undertaken. The place receives an annual rainfall of 1,000-4,000 mm annually. It enjoys the south-west and north-east monsoon. The best season is from October to January. The nearest airport is at Madurai, 200 km away. The nearest railway station is Ambasamudram only six kms away.

3.22 Overview of the Industrial Scenario

- Limestone is the major mineral available in Rastha, Thalaiyoothu, Sankar nagar and Padmaneri.
- Limestone available here contains Calcium oxide (CaO) from 34.57 per cent to 55.49 per cent, Magnesium Oxide (MgO) from 0.31 per cent to 7.24 per cent.
- Lime industries manufacturing lime powder, burnt lime and Cempowder numbering about 65 are available in Manur block.
- Red garnet sands and ilmenite are available in the river beds of Nambiyar, as well as in seashore lands of Radhapuram taluk.
- Garnet sand and abrasives are separated and exported.
- There are 25 numbers of medium and major industries functioning.
- Major products are cement, cotton yarn, sugar, cotton seed oil, printing paper and flour products.

3.23 Cottage and Handicraft Industry

- Handloom, mat weaving, basket making, palmirah products, poultry.

- Country bricks, tiles making, blacksmithing, carpentry.
- Metal and allied works, terracota products.
- Lacquer ware and wet grinding stone.

3.24 Infrastructure

- Electric power is sufficiently available.
- Thamirabarani, a perennial river is the main source of water.
- Well connected by roads and rails.
- Thoothukudi port is just 50 kms away from Tirunelveli.
- Air port is situated 30 kms away from Tirunelveli.
- Thoothukudi is connected by four way lane.
- Due to the literacy ratio of 77 per cent, sufficient educated manpower is sufficiently available.

3.25 Power Scenario

3.25.1 Kudankulam Atomic Power Project

- Location : Kudankulam, Tirunelveli district.
- Capacity : 2 × 1, 000 MW.

3.25.2 Wind Turbines

- Nos : 3, 622.
- Installed capacity : 1,555 MW.

3.25.3 Hydro Electric Power Plants

- Installed capacity : 233 MW.

3.26 Export Potentials of Tirunelveli District

- Coir pith block/coir products.
- Processed gherkins.
- Cashew products.
- Korai mat.
- Readymade garments.
- Terry towels and lungies.
- Herbal products.
- Ornamental wooden products.

3.27.1 Special Economic Zone Nanguneri

- A multi product SEZ is being formed in Nanguneri.
- Government of India granted formal approval AMR Construction and its associates are the JV partner with TIDCO.
- AMRL International Tech City Ltd., the JV of TIDCO, would implement this project in two phases.
- Project cost for creating infrastructure estimated at Rs 630 crore.
- Preliminary construction activities would commence by end of 2008
- Basic infrastructure proposed to be made in place by end of 2008.
- Nearest sea (major) port is Tuticorin @ 82 kms.
- Nearest domestic airport is Tuticorin @50 kms.
- Nearest international airports are Thiruvananthapuram and Chennai@ 135 kms and 600 kms respectively.

3.27.2 Sipcot Industrial Growth Centre - Gangaikondan

- Location : Gangaikondan village, Tirunelveli district.
- Total area of the complex : 1994.59 Acres.
- Area available for industrial plots : 1,543 Acres.
- Area, allotted so far : 729.57 Acres.
- Industries started production : 7 Nos.
- Products manufactured : Calcite powder, textiles, burnt lime, industrial Oxygen and bottling unit.
- Area for ELCOT IT Park : 400 Acres.

3.27.3 SIDCO Industrial Estate, Pettai

- Pettai Industrial Estate is having 54 sheds, 10 tiny sheds and 18 developed plots occupied fully.
- Pressure cooker utensils, coir mattress.
- Foundries, Engineering worksshop.
- Corrugated boxes, PVC, Plastic products.
- Strapping.

3.27.4 SIDCO Industrial Estate, Kadayanallur

- Have 10 sheds and 12 plots. Except five developed plots all sheds and plots have been occupied.
- Wooden furniture and c urled coir are the major products.

3.27.5 SIDCO Industrial Estate, Valliyoor

- Have 54 developed plots out of which 50 have been filled.

3.27.6 Overall Scenario After five Years

- Tirunelveli the expected fast developing "Information Technology Hub of the South" would bring more employment opportunities and related Industrial activities.
- The proposed IT Park at Gangaikondan and High Tech Park at Nanguneri would bring about change in the industrial climate and further opportunities under this sector.
- The district has been identified as one of the six districts under Agri Export Zone for Mango. More number of agro based and food processing industries would come up once AEZ will be set up.
- The New MSME Policy, 2008 would encourage the potential entrepreneurs to set up new ventures in Industrially backward blocks of this district, *viz,* Alangulam, Kadayam, Pappakudi, Kuruvikulam, Meelaneelithanallur, Nanguneri and other areas.

3.28 Conclusion

The district has diverse geographical and physical features such as lofty mountains and low plains, rivers and cascades, seacoast and thick inland forest, sandy soils and fertile alluvium, a variety of flora, fauna, and protected wild life. The glory of Tirunelveli district is the pride of Tamils. The crawling clouds on the western ghats, the picturesque Pothigai hills and the Courtallam waterfalls are the special features which make Tirunelveli unique. The district consists of all the five geographical divisions referred to in Tamil literature. The western ghats form the Kurinji (mountainous) region; the Kalakkadu and Mundanthurai forests form the Mullai (forest) region; the lands watered by the Tamiraparani and other rivers fall under Marudham (paddy fields); the Radhapuram sea coast is its neithal land (coastal) and the teri land forms the Palai (desert) region. The district is dotted with centres of natural beauty, pilgrimage, architectural eminence and memorials to great warriors of Indian independence. A brief profile of the study area is given above to get a better understanding of the study and the other analysis that follows.

Chapter-IV

Investment Avenues: An Overview

4.1 Introduction

Investing in various types of assets is an interesting activity that attracts people from all walks of life irrespective of their occupation, economic status, education and family background. When a person has more money than he requires for current consumption, he would be coined as a potential investor. The investor who is having extra cash could invest it in securities or in any other assets like gold or real estate or could simply deposit it in his bank account. The companies that have extra income may like to invest their money in the extension of the existing firm or undertake new venture. All of these activities in a broader sense mean investment.

Investment is the employment of funds on assets with the aim of earning income or capital appreciation. Investment has two attributes namely time and risk. Present consumption is sacrificed to get a return in the future. The sacrifice that has to be borne is certain but the return in the future may be uncertain. This attribute of investment indicates the risk factor. The risk is undertaken with a view to reap some return from the investment. For a layman, investment means some monetary commitment. A person's commitment to buy a flat or a house for his personal use may be an investment from his point of view. This cannot be considered as an actual investment as it involves sacrifice but does not yield any financial return. To the economist, investment is the net addition made to the nation's capital stock that consists of goods and services that are used in the production process. A net addition to the capital stock means an increase in the buildings, equipments or inventories. These capital stocks are used to produce other goods and services. Financial investment is the allocation of money to assets that are expected to yield some gain over a period of time. It is an exchange of financial claims such as stocks and bonds for money. They are expected to yield returns and experience capital growth over the years.

The financial and economic meanings are related to each other because the savings of the individual flow into the capital market as financial investments, to be used in economic investment. Even though they are related to each other, the study is concerned only about the financial investment made on securities.

4.2 Speculation

Speculation means taking up the business risk in the hope of getting short term gain. Speculation essentially involves buying and selling activities with the expectation of getting profit from the price fluctuations. For example, if a spouse buys a stock for its dividend, she may be termed as an investor. If she buys with the anticipation of price rise in the near future and the hope of selling it at a gain price she would be termed as a speculator. The dividing line between speculation and investment is very thin because people buy stocks for dividends and capital appreciation.

The time factor involved, in the speculation and investment is different. The investor is interested in consistent good rate of return for a longer period. He is primarily concerned with the direct benefits provided by the securities in the long run. The speculator is interested in getting abnormal return, i.e., extremely high rate of return than the normal return in the short run. Speculator's investments are made for short term. The speculator is more interested in the market action and its price movement. The investor constantly evaluates the worth of security whereas the speculator evaluates the price movement. He is not worried about the fundamental factors like his counterpart, the investor.

The investor would try to match the risk and return. The speculator would like to assume greater risk than the investors. Risk refers to the possibility of incurring loss in a financial transaction. The negative short term fluctuations affect the speculators in a worse manner than the investors. The risk factor involved in the investments is also limited. After studying the factors related with the concerned company's stock, the investor buys it and hence the risk exposure is limited. The investor likes to invest in securities where his principal would be safe.

Table 4.1: Investor Vs Speculator

Investor	*Investor*	*Investor*
Time	Plans for a longer time horizon.	Plans for a very short period. Holding period varies.
Horizon	His holding period may be from one year to few years.	From few days to months.
Risk	Assumes moderate risk.	Willing to undertake high risk.
Return	Likes to have moderate rate of return associated with limited risk.	Like to have high returns for assuming high risk.
Decision	Considers fundamental factors and evaluates the performance of the company regularly.	Considers inside information, hearsays and market behaviour.
Funds	Uses his own funds and avoids borrowed funds.	Uses borrowed funds to supplement his personal resources.

Source:

4.3 Gambling and Investment

A gamble is usually a very short term investment in a game or chance. Gambling is different from speculation and investment. The time horizon involved in gambling is shorter than speculation and investment. The results are determined by the roll of dice or the turn of a card. Secondly, people gamble as a way to entertain themselves, earning incomes would be the secondary factor. Thirdly, the risk in gambling is different from risk of the investment. Gambling employs artificial risks whereas commercial risks are present in the investment activity. There is no risk and return trade off in the gambling and the negative outcomes are expected. But in the investment, there is an analysis of risk and return. Positive returns are expected by the investors. Finally, the financial analysis does not reduce the risk proportion involved in the gambling.

4.4 Investment Objectives

The main investment objectives are increasing the rate of return and reducing the risk. Other objectives like safety, liquidity and hedge against inflation can be considered as subsidiary objectives.

Return: Investors always expect a good rate of return from their investments. Rate of return could be defined as the total income the investor receives during the holding period stated as a percentage of the purchasing price at the beginning of the holding period.

$$\text{Return} = \frac{\text{End period value-Beginning period value} + \text{Dividend}}{\text{Beginning period value}} \times 100.$$

Rate of return is stated semi-annually or annually to help comparison among the different investment alternatives. If it is a stock, the investor gets the dividend as well as the capital appreciation as returns. Market return of the stock indicates the price appreciation for the particular stock. If a particular share is purchased in 1998 at Rs 50, disposed at Rs 60 in 1999 and the dividend yield is Rs 5, then the return would be calculated as follows:

$$\text{Return} = \frac{\text{Capital appreciation and dividend}}{\text{Purchase price}} \times 100.$$

$$\text{Return} = \frac{10.5}{50} \times 100 = 30 \text{ per cent.}$$

Risk: Risk of holding securities is related with the probability of actual return becoming less than the expected return. The word risk is synonymous with the phrase variability of return. Investments' risk is just as important as measuring its expected rate of return because minimising risk and maximising the rate of return are interrelated objectives in the investment management. An investment whose rate of return varies widely from period to period is risky than whose return that does not change much. Every investor likes to reduce the risk of his investment by proper combination of different securities.

Liquidity: Marketability of the investment provides liquidity to the investment. The liquidity depends upon the marketing and trading facility. If a portion of the investment could be converted into cash without much loss of time, it would help the investor meet the emergencies. Stocks are liquid only if they command good market by providing adequate return through dividends and capital appreciation.

Hedge against Inflation: As there is inflation in almost all the economy, the rate of return should ensure a cover against the inflation. The return rate should be higher than the rate of inflation; otherwise the investor will sustain loss in real terms. Growth stocks would appreciate in their values overtime and provide a protection against inflation. The return thus earned should assure the safety of the principal amount, regular flow of income and be a hedge against inflation.

Safety: The selected investment avenue should be under the legal and regulatory frame work. If it is not under the legal frame work, it is difficult to represent the grievances, if any. Approval of the law itself adds a flavour of safety. Even though approved by law, the safety of the principal differs from one mode of investment to another. Investments done with the government assure more safety than with the private party. From the safety point of view investments can be ranked as follows: bank deposits, government bonds, UTI units, non-convertible debentures, convertible debentures, equity shares and deposits with the non-banking financial companies.

4.5 Financial Investments vs. Physical Investment

Many savers will have their first preference for physical investments which are less productive and rarely income earning. Such investments are in consumer goods - non-durables or durables, gold, silver, cars and antiques and 'curios.' These are satisfying the immediate consumer needs, for comfort, luxuries, social status, ego satisfaction, etc. Some investments of physical nature are more in real estate, land, buildings, etc. Some of them if rented out to others give income and sometimes capital appreciation also, if the location is at good places or commercial areas. Similarly, gold, silver and other metals, diamonds, and antiques may present capital appreciation, without giving any regular income. Some investments are for social status and prestige as gold, diamonds, jewellery, etc.

4.6 The Investment Process

The investment process involves a series of activities leading to the purchase of securities or other investment alternatives. The investment process can be divided into five stages: (i) framing of investment policy (ii) investment analysis (iii) valuation (iv) portfolio construction (v) portfolio evaluation. The flowchart 4.1 explains the stages and factors connected thereof.

Flow Chart 4.1: Investment Process

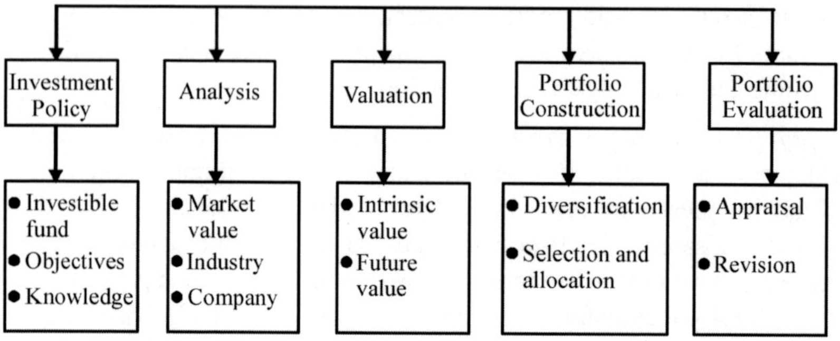

4.6.1 Investment Policy

The government or the investor before proceeding into investment formulates the policy for the systematic functioning. The essential ingredients of the policy are the investible funds objectives and the knowledge about the investments alternatives and market.

Investible Funds: The entire investment procedure revolves around the availability of investible funds. The fund may be generated through savings or from borrowings. If the funds are borrowed, the investor has to be extra careful in the selection of investment alternatives. The return should be higher than the interest he pays. Mutual funds invest their owner's money in securities.

Objectives: The objectives are framed on the premises of the required rate of return in the form of capital appreciation, whereas the primary objective of the risk averse is the safety of the principal.

Knowledge: The knowledge about the investment alternatives and markets plays a key role in the policy-formulation. The investment alternatives range from security to real estate. The risk and return associated with investment alternatives differ from each other. Investment in equity is high yielding but has more risk than the fixed income securities. The tax sheltered schemes offer tax benefits to the investors.

The investor should be aware of the stock market structure and the functions of the brokers. The mode of operation varies among BSE, NSE and OTCEI. Brokerage charges are also different. The knowledge about the stock exchanges enables him to trade the stock intelligently.

4.6.2 Security Analysis

After formulating the investment policy, the securities to be bought have to be scrutinised through the market, industry and company analysis.

Market Analysis: The stock market mirrors the general economic scenario. The growth in gross domestic product and inflation are reflected in the stock prices. The recession in the economy results in a bear market. The stock prices may be fluctuating in the short run but in the long run they move in trends, i.e., either upwards or downwards. The investor can fix his entry and exit points through technical analysis.

Industry Analysis: The industries that contribute to the output of the major segments of the economy vary in their growth rates and their overall contribution to economic activity. Some industries grow faster than the GDP and are expected to continue in their growth. For example. the information technology industry has experienced higher growth rate than the GDP in 1998. The economic significance and the growth potential of the industry have to be analysed.

Company Analysis: The purpose of company analysis is to help the investors to make better decisions. The company's earnings, profitability, operating efficiency, capital structure and management have to be screened. These factors have direct bearing on the stock prices and the return of the investors. Appreciation of the stock value is a function of the performance of the company. Company with high product market share is able to create wealth to the investors in the form of capital appreciation.

4.6.3 Valuation

The valuation helps the investor to determine the return and risk expected from an investment in the common stock. The intrinsic value of the share is measured through the book value of the share and price earnings ratio. Simple discounting models also can be adopted to value the shares. The stock market analysts have developed many advanced models to value the shares. The real worth of the share is compared with the market price and then the investment decisions are made.

Future Value: Future value of the securities could be estimated by using a simple statistical technique like trend analysis. The analysis of the historical behaviour of the price enables the investor to predict the future value.

4.6.4 Construction of Portfolio

A portfolio is a combination of securities. The portfolio is constructed in such a manner to meet the investor's goals and objectives. The investor should decide how best to reach the goals with the securities available. The investor tries to attain maximum return with minimum risk. Towards this end he diversifies his portfolio and allocates funds among the securities.

Diversification: The main objective of diversification is the reduction of risk in the loss of capital and income. A diversified portfolio is comparatively less risky than holding a single portfolio. There are several ways to diversify the portfolio.

Debt and Equity Diversification: Debt instruments provide assured return with limited capital appreciation. Common stocks provide income and capital gain but with the flavour of uncertainty. Both debt instruments and equity are combined to complement each other.

Industry Diversification: Industries' growth and their reaction to government policies differ from the other. Banking industry shares may provide regular returns but with limited capital appreciation. The information technology stock yields high return and capital appreciation. Thus, industry diversification is needed and it reduces risk.

Company Diversification: Securities from different companies are purchased to reduce risk. Technical analysts suggest the investors to buy securities based on the price movement. Fundamental analysts suggest the selection of financially sound and investor friendly companies.

Selection: Based on the diversification level, industry and company analyses the securities to be selected. Funds are allocated for the selected securities. Selection of securities and the allocation of funds constitute the construction of portfolio.

4.6.5 Evaluation

The portfolio has to be managed efficiently. The efficient management calls for evaluation of the portfolio. This process consists of portfolio appraisal and revision.

Appraisal: The return and risk performance of the security vary from time to time. The variability in returns of the securities is measured and compared. The developments in the economy, industry and relevant companies from which the stocks are bought have to be appraised. The appraisal warns the loss and steps can taken to avoid such losses.

Revision: Revision depends on the results of the appraisal. The low yielding securities with high risk are replaced with high yielding securities with low risk factor. To keep the return at a particular level necessitates the investor to revise the components of the portfolio periodically.

4.7 Investment Avenues

A bewildering range of investment alternatives is available. There are different methods of classifying the investment avenues. A major classification is Physical Investments and Financial Investments.

Flow Chart 4.2: Investment Activity

(Acquisition of Assets)

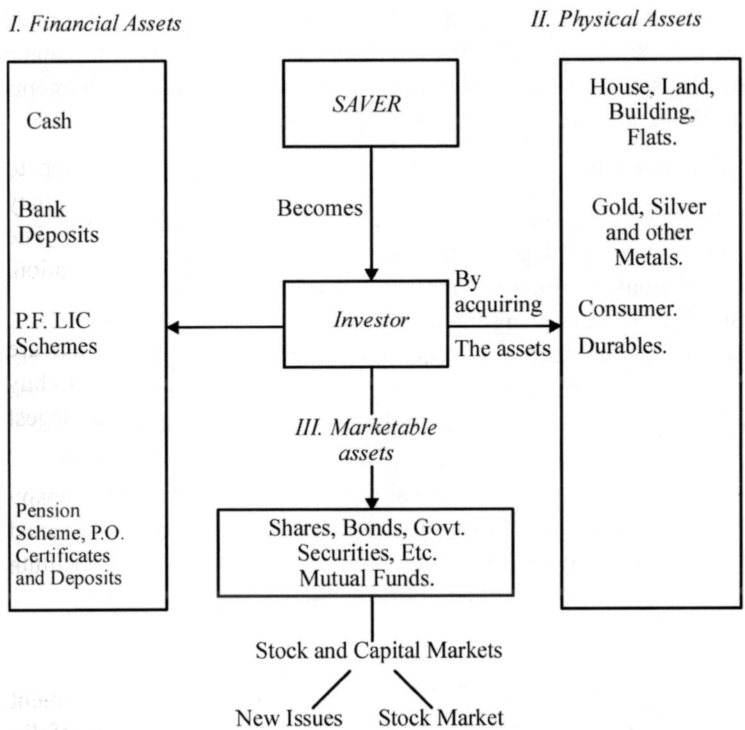

If savings are used to acquire physical assets, they are useful for consumption or production. Some physical assets like ploughs, tractors are useful in agricultural production. A few physical assets like lorries, cars, jeeps, etc, are useful to business. Many items of physical assets are not useful for further production of goods or to create income as in the case of consumer durables, gold, silver, etc. But most of the financial assets, barring cash are used for production or consumption or further creation of assets, useful for production of goods and services. Among different types of investment, some are marketable and transferable and others are not. Examples of marketable assets are shares and debentures of public limited companies, particularly the listed companies on Stock exchanges, bonds of PSUs, government securities, etc. Non-marketable securities or investments are bank deposits, provident and pension funds, insurance certificates, post office deposits, national savings certificates, company deposits, etc. These three types of assets are detailed in the chart above.

4.8. Financial Assets

Financial assets are intangible assets that derives value because of a contractual claim. Examples include bank deposits, bonds, and stocks. Financial assets are usually more liquid than tangible assets, such as land or real estate, and are traded on financial markets.

4.8.1 Bank Deposits

It is the simple investment avenue open for the investors. He has to open an account and deposit the money. Traditionally, the banks offered current account, savings account and fixed deposit account. Current account does not offer any interest rate. The drawback of having large amounts in savings accounts is that the return is just four and a half per cent. The savings account interest rate is regulated by the Reserve Bank of India and is kept low because of the high cost of servicing them. The savings account is more liquid and convenient to handle. The fixed account carries high interest rate and the money is locked up for a fixed period. With increasing competition among the banks, the banks have bundled the plain savings account with the fixed account to cater to the needs of the small savers. Some of the hybrid accounts are given below in the Table 4.2.

Table 4.2: Hybrid Accounts Offered by Banks

Bank	*Product*	*Nature*	*Min. Dep. (Rs.)*	*Other benefits*
ICICI Bank	Maxi cash	Savings account, savings with Auto-sweep facility through which standing instructions can be issued to transfer surplus funds of FD.	10, 000	ATM card, Internet banking and assistance in investing funds in money market instruments, anywhere banking and cheque book.

	Quantum-Optima	FD linked to savings account with Auto-sweep Reverse-sweep, Auto Renewal facilities.	25, 000	ATM card, Anywhere banking, Internet Banking, and overdraft facility.
IndusInd Bank	2-in-1 Account	Savings account with link to FD.	25, 000	Cheque book and overdraft facility.
	Cluster Deposits	Savings linked FD with Auto-sweep and Reverse-sweep.	25, 000	Cheque book.
HDFC Bank	Super saver account	Savings linked to FD.	25, 000	Overdraft, cheque book, ATM and phone banking.
	Sweep-in-account	Savings linked to FD with Reverse-Sweep and add-on-deposit.	25, 000	ATM, Cheque book and phone banking.

The deposits in the banks are considered to be safe because of the RBI regulation. The risk averse investors prefer the bank deposits.

4.8.2 NBFC Deposits

In recent years, there has been a significant increase in the importance of non-banking financial companies in the process of financial intermediation. The NBFC comes under the purview of the RBI. The amendment of RBI Act in January, 1997 made registration compulsory for the NBFCs.

(i) Period: The maturity period ranges from few months to five years. It varies from company to company. For example, the Birla Global Finance, the company belonging to Aditya Birla group accepts deposits with maturity from three to five years.

(ii) Maximum limit: The limit for acceptance of deposit has been based on the credit rating of the company. The NBFCs not having net owned funds of Rs 25 lakh are not entitled to accept deposits.

(iii) Interest: NBFCs offer interest rate higher than the commercial bank on public deposit. The interest rate differs according to maturity period. There is a disparity in the interest rate among the companies in accordance with the credit ratings and policies of the companies. Even the companies with similar credit ratings provide different interest rates for their deposits. Generally, companies with lower credit ratings offer higher interest rates to cover the risk.

(iv) Security: The deposits of the NBFCs is much lower than the deposits with banks. To improve the liquidity of NBFCs the percentage of liquid assets required to be maintained by them has been enhanced from 12.5 per cent to 15 per cent with effect from April 1999 respectively. Company Law Board is authorised to direct the defaulting NBFCs to repay the deposits. In spite of the strict rules and regulations laid down by RBI the default rate is high in the case of NBFCs.

4.8.3 Postal Savings and Deposits

1. Post office savings account

A post office savings account is similar to a savings bank account. It serves the need of regular deposits and withdrawals. Cheque facility is also available.

Its salient features are as follows:

- Interest payable is four per cent per annum on individual (or) joint accounts.
- Minimum Amount for opening of account Rs 20.
- Account can be opened by cash only.
- The interest is tax exempt.
- Cheque facility is available if an account is opened with Rs 500 and for this purpose minimum balance of Rs 500 is to be maintained.
- Minimum balance to be maintained in a non-cheque facility account is Rs 50.
- The maximum balance that can be held is Rs 50,000 for a single account and Rs 1,00,000 for a joint account.

2. Post Office Time Deposits (POTDS)

Similar to fixed deposits of commercial banks POTDS have the following features:

- Deposits can be made in multiplies of Rs 50 without any limit.
- The interest rates on POTDs are, in general, slightly higher than those on bank deposits.
- The interest is calculated half-yearly and paid annually. No withdrawal is permitted upto six months.
- Rate of interest - 8.20 per cent, 8.20 per cent, 8.30 per cent, 8.40 per cent compounded quarterly for one, two, three and five years Time Deposits account respectively.
- After six months, withdrawals are permitted. However, on withdrawals made between six months and one year, no interest is payable. On

withdrawals after one year, but before the term of deposit, interest is paid for the period the deposit has been held, subject to a penal deduction of two per cent.

- A POTD account can be pledged.
- Deposits in 10 years to 15 years Post Office Cumulative Time Deposit Account can be deducted before computing the taxable income under Section 80 C of the Income Tax Act, 1961.

3. Monthly Income Scheme of the Post Office (MISPO)

A popular scheme of the post office, the MISPO is meant to provide regular monthly income to the depositors. The salient features of this scheme are as follows:

- The term of the scheme is six years.
- The minimum amount of investment is Rs 1,000. The maximum investment can be Rs 3,00,000 in a single account or Rs 6,00,000 in a joint account.
- The interest rate is eight per cent per annum, payable monthly. A bonus of 10 per cent is payable on maturity. There is no tax deduction at source.
- There is a facility of premature withdrawal after one year, with five per cent deduction before three years.

4. Kisan Vikas Patra (KVP)

This deposit scheme was dropped from 1st December, 2011 onwards.

5. National Savings Certificate

(a) National savings certificates (NSC)(VIII) issue

- It is a fixed investment for five years on certificates of varied denominations.
- Pledging facility available for availing loan from Banks.
- From 1.4.2013, interest rates are as follows- eight and a half per cent compounded six monthly but payable at maturity. Rs 100 grows to Rs 151.62 after five years.
- Minimum Rs 100. No maximum limit. Available in denominations of Rs 100, 500, 1000, 5000 and Rs 10,000.
- Deposits qualify for tax rebate under Section 80 C of IT Act.

(b) National Savings certificates (IX) issue

- Fixed investment tenure of 10 years.
- 8.80 per cent compounded six monthly but payable at maturity. Rs 100 grows to INR 236.60 after 10 years.

- Minimum Rs 100 No maximum limit. Available in denominations of Rs 100, 500, 1000, 5000 and Rs 10,000.
- Deposits qualify for tax rebate under Section 80 C of IT Act.

6. Postal Life Insurance (PLI)

It was introduced on 1st February, 1884 with the express approval of the Secretary of State (for India) to Her Majesty, the Queen Empress of India. It was essentially a scheme of State Insurance mooted by the then Director General of Post Offices, Mr F.R. Hogg in 1881 as a welfare scheme for the benefit of postal employees and later extended to the employees of telegraph department in 1888. In 1894, PLI extended insurance cover to female employees of P and T Department at a time when no other insurance company covered female lives. It is the oldest life insurer in this country.

In the beginning, the upper limit of life insurance was only Rs 4,000 which has now increased to Rs 10 lacs (Rupees Ten Lacs) for all schemes combined—Endowment Assurance and Whole Life Assurance. Over the years, PLI has grown substantially from a few hundred policies in 1884 to 42,83,302 policies as on 31.03.2010. It now covers employees of Centre and State Governments, Centre and state public sector undertakings, universities, government aided educational institutions, nationalised banks, local bodies, etc. PLI also extends the facility of insurance to the officers and staff of the defence services and para-military forces. Apart from single insurance policies, postal life insurance also manages a group insurance scheme for the extra departmental employees (*Gramin Dak Sevaks*) of the Department of Posts.

PLI is an exempted insurer under Section 118 (c) of the Insurance Act of 1938. It is also exempted under Section 44 (d) of LIC Act, 1956.

PLI offers Seven types of plans:

1. Whole Life Assurance (Suraksha).
2. Convertible Whole Life Assurance (Suvidha)
3. Endowment Assurance (Santosh).
4. Anticipated Endowment Assurance (Sumangal).
5. Joint Life Assurance (Yugal Suraksha).
6. Scheme for Physically handicapped persons.
7. Children Policy.

PLI is the only insurer in the indian life insurance market today, which gives the highest return (bonus) with the lowest premium charged for any product in the market.

7. Rural Postal Life Insurance (RPLI)

It came into being as a sequel to the recommendations of the Official Committee for Reforms in the insurance sector (Malhotra Committee). The Committee had observed in 1993 that only 22 per cent of the insurable population in this country had been insured; life insurance funds accounted for only 10 per cent of the gross household savings. The Committee understands that rural branch postmasters who enjoy a position of trust in the community have the capacity to canvass life insurance business within their respective areas.

The government accepted the recommendations of Malhotra Committee and allowed postal life insurance to extend its coverage to the rural areas to transact life insurance business with effect from 24.3.1995, mainly because of the vast network of post offices in the rural areas and low cost of operations. The prime objective of the scheme is to provide insurance cover to the rural public in general and to benefit weaker sections and women workers of rural areas in particular and also to spread insurance awareness among the rural population.

RPLI offers following types of plans:

1. Whole Life Assurance (Grama Suraksha).
2. Convertible Whole Life Assurance (Grama Suvidha).
3. Endowment Assurance (Grama Santosh).
4. Anticipated Endowment Assurance (Grama Sumangal).
5. Gram Priya.
6. Scheme for Physically handicapped persons.

Table 4.3: Growth Rate of RPLI

	Rural Postal Life Insurance (RPLI)		
Year	*No. of Policies in Force*	*Sum Assured (in Rs Crore)*	*Corpus of Fund (in Rs Crore)*
2001-2002	11,33,013	4,403.92	341.05
2002-2003	17,95,070	7,464.53	510.69
2003-2004	26,66,485	12,385.11	756.48
2004-2005	37,38,798	18,520.93	1,127.61

2005-2006	47,02,776	25,229.66	1,624.77
2006-2007	52,46,673	33,865.65	2,284.92
2007-2008	61,67,928	41,846.09	3,003.78
2008-2009	73,56,446	53,072.10	3,994.36

Source: *Postal Annual Report, 2010.*

4.8.4 Life Insurance

1. Introduction

A contract in which the insurer undertakes to pay a certain sum of money to the insured, either on the expiry of a specified period, or on the death of the insured, in consideration of payment of 'premium' for a certain period of time, is known as 'life insurance'. It is typically called 'life assurance'. Life insurance serves the purpose of protection, as well as an investment contract. It is a protection contract because it gives protection to the assured in the event of death, by making payment of the entire amount of the 'sum assured'. It is an investment contract, too, as it gives the assured/investor the advantage of regaining the money with interest and bonus at the end of the policy.

2. Insurance Contract

A contract whereby one party, called the 'insurer or insurance company', undertakes to compensate the other party called the 'insured', for any loss or damage suffered by the latter, in consideration of payment of 'premium' for a certain period of time, is known as 'insurance'.

3. Basic Principles of Insurance

A contract of insurance is required to possess the following essential characteristics:

(a) Good Faith: A contract of insurance is based on the principle of 'utmost good faith'. Accordingly, both parties to the contract are required to disclose all material facts. The rule of 'caveat emptor' is not applicable in the case of insurance.

(b) Insurable Interest: The insured party is required to have an insurable interest on the object on which the insurance policy is taken. Insurable interest is required to be present both at the time of the contract, as well as at the time of loss. Insurance interest refers to the pecuniary or financial interest possessed by the beneficiary, which is the insured party, on the object being insured for. This implies that loss or damage caused to such an object would cause financial loss to the insured party.

(c) Compensation: An insurance contract undertakes to indemnify the insured for any loss or damage sustained due to the risk against which it is insured. This is applicable only to the general insurance business, where it is possible to calculate the loss or the damage in terms of money. The amount of compensation depends on the value of the insurance policy, and not on the value of the object insured.

(d) Subrogation: The term 'subrogation' refers to stepping into the shoes of others. Accordingly, an insurer can step into the shoes of an insured, and become entitled to all the rights and privileges of the insured in relation to the insured object, after making payment to the insured. Under this doctrine, the property in the object will pass on to the insurance company after the payment of insurance claims.

(e) Contribution: According to this principle, the amount of compensation forthcoming from an insurance company would depend proportionately on the amount for which the insurance policy has undertaken to compensate for the loss. This is applicable in the case of 'double insurance', whereby the insured insures the object with more than one insurance company.

(f) Loss Mitigation: In order that the insurance company makes a reasonable payment of claims, it is necessary that the insured party takes all the necessary steps to mitigate the risk of loss in the event that the contingency insured against occurs. The insured must act as a person of ordinary prudence, and should make all reasonable efforts to minimise the loss.

(g) Causa Proxima: According to this principle, risk coverage is available to the insured party, provided the loss has occurred directly from such events as specified in the insurance policy.

4.8.4.1 Life Insurance Policies

Some of the popular types of life assurance policies are as follows:

1. *Whole Life Policy:* An ordinary policy which runs throughout the life of the assured is known as 'whole life policy'. The sum assured under this policy is payable only after the death of the assured. The premium payable is low, and is meant to protect the family. This policy offers the advantage of an investment for a life term.

2. *Endowment Policy:* The policy runs for a period as specified in the policy document. The sum assured along with the bonuses, are payable either on the date of maturity of the policy, or on the death of the assured whichever occurs earlier. This policy offers the advantage of both protection and investment.

3. ***Annuity Policy:*** Under this policy, the amount of the policy is paid in the form of annuities for a specified number of years, or till the death of the assured.

4. ***Joint Life Policy:*** When the insurance policy covers the lives of two or more persons, it is called 'Joint life policy'.

5. ***Group Insurance Policy:*** When an insurance policy is taken out on the lives of the members of a family, or the employees of a business concern, it is called 'group insurance policy'.

4.8.4.2 Life Insurers

In addition to the LIC of India, the following companies have been registered with the IRDA for providing life insurance services:

Table 4.4: Registered Life Insurers in India

Sl.No.	*Name of the Life Insurance Companies*	*Date of Registration*
1.	HDFC Standard Life Insurance Company Ltd	23.10.2000
2.	Max New York Insurance Company Limited	15.11.2000
3.	ICICI Prudential Life Insurance Co. Limited	24.11.2000
4.	Kotak Mahindra Life Insurance Co Ltd	10.01.2001
5.	Birla Sun Life Insurance Company Limited	12.01.2001
6.	Tata AIG Life Insurance Company Limited	12.02.2001
7.	SBI Life Insurance Company Limited	30.03.2001
8.	ING Vysya Life Insurance Company Limited	02.08.2001
9.	Allianz Bajaj Life Insurance Company Limited	03.08.2002
10.	Metlife India Insurance Company Pvt Ltd	06.08.2001
11.	AMP SANMAR Assurance Company Limited	03.01.2002
12.	Dabur CGU Life Insurance Company Pvt Ltd	14.05.2002

Source: *IRDA Annual Report, 2010.*

4.8.4.3 Life Insurance Corporation of India (LIC)

The Insurance Act, 1938 was the first legislation governing not only life insurance but also non-life insurance to provide strict state control over insurance business. The demand for nationalisation of life insurance industry was made repeatedly in the past but it gathered momentum in 1944 when a bill to amend the Life Insurance Act, 1938 was introduced in the legislative assembly. However, it was much later on the

19th of January, 1956, that life insurance in India was nationalised. About 154 Indian insurance companies, 16 non-Indian companies and 75 provident were operating in India at the time of nationalisation. Nationalisation was accomplished in two stages; initially the management of the companies was taken over by means of an Ordinance, and later, the ownership, too, by means of a comprehensive bill. The Parliament of India passed the Life Insurance Corporation Act on the 19th of June 1956, and the Life Insurance Corporation of India was created on 1st September, 1956, with the objective of spreading life insurance much more widely and in particular to the rural areas with a view to reach all insurable persons in the country, providing them adequate financial cover at a reasonable cost.

4.8.4.4 Objectives

The LIC of India was set up to achieve the following objectives:

1. ***Wide Coverage:*** To spread life insurance widely, in particular to the rural areas and to the socially and economically backward classes, with a view to reaching all insurable persons in the country and in order to provide them adequate financial cover at a reasonable cost against death.

2. ***Savings Mobilisation:*** To maximise mobilisation of people's savings by making insurance-linked savings adequately attractive.

3. ***Funds Investment:*** To make a judicious investment of funds to the best advantage of investors as well as the community as a whole, keeping in view national priorities and the obligations of an attractive return.

4. ***Economy:*** To conduct business with utmost economy, and with the full realisation that the amount belong to the policy holders.

5. ***Trustee:*** To act as a trustee of the insured public in their individual and collective capacities.

6. ***Meeting Growing Needs:*** To meet the various life insurance needs of the community that would arise in the changing social and economic environment.

7. ***Efficient Service:*** Involve all people working in the Corporation to the best of their capability in furthering the interests of the insured public by providing efficient service with courtesy.

8. ***Motivating People:*** To promote amongst all agents and employees of the Corporation a sense of participation, pride and job satisfaction through discharge of their duties with dedication towards achievement of the corporation's objective.

4.8.4.5 Superiority of Life Insurance

The various policies offered by LIC are considered superior on account of the following reasons:

1. ***Protection:*** Savings through life insurance guarantees full protection to the insured against risk of death. In life insurance, the full sum assured is payable in the event of death, (with bonuses wherever applicable) whereas in other savings schemes, only the amount saved (with interest) is payable.

2. ***Aid to Thrift:*** Life insurance encourages 'thrift'. Long-term savings can be made in a relatively 'painless' manner because of the 'easy installment' facility built into the scheme (method of paying premium is monthly, quarterly, half-yearly or yearly.

3. ***Liquidity:*** Loans can be raised on the sole security of a policy which has acquired loan value. Besides, a life insurance policy is also generally accepted as security even for a commercial loan.

4. ***Tax Relief:*** Tax relief from income tax and wealth tax is also available for amounts paid as premium for life insurance, subject to income tax rates in force. Assessee can avail tax relief in accordance of the provisions in the law. In such cases, the assured pays in effect a lower premium for insurance than that would have to be paid otherwise.

5. **Easy Money:** A suitable insurance plan, or a combination of different plans, can be taken out to meet specific needs that are likely to arise in future, such as children's education, start-in-life or marriage provision or even periodical needs for cash over a stretch of time.

Medical and Non-medical Schemes

Life insurance normally requires a medical examination. However, to facilitate greater spread of insurance, and as a measure of relaxation, LIC has been extending insurance cover without any medical examination, subject to certain conditions.

With Profit and Without Profit Plans

An insurance policy can be 'with' or 'without' profit. In the former, bonuses disclosed, if any, after periodical valuations are allotted to the policy, and are payable to the assured along with the contracted amount. In 'without' profit plan, the contracted amount is paid without any addition. The premium rate charged for a 'with profit policy, is, therefore, higher than a 'without profit policy'.

4.8.5 Employee Provident Fund

Each employee has a separate provident fund account in which both the employer and employee are required to contribute a certain minimum amount on a monthly basis.

- The employee can choose to contribute additional amounts, subject to certain restrictions.
- While the contribution made by the employer is fully tax exempt (from the point of view of the employee), the contributions made by the employee can be deducted before computing the taxable income under Section 80 C of the Income Tax Act, 1961.
- Provident fund contributions currently earn a compound interest rate of eight and a half per cent per annum that is totally exempt from taxes. The interest however is accumulated in the provident fund account and is not paid annually to the employee.
- The balance in the provident fund account is fully exempt from wealth tax. Further, it is not subject to attachment under any order or decree of a court. Within certain limits, the employee is eligible to take a loan against the provident fund balance pertaining to his contributions only.

4.8.6 Public Provident Fund Scheme

One of the most attractive investment avenues available in India is the Public Provident Fund (PPF) Scheme which has the following features:

- Individuals and HUFs can participate in this scheme. A PPF account may be opened at any branch of the State Bank of India or its subsidiaries or at specified branches of the other public sector banks.
- Though the period of a PPF account is stated to be 15 years, the number of contribution-year has to be 16. This is because the 15 years period is calculated from the financial year following the date on which the account is opened. Thus, a PPF account matures on the first day of the 17th year.
- The subscriber to a PPF account is required to make a minimum deposit of Rs 100 per year. The maximum permissible deposit per year is Rs 70,000. Deposits in a PPF account can be deducted before computing the taxable income under Section 80 C.
- PPF deposits currently earn a compound interest rate of eight per cent per annum, which is totally exempt from taxes. The interest, however, is accumulated in the PPF account and is not paid annually to the subscriber.

- The balance in a PPF account is fully exempt from wealth tax. Further, it is not subject to attachment under any order or decree of a court.
- The subscriber to a PPF account is eligible to take a loan from the third year to the sixth year after opening the PPF account. The amount of loan cannot exceed 25 per cent of the balance standing to the credit of the PPF account at the end of the second preceding financial year. The interest payable on such a loan is one per cent higher than the PPF account interest rate.
- The subscriber to a PPF account can make one withdrawal every year from the sixth year to the 15th year. The amount of withdrawal cannot exceed 50 per cent of the balance at the end of the fourth preceding year or the year immediately preceding the year of withdrawal, whichever is lower, less the amount of loan, if any. The withdrawal can be put to any use and is not required to be refunded.
- On maturity, the credit balance in a PPF account can be withdrawn. However, at the option of the subscriber, the account can be continued for three successive block periods of five years each, with or without deposits. During the extensions the account holder can make one withdrawal per year, subject to the condition that the total amount withdrawn during a five-year block does not exceed 60 per cent of the balance to the credit of the account at the beginning,

4.8.7 Pension Plan

A pension plan or an annuity is an investment that is made either in a single lump sum payment or through installments paid over a certain number of years, in return for a specific sum that is received every year, every half-year or every month, either for life or for a fixed number of years. Annuities differ from all the other forms of life insurance. In that an annuity does not provide any life insurance cover but offers a guaranteed income either for life or a certain period.

Typically, annuities are bought to generate income during one's retired life, which is why they are also called pension plans. By buying an annuity or a pension plan, the annuitant receives guaranteed income throughout his life. He also receives lump sum benefits for the annuitant's estate in addition to the payments during the annuitant's lifetime. Pension plans are perfect investment instrument for a person who after retiring from service has received a large sum as superannuation benefit. He can invest the proceeds in a pension plan as it is safest way of secured income for the rest of his life. One can pay for a pension plan either through an annuity or through installments that are annual in most cases.

4.8.8 Types of Annuities/Pension Plans

Life Annuity

It guarantees the investor a specified amount of income for his life. After death, the amount invested is refunded to his nominee.

Guaranteed Period Annuity

It provides specified income for the investor's lifetime and guarantees that his nominee will receive payments for a certain minimum number of years, even if the investor die earlier. In case the investor lives longer than the specified minimum number of years, the investor is entitled to receive annuity payments for his lifetime.

Annuity Certain

Under this plan, the stipulated annuity is paid for a fixed number of years. The annuity payments stop at the end of that period, irrespective of how much longer the investor may live.

Deferred Annuities

The premiums paid into such plans may be deducted from one's taxable income at the time of payment. In addition, the interest earned on the annuities is not taxed immediately. But the proceeds of the annuity will be taxable when they are paid to the investor.

Pension Fund Regulatory and Development Authority (PFRDA)

In India, formal pension schemes only cover 12 per cent of the working population. Only government employees and workers in the organised private sector were covered by these schemes. It was felt necessary to increase the coverage of the government pension scheme. But the existing form of pension support for government employees was also putting fiscal pressure on the government. These two considerations led to pension reforms in India for both Central Government and for unorganised sectors. On January 1, 2004 the government launched a New Pension System (NPS). The move shifted all new Central Government employees (except for armed forces) to a defined contribution plan from the current noncontributory defined benefit scheme, shifting the risk of retirement financing from the government to individuals. Participants in the new scheme will have access to a range of investment products from selected private sector companies. The NPS would be open on a voluntary basis to non-government workers, including those in the unorganised private sector. An important element of the reform was to set up a proper regulatory framework. The role of Pension Fund Regulatory and Development Authority (PFRDA) is to consolidate the initiatives taken so far regarding the full New Pension System and expanding the reach of the distribution network of NPS. The NPS architecture allows a subscriber to monitor his/her investments and returns under NPS, the choice of Pension Fund Manager (PFM) and the investment option would also rest with the subscriber. The design allows the subscriber to switch his/her investment options as well as pension funds. PFRDA has set up a Trust under the Indian Trusts Act, 1882 to oversee the functions of the PFMs. PFRDA also intends to intensify its effort towards financial education and awareness as a part of its strategy to protect the interest of the subscribers. PFRDA's efforts are an important milestone in the development of a sustainable and efficient voluntarily defined contribution based pension system in India. However, PFRDA set up as a regulatory body for pension sector, is yet to get statutory powers as the Bill pertaining to that effect lapsed in Parliament with the expiry of last Lok Sabha in 2009.

4.8.9 Chit Funds

Origin

The concept of chit funds originated more than 1,000 years ago. Initially, it was in the form of an informal association of traders and households within communities, wherein the members contributed some money in return for an accumulated sum at the end of the tenure. Participation in chit funds were mainly for the purpose of purchasing some property, or in other words, for 'consumption' purposes. However, in recent times, there has been tremendous alteration in the constitution and functioning of chit funds. With the advent of the Chit Funds Act, initially in the year 1961 (Madras Act) and amended subsequently in the year 1982 (Central Act). Chit funds have been highly regulated and governed by stringent rules. The purpose of the said Act and its proposed benefit to the chit funds industry is, however, questionable.

Workings of Chits

A chit scheme generally has a predetermined value and duration. Each scheme admits a particular number of members (generally equal to the duration of the scheme), who contribute a certain sum of money every month (or everyday) to the 'pot'. The 'pot' is then auctioned out every month. The highest bidder (also known as the prized subscriber) wins the 'pot' for that month. The bid amount is also called the 'discount' and the prized subscriber wins the sum of money equal to the chit value less the discount. The discount money is then distributed among the rest of the members (or the non-prized subscribers) as 'dividend' and in the subsequent month, the required contribution is brought down by the amount of dividend.

Regulations and Costs of Registration

Registration of a chit scheme entails numerous fee payments and other formalities, such as filing of returns, maintaining minutes of the meeting, auditing of accounts and soon, that need to be satisfied by the chit manager. The Registrar of Chits of a particular jurisdiction is responsible for registering the chit funds in that jurisdiction. As a firststep in the formation of a group or scheme, prior sanction needs to be obtained from the Registrar. The prior sanction is granted at the filing of an application and at the payment of fees of Rs 50. Subsequently, the company needs to file a chit agreement with every member in that particular group. The fee for the purpose is around Rs 20 per member. Once the chit agreement is filed and approved, the certificate for commencement of the scheme is issued.

The chit manager needs to deposit 100 per cent of the chit value with the Registrar prior to the commencement of the scheme. This deposit will be refunded to the chit manager on the successful completion of the chit cycle. Normally, in the first month of each scheme, there will be no auction, and the amount collected from the members would be taken by the company to compensate for the deposit made. However, as this would be considered unfair to the members (who will lose the entire contribution in that particular month) the chit manager also takes part in the group and makes regular monthly contributions to the scheme. Therefore, in essence, the chit manager is the bidder in the first month who takes a loan to make the deposit.

The registration process generally takes around two months to complete. There is no subsequent requirement for renewal of the registration. Once the scheme commences, the chit manager has to file the minutes of each auction with the Registrar every month along with a fee of around Rs four. Other costs of registration include fees payable on transfer of membership and on any other filing requirement that may arise during the course of the scheme. The total quantum of fees to be paid by a chit manager was raised by 200 per cent in 2003 by the Tamil Nadu Government's Order Revision of Fees under Chit Funds Act, 1982.

A registered chit fund needs to have its accounts audited by a qualified Chartered Accountant. The fixed deposit made at the beginning of the scheme will be refunded only on the submission of the audited Balance Sheet and Statement of Accounts. The Act also requires all registered chit funds to impose a 30 per cent (now increased to 40 per cent) cap on the bidding amount. This 30 per cent (or 40 per cent) is calculated on the chit value of the scheme. This bid-cap is administered to ensure that the bid does not rise uncontrollably leading to subsequent default by the bidder. The minimum bid is restricted to five per cent of the chit value which is the foreman's commission.

According to the chit managers, the registration of chit funds ensures more transparency and accountability in its operations, which in turn helps to boost the confidence of the members. The risk involved in a registered chit fund is far less than in an unregistered fund, even though the cost involved is higher. And of course, in case of defaults by the parties involved, there is the possibility of legal recourse. More importantly, registration of chit funds leads to more revenue for the exchequer.

Use of the Chit Money to the Investors

Chit managers do not require the members to specify the purpose to which they deploy the funds. Generally, chit loans are used by households for consumption purposes like marriages, buying property (land, vehicle etc.) and education. It is primarily considered a means to saving free cash by the women of the household in order to provide for any contingencies that may arise in the future. Sometimes, the chit fund loans may also be used to settle outstanding loans with the money lenders. The chit member may use the 'pot' to pay off the money lender loan which is at a much higher rate and thus save money. Such members, who have several loans from varied sources, may run the risk of defaulting in some cases, as they may be caught in the 'vicious circle of debt' or the 'debt trap'.

4.9 Physical Assets

Definition

Physical assets are defined as an item of economic, commercial or exchange value that has a tangible or material existence. For most businesses, physical assets usually refer to cash, equipment, inventory and properties owned by the business. Physical assets are the opposite of intangible assets, which are non-physical assets such as leases, computer programmes or agreements.

4.9.1 Gold

Gold, the shining yellow metal is one of the most popular investment options. It is considered as a safe instrument against all national, political and cultural crises. Traditionally, gold has been considered as the most favoured currency of the world's population. The value of gold is negatively correlated to shares. When the economy is not stable, the price of gold appreciates. The advantage of investing in gold is it improves the consistency of the investments. A majority of the financial planners recommends around 15-20 per cent allocation of the total portfolio in Gold.

Reasons for Investing in Gold

From time immemorial, gold and silver has been purchased and owned by us in the form of ornaments and jewellery but these metals were never treated at par with conventional investment products like shares, debentures, FDs, PPF, and mutual funds etc. But in the changing investment scenario, gold is now taking a prominent place among investment products.

Broad Four Reasons for Investing in Gold

(a) Risky Stock Markets

Owing to wild fluctuations in stock market, people are uncertain about their investments. Almost all financial markets are now a days uncertain and volatile and factors like inflation rising cost of fuel, a decreasing index in GDP etc., would also affect the investments adversely.

(b) Gold Acts as a Deterrent Towards Inflation and Dollar

Often Gold acts a deterrent towards rising inflation and controls Indian currency against fluctuating foreign currency as gold is inversely related with Dollar. That is to say, when Dollar weakens, gold gains.

(c) High Rate of Return

Though gold has been a popular investment option so far, the present trend of rising gold prices has been valid reason for investing in gold for better returns.

(d) The Demand-Supply Gap

The international demand for gold has been increasing steadily like 15 per cent an year and the annual domestic demand for gold has reached 23 per cent which is the highest in the world. Since the yellow metal is less in supply and high in demand in India, gold prices have been soaring high (close to Rs 30,800) in June 2012.

Apart from the reasons mentioned above, if you want to diversify your portfolio from the conventional mode of investment instruments, then investing in gold is a valid option available to an investor.

Form of Invest in Gold

Investment in gold can be made in two forms, i.e., in Physical form and in non-physical form. Investment in physical gold is in form of coins/bars in addition to the jewellery which every household use. Whereas non-physical form of investment should be in the form of Gold Exchange Traded Fund (A Financial product designed to give an opportunity to the investors to invest in gold without taking the physical custody of the yellow metal). Most of the banks are selling gold coins/ bars where one can invest to get healthy returns. Many banks and few private organisations also provide the option of gold loans to their customers.

Trading in Gold can be Made in Three Ways

(a) ***Trade in Gold—Spot Market:*** For the first time in the history of Indian commodity market, National Spot Exchange has launched a unique investment product in gold on its platform. NSEL has launched its first product under the e-Series as e-Gold on Wednesday, the 17th March, 2010. NSEL has made necessary arrangements with National Securities Depository Limited (NSDL) and Central Services Depository (India) Ltd (CDSL) as the depository for holding commodity units in the electronic form. It provides an opportunity for small investors to invest in gold in smaller denominations like one gram and multiple thereof in demat form. Trading in spot market is offered by National Spot Exchange Ltd (NSEL). NSEL provides a product 'e-Gold' which can be purchased and sold online through a trading account like shares. NSEL came with the objective to develop a convenient and cost effective platform for buying and selling physical gold by providing an option of holding gold electronically (in Demat account). This contract can be purchased in multiples of 1 gram and the settlement period of e-Gold contract is T + 2 system. One has to pay the full amount of the contract. You can either take delivery of the gold or can keep the gold with the exchange custody by paying nominal charges. Example of broking houses who deals in e-Gold are Globe, Religare, Karvy, Alankit, BNP Paribas, Master Capital, India Infoline and Aditya Birla. Liquidity, i.e., any time buying and selling of commodity is possible with hassle free low cost transaction in physical commodity. There is no risk of commodity custody/theft. The storage charges of holding gold in demat form is Rs 0.50 to 0.60 per unit/month app. The price of the three contracts is visible on the website of NSEL, and once you buy a contract, it will be credited to your demat account after settlement. One can hold the e-Series products in Demat form, and always have the option of converting it into physical form—this is known as rematerialisation. There are 89 registered members till now in different parts of the country who are authorised to convert e-gold certificates into physical form.

(b) *Trade in Gold—Future Market:* It started operations in November 2003, today; MCX holds a market share of over 85 per cent (as on March 31, 2012 MCX had a market share of 86 per cent) of the Indian commodity futures market. The Exchange has more than 2,170 registered members operating through over 3,46,000 including CTCL trading terminals spread over 1,577 cities and towns across India. MCX was the third largest commodity futures exchange in the world, in terms of the number of contracts traded in the 2011. Gold futures trading happens in the Multi-commodity Exchange and also in the National Commodity (MCX) and Derivatives Exchange (NCDEX). The Exchange is the world's largest exchange in silver and gold, second largest in natural gas and the third largest in crude oil with respect to the number of futures contracts traded. In MCX, there are six contracts in gold. Gold (one kg), Gold Guinea (eight gram), Gold HNI (10 gram), Gold M (100 gram) and Gold Petal (one gram) and Gold Mini (10 gram). The contract is settled on the expiry date before which the trader has to settle the contract amount by selling it or by paying the full value to take full delivery of the commodity. If anyone wants to trade in volumes, trading in futures market is the best option available. The initial margin money requirement on a 100 gram gold future is Rs 9,000.

(c) *Trade in Gold- ETF:* ETF or Exchange Traded Funds are mutual fund scheme which invest in gold. Gold ETFs are listed on the stock exchange and can be bought and sold during the stock market trading hours. Exchange-traded funds, or ETFs, are so hot right now because they give good returns. ETFs allow investors to purchase an entire index with the, same convenience and cost of buying a single stock. ETFs are defined as the 'exchange-traded' part of exchange-traded fund means that investors can buy and sell ETF shares on major stock markets all day long. An ETF is an Exchange Traded Fund that is traded on major stock exchanges like NSE or BSE. Unlike individual stocks, however, ETFs hold numerous companies that share a common bond. Stocks comprising an ETF may belong to the same index (like the Dow Jones Industrial Average) or all share the same size and industry (for example, small-cap financial stocks). The Gold ETF Scheme will purchase a large amount of physical gold and store it. Shares are issued based on the value of gold holdings. The value of the shares will increase/decrease with the rise/fall in price of gold bullion. If the price of gold goes up by 10 per cent, then individual shares would increase in value by the same 10 per cent and vice versa. There are thirty seven gold ETF'S available in India (as on July 25th, 2012) out of which the ETF'S which gives more than eight per cent six monthly returns are selected which are as follows:

Table 4.5: Indian Best Gold Exchange Traded Funds on 25.07.2012

Sl. No.	*Name of the Gold Exchange Traded Fund*	*Rate of return*
1.	SBI Gold ETF	9.31 per cent
2.	Gold Benchmark ETF	9.47 per cent
3.	UTI Gold ETF	9.26 per cent
4.	Kotak Gold ETF	9.46 per cent
5.	Reliance Gold ETF	9.47 per cent
6.	Quantum Gold ETF	9.21 per cent
7.	Religare Gold	9.33 per cent
8.	HDFC Gold ETFs	9.45 per cent
9.	ICICI Prudential Gold ETF	9.34 per cent
10.	Birla Sun Life Gold ETFs	9.37 per cent
11.	Axis Gold ETF	9.12 per cent

Source: money.rediff.com.

Before an investor decides to invest in gold ETF; he needs to understand 'gold as an investment option'. Basically every portfolio should have exposure to gold ETF as it reduces volatility in a well-diversified portfolio. It also protects the capital against inflation and provides inflation plus returns to the investors.

Gold ETFs and Tax under Income Tax Act, 1961

Under the Income Tax Act, gains from Gold ETFs are treated like non-equity mutual funds. If the Gold ETF is held for less than one year, it attracts Short Term Capital Gains (STCG) tax @ 15 per cent. If the Gold

ETF is held for a period of more than a year, long term capital tax is applicable @10 per cent.

Gold ETFs *vs* Physical Gold

Gold ETFs are held in demat/electronic form and normally are traded on a stock exchange similar to stocks. Gold ETFs are also called as paper gold as it is gold held by investor in a paper form. However, in case of physical gold, the buyer takes possession of the gold. Returns from Gold ETFs are almost similar to returns from physical gold as they are passively managed and the fund closely tracks the performance and yield of gold in the spot market. Investing in gold ETFs gives investors tax advantages over investing in physical gold. Gold ETF units held for more than one year qualify for long-term capital gains, whereas the holding period in physical form has to be three years to qualify for long-term capital gains. Gold held in paper form is not liable for wealth tax as per Income Tax Act, 1961.

4.9.2 Real Estate

The real estate market offers a high return to the investors. The word real estate means land and buildings. There is a normal notion that the price of the real estate has increased by more than 12 per cent over the past ten years. The population growth and the exodus of people towards the urban cities have made the prices to increase manifold. The price of the residential area land generally in South Mumbai ranges from a high of Rs 19,400 per sqft at Kemps Corner to a low of Rs 8,400 per sqft at Cuffe Park in 1998. Recently, the recession in the economy has affected the price of the real estate. Prices marked a substantial fall in 1998 from the 1997 prices.

Reasons for investing in real estate are given below:

- High capital appreciation compared to gold or silver particularly in the urban area.
- Availability of loans for the construction of houses. The 1999-2000 budget provides huge incentives to the middle class to avail of housing loans. Scheduled banks now have to disburse three per cent of their incremental deposits in housing finance.
- Tax rebate is given to the interest paid on the housing loan. Further Rs 75,000 tax rebate on a loan upto Rs five lakhs which is availed of after April 1999. If an investor invests in a house for about Rs six-seven lakh, he provides a seed capital of about Rs one-two lakh.

The Rs five lakh loan, which draws an interest rate of 15 per cent, will work out to be less than 9.6 per cent because of the Rs 75,000 exempted from tax annually. In assessing the wealth tax, the value of the residential home is estimated at its historical cost and not on its present market value.

- The possession of a house gives an investor a psychologically secure feeling and a standing among his friends and relatives.

Apart from making investment in the residential houses, the people in the higher income bracket invest their money in time share plans of the holiday resorts and land situated near the city limit with the anticipation of a capital appreciation. Farm houses and plantations also fall in the line. In spite of the fast capital appreciation investors generally do not invest in the real estate apart from owning one or two houses. The reasons are:

Requirement of Huge Capital: To purchase a land or house in the urban area, the investor needs money in lakhs whereas he can buy equity, gold or other form of investment by investing thousands of rupees.

- ***Malpractices:*** Often-gullible investors become cheated in the purchase of land. The properties already sold are resold to the investors. The investor has to lose the hard-earned money.
- ***Restriction of the Purchase:*** The land ceiling Act restricts the purchase of agricultural land beyond a limit.
- ***Lack of liquidity:*** If the investor wants to sell the property, he cannot immediately realise the money. The waiting period may be months or years.

The points to be taken care of while purchasing the real estate are:

- The plots should be approved by the local authority because in the unapproved layout construction of a house is not permitted.
- Possibility of capital appreciation. It depends upon the locality and other facilities of the site.
- Originality of title deeds. The site should be free from encumbrance. Encumbrance certificate for a minimum period of latest 15 years should be obtained from the Registrar Office.
- Plinth area should be verified. Credibility of the broker is important. The role of broker cannot be undermined because it is he who introduces to the parties and the location of site. He should be faithful and loyal otherwise the investor finds himself in trouble.

4.9.3 Art

Paintings are the most sought after form of art. The prices in the art market are rising and this rise is expected to continue. The trend in the art market today is to invest in young upcoming painters whose prices will soar over the years. People who have bought paintings from young painters in the last few years are happy with the kind of financial as well aesthetic appreciation they have received over the years. For example Manash Kamal Bishwash who used to sell A 22" × 30" mixed media on paper for Rs 30,000 in 1997, commands a price of Rs 45,000 in 1999. If an investor likes to buy paintings as a form of investments he has to consider the following points:

- Paintings of the young painters. The works of established painters are costly and scopes for appreciation in their values are limited. But prices of the good quality paintings of the young painters may increase quickly.
- Should possess the basic idea of the painting. This is needed to decide the quality of the paintings. He should be able to judge the primary attributes of the paintings such as spontaneity, nature of strokes, colour combination and originality.
- The investor should have aesthetic sense because he may or may not be able to resell the paintings. Therefore when he possesses the art piece the investor should have a sense of fulfillment.

4.9.4 Antiques

In western countries' investment in antiques is more common than in India. The antique is an object of historical interest. It may be a coin, sculpture, manuscript or any other object of olden days. The owner of the antique has to register himself with Archeological Society of India. The society after examining the authenticity of the antique issues a 'Certificate of Registration'. Any dealings, i.e., purchase and sale of antique should be informed to the society. The government has the right to buy the antique from the owner, if it wants to keep it in the museum. In the case of investment, the investor has to be careful about the fake antique and the rise in the price of the antique is uncertain.

4.10 Marketable Assets

Marketable assets or securities are those assets that are to be sold or redeemed within a year. These are financial instruments that can be easily converted to cash such as government securities, common stock and mutual funds.

4.10.1 Mutual Fund

Definition

According to the *Mutual Fund Fact Book* (published by the Investment Company Institute of US), "A Mutual Fund is a Financial Service Organisation that receives money from shareholders, invests it, earns returns on it, attempts to make it grow and agrees to pay the shareholder cash on demand for the current value of his investment".

A trust that pools the savings of investors who share a common financial goal is known as a 'Mutual Fund'. The money thus collected is then invested in financial market instruments such as shares, debentures and other securities like government paper, etc. The income earned through these investments, and the capital appreciation realised, are shared by its unit holders in proportion to the 'number of units owned by them. Investments in securities are spread over a wide cross-section of industries and sectors, thus allowing risk reduction to take place. Diversification reduces the risk because all stocks and/or debt instruments may not move in the same direction and in the same proportion at the same time.

A special type of institution that acts as an investment conduit is called a 'Mutual Fund'. It is essentially a I mechanism of pooling together the savings of a large number of investors for collective investments with the objective of attractive yields and appreciation in their value. Mutual Funds are an important segment of the financial system. It is a non-depository financial intermediary. Mutual funds are mobilisers of savings, particularly of the small and household sectors, for investment in the stock and money market.

A non-depository or non-banking financial intermediary which acts as an important vehicle for bringing wealth holders and deficit units together, indirectly, is known as 'Mutual Fund'. Mutual funds are corporations that accept money from savers and then use this money to buy stocks, long-term bonds, and short-term debt instruments issued by business or government units. These corporations pool funds and thus reduce risk by diversification.

Features/Role/Benefits

1. ***Mobilising Small Saving:*** Mutual funds mobilise funds by selling their own shares, known as units. To an investor, a unit in mutual funds means ownership of a proportional share of securities in the portfolio of,

mutual fund. This gives the benefit of convenience and the satisfaction of owning shares in many industries Thus, mutual funds are primarily investment intermediaries to acquire individual investments and pass on the returns to small fund investors.

2. *Investment Avenue:* One of the basic characteristics of a mutual fund is that it provides an ideal avenue for investment for persons of small means, and enables them to earn a reasonable return with the advantages of relatively better liquidity. It offers investors a proportionate claim on the portfolio of assets that fluctuate in value in comparison to the value of the assets that comprise the portfolio.

3. *Professional Management:* It is possible for the small investors to have the benefit of professional and expert management of their funds. Mutual Funds employ professional experts who manage the investment portfolios efficiently and profitably.

Investors are relieved of the emotional stress involved in buying or selling securities since mutual funds take care of this function. With their professional knowledge and experience, they act scientifically with the right timing to buy and sell for their clients. Moreover, automatic reinvestment of dividends and capital gains provides relief to the members of mutual funds. Expertise in stock selection and timing is made available to investors so that the invested funds generate returns.

4. *Diversified Investment:* Mutual funds have the advantage of diversified investment of funds in various industry segments spread across the country. This is advantageous to small investors who cannot afford having the shares of highly established corporate because of high market price. Thus, mutual funds allow millions of investors to have investment in a variety of securities of many different companies. Small investors therefore share the benefits of an efficiently managed portfolio and are free of the problem of keeping track of share certificates etc of various companies, tax rules, etc.

5. *Better Liquidity:* Mutual funds have the distinct advantage of offering to its investors the benefit of better liquidity of investment. There is always a ready market available for the mutual funds units. In addition, there is also an obligation imposed by SEBI guidelines. For instance, in the case of open-ended mutual fund units, it is possible for the investor to divest holdings any time during the year at the Net Asset Value (NAV). In the case of close-ended mutual funds, it is obligatory that units are listed and traded, thus offering a secondary market for the units.

Further, a high level of liquidity is possible for the fund holders because of more liquid securities in the mutual fund portfolio. These securities could be converted into cash at any time. Moreover, mutual fund schemes provide the advantage of an active secondary market by allowing the units to be listed and traded in the stock exchange. This is in sharp contrast to the fact that many of the corporate entities do not have their scrips traded at all.

6. *Reduced Risks:* There is only a minimum risk attached to the principal amount and return for the investments made in mutual fund schemes. This is usually made possible by expert supervision, diversification and liquidity of units. Mutual funds provide small investors the access to a reduced investment risk resulting from diversification, economies of scale in transaction cost and professional finance management.

7. *Investment Protection:* Mutual funds in India are largely regulated by guidelines and legislative provisions put in place by regulatory agencies such as the SEBI. The Securities Exchange Commission (SEC) in the USA allows for the provision of safety of investments. In order to protect the investor interest, it is incumbent on the part of mutual funds to broadly follow the provisions laid down in this regard.

8. *Switching Facility:* Mutual funds provide investors with flexible investment opportunities, whereby it is possible to switch from one scheme to another. This flexibility enables investors to shift from income scheme to growth scheme, or vice-versa, or from a close-ended scheme to an open ended scheme, all at will.

9. *Tax Benefits:* An attractive benefit of mutual funds is that the various schemes offered by them provide tax shelter to the investor. This benefit is available under the provisions of the Income Tax Act.

10. *Low Transaction Costs:* The cost of purchase and sale of mutual fund units is relatively lower. This is due to the large volume of money being handled by mutual funds in the capital market. The fees payable, such as brokerage fees or trading commissions etc are lower. This obviously enhances the quantum of distributable income available for investors.

11. *Economic Development:* Mutual funds make contribution to the development of a country's economy. For instance, the efficient functioning of mutual funds contributes to an efficient financial system. This in turn paves the way for efficient allocation of the financial resources of the country, thus contributing to the economic development. This is made possible through the mobilisation of more savings and channelising them to the more productive sectors of the economy.

12. Convenience: Mutual fund units can be traded easily and with little or no transaction costs. No brokerage is incurred.

13. Other benefits: In addition to the above mentioned advantages, mutual funds also offer the following benefits, as compared to a personal portfolio:

(a) Option to reinvest dividends.

(b) Strong possibility of capital appreciation.

(c) Regular returns.

Products/Schemes

Investors have the option of choosing from a wide variety of schemes in a mutual fund, depending upon their requirements. Mutual funds adopt different strategies to achieve these objectives, and accordingly offer different schemes of investments. Following section presents a detailed classification of mutual funds:

Operational Classification

1. Open-ended Scheme: When a fund is accepted and liquidated on a continuous basis by a mutual fund manager, it is called 'open-ended scheme'. The fund manager buys and sells units constantly on demand by the investors. Under this scheme, the capitalisation of the fund will constantly change, since it is always open for the investors to sell or buy their share units (shares in USA, units in India). The scheme provides an excellent liquidity facility to investors, although the units of such scheme are not listed. No intermediaries are required. There is a certainty in repurchase price, which takes place in accordance with the declared NAV.

2. Close-ended Scheme: When units of a scheme are liquidated (repurchased) only after the expiry of a specified period, it is known as a close-ended scheme. Accordingly, such funds have fixed capitalisation and remain as a corpus with the mutual fund manager. Units of close-ended scheme are to be quoted, and therefore traded, on the floors of a stock exchange in the secondary market. The price is determined on the basis of demand and supply. Therefore, there will be, two prices, one that is market determined and the other, which is NAV-based. The market price may be either above or below NAV. Managing a close-ended scheme is comparatively easy as it gives fund managers ample opportunity to evolve and adopt long-term investment strategies depending on the life of the scheme. Need for liquidity arises after a comparatively longer period, i.e., normally at the time of redemption. The main points of distinction between the Open-ended and Closed-end Schemes are as follows:

Table 4.6: Distinction Between the Open-ended and Close-ended Schemes

Feature	*Open-ended*	*Close-ended*
Subscription	Open for public subscription throughout the currency of the scheme.	Open for subscription only for a limited period.
Corpus	The fund raised from public keeps varying.	The corpus of the scheme is fixed for all time to come.
Exit	Easy and convenient exit, any time.	No exit possible till the closure of the scheme.
Liquidation	Units can be liquidated any time.	Units can be liquidated only at the end of specified period.
Maturity	No maturity period.	Fixed maturity period.
Listing	No listing and hence not traded in stock exchange.	Listed in stock exchange and traded.
Liquidity	Through re-purchase by MF at NAV or at any other price as may be determined.	Through trading in a stock exchange at the current market price.

Source:

Interval Scheme: It is a kind of close-ended scheme with a peculiar feature that it remains open during a particular part of the year for the benefit of investors, either to off-load their holdings or to undertake purchase of units at the NAV. Under SEBI (MF) Regulations, every mutual fund is free to launch any or both types of schemes, including interval scheme. In the USA, UK and Canada, close-ended funds are popularly known as investment companies/trust, whereas open-ended funds are known as mutual funds.

Return-based Classification

Under this classification fall those mutual fund schemes that are designed to meet the diverse needs of investors and to earn a good return. Returns expected are in the form of regular dividends or capital appreciation, or a combination of these two.

1. Income Fund Scheme: The scheme that is tailored to suit the needs of investors who are particular about regular returns is known as 'income fund scheme'. The scheme offers the maximum current income, whereby the income earned by units is distributed periodically. Such funds are offered in two forms. The first scheme earns a target constant income at relatively low risk, while the second scheme offers the maximum possible income. This obviously implies that the higher expected return comes with a higher potential risk of the investment.

2. Growth Fund Scheme: It is a mutual fund scheme that offers the advantage of capital appreciation of the underlying investment. For such funds, investment is made in growth-oriented securities that are capable of appreciating in the long run. Growth funds are also known as nest eggs or long haul investments. In proportion to such capital appreciation, the amount of risks to be assumed would be far greater.

3. Conservative Fund Scheme: A scheme that aims at providing a reasonable rate of return, protecting the value of the investment and achieving capital appreciation, may be designated as 'conservative fund scheme'. These are also known as middle-of-the-road funds, since such funds offer a blend of all these features. Further, such funds divide their portfolio in common stocks and bonds in such a way as to achieve the desired objectives.

Investment-based Classification

1. ***Equity Fund Scheme:*** A kind of mutual fund whose strength is derived from equity-based investments is called 'equity fund scheme'. They carry a high degree of risk. Such funds do well in periods of favourable capital market trends. A variation of the equity fund scheme is the 'Index Fund' or 'Never beat market fund' which are involved in transacting only those scrips which are included in any specific index e.g., the scrips which constitute the BSE-30 Sensex or 100-shares National index. These funds involve low transaction costs.

2. ***Bond Fund Scheme:*** It is a type of mutual fund whose strength is derived from bond-based investment The portfolio of such funds comprises bonds, debentures, etc. This type of fund carries the advantage of secure and steady income. However, such funds have little or no chance of capital appreciation, and carry risk. A variant of this type of fund is called 'Liquid Funds' which specialises in investing in short-term money market instruments. This focus on liquidity delivers the twin features of lower risks and low returns.

3. *Balanced Fund Scheme:* A scheme of mutual fund that has a mix of debt and equity in the portfolio of investments may be referred to as a 'balanced fund scheme'. The portfolio of such funds will be often shifted between debt and equity, depending upon the prevailing market trends.

4. *Sectoral Fund Schemes:* When the managers of mutual funds invest the amount collected from a wide variety of small investors directly in various specific sectors of the economy, such funds are called sectoral mutual funds. The specialised sectors may include gold and silver, real estate, specific industry such as oil and gas companies, offshore investments, etc.

5. *Fund-of-fund Scheme:* There can also be Funds of Funds, where funds of one mutual fund are invested in the units of other mutual funds. There are a number of funds that direct investment into a specified sector of the economy. This makes diversified and yet intensive investment of funds possible.

6. *Leverage-fund Scheme:* The funds that are created out of investments, with not only the amount mobilised from small savers but also the fund managers who borrow money from the capital market, are known as 'Leverage-fund Scheme'. This way, fund managers pass on the benefit of leverage to the mutual fund investors. In order to operate such schemes, there must be provisions available. Normally, leverage funds use short sale, whereby the management controlling the fund avails of the advantage of declining markets in order to realise gains in the portfolio. Options, especially call options are used by the leverage funds.

7. *Gilt Funds:* These funds seek to generate returns through investment in gilts. Under this scheme, funds are invested only in Central and State Government securities and repos/reverse repo in such securities, and not in equity or corporate debt securities. A portion of the corpus may be invested in the call money market or RBI to meet liquidity requirement. This may provide an alternative investment for the call money market. Government Securities carry zero credit risk or default risk. Their prices are however, influenced only by movement in interest rates in the financial system.

8. *Index Funds:* These funds are also known as growth funds, but they are linked to a specific index of share prices. It means that the funds mobilised under such scheme are invested principally in the securities of companies whose securities are included in the index concerned and in the same weightage. Thus, the fund's performance is linked to the growth in the concerned index. Such funds endeavour to attain results commensurate with that of the index concerned, subject to tracking errors.

9. *Tax Saving Schemes:* Certain mutual fund schemes offer tax rebate on investments made in equity shares, under Section 88 of the Income Tax Act 1961. Income may also be periodically distributed, depending upon surplus. Subscriptions made upto Rs10,000 in an assessment year are eligible for tax rebate under Section 88. The broad investment pattern of the scheme includes investment in equities, cumulative convertible preference scares, and fully convertible debentures and bonds to the extent of 80 per cent to 100 per cent and the rest in money market instruments.

10. *Other Funds:* In addition to the schemes mentioned above, following are some of the other schemes that are designed and operated by mutual fund managers.

(a) Load Funds, where mutual fund managers charge a fee over and above the NAV from the purchaser.

(b) No Load Funds, where no load-fee is charged because very little effort is made to promote the sale of the funds unit, except through direct advertising MMMF, which is designed to offer tax sops.

(c) Offshore Mutual Funds, also known as regional or country funds, where the funds are mobilised from abroad for deployment in the Indian market.

(d) Other Funds, such as property funds, art funds, commodity funds, energy funds, etc.

Mutual Funds in India

The mutual fund industry in India made its debut with the setting up of the largest public sector mutual fund n the world, namely the Unit Trust of India (UTI). It was set up in the year 1964 by a special Act of Parliament. The first unit scheme offered was the 'US-64'. A host of other fund schemes were subsequently introduced by the UTI. The basic objective behind the setting up of the Trust was to mobilise small savings and to allow channeling of those savings into productive sectors of the economy, so as to accelerate the industrial and economic development of the country.

The monopoly of the UTI ended in the year 1987, when the Government of India permitted commercial banks in the public sector to set up subsidiaries operating as trusts to perform the functions of mutual fund? by amending the Banking Regulation Act. SBI set up the first mutual fund, which was followed by Canara Bank. Later, many large financial institutions under government control also came out with mutual funds subsidiaries. Recently, with the beginning of the economic reforms and liberalisation of the economy, based on the recommendations of the Abid Hussain Committee, foreign companies were also permitted to start mutual funds in India. The government introduced a number of regulatory measures, through various agencies such as the SEBI, for the purpose of allowing the growth of the mutual funds industry in an orderly fashion for the benefit of the investors, especially the small investors.

4.10.2 Equity Shares

Equity shares are commonly referred to common stock or ordinary shares. Even though the words shares and stocks are interchangeably used, there is a difference between them. Share capital of a company is divided into a number of small units of equal value called shares. The term stock is the aggregate of a member's fully paid up shares of equal value merged into one fund. It is a set of shares put together in a bundle. The 'stock' is expressed in terms of money and not as many shares. Stock can be divided into fractions of any amount and such fractions may be transferred like shares.

Share certificate means a certificate under the common seal of the company specifying the number of shares held by any member. Share certificate provides the prima facie evidence of title of the members to such shares. This gives the shareholder the facility of dealing more easily with his shares in the market. It enables him to sell his shares by showing marketable title.

Equity shares have the following rights according to section 85 (2) of the Companies Act, 1956:

1. Right to vote at the general body meetings of the company.
2. Right to control the management of the company.
3. Right to share in the profits in the form of dividends and bonus shares.
4. Right to claim on the residual after repayment of all the claims in the case of winding up of company.
5. Right of pre-emption in the matter of issue of new capital.
6. Right to apply to court if there is any discrepancy in the rights set aside.

7. Right to receive a copy of the statutory report, copies of annual accounts along with audited report.
8. Right to apply the central government to call an annual meeting when a company fails to call such a meeting.
9. Right to apply the Company Law Board for calling an extraordinary general meeting.

In a limited company the equity shareholders are liable to pay the company's debt only to the extent of their share in the paid up capital. The equity shares have certain advantages. The main advantages are:

- Capital appreciation,
- Limited liability,
- Free tradeability,
- Tax advantages (in certain cases), and
- Hedge against inflation.

Stock Market Classification: In stock market parlance, it is customary to classify equity shares as follows:

Table 4.7: Stock Market Classification

Share Types	*Characteristics*
Blue-chip Shares	Shares of large, well-established, and financially strong companies with an impressive record of earnings and dividends.
Growth Shares	Shares of companies that have a fairly entrenched position in a growing market and which enjoy an above average rate of growth as well as profitability.
Income Shares	Shares of companies that have fairly stable operations, relatively limited growth opportunities, and high dividend payout ratios.
Cyclical Shares	Shares of companies that have a pronounced cyclically in their operations.
Defensive Shares	Shares of companies that are relatively unaffected by the ups and downs in general business conditions.
Speculative Shares	Shares that tend to fluctuate widely because there is a lot of speculative trading in them.

Source:

Note that the above classification is only indicative. It should not be regarded as rigid and straitjacketed. Often you can't pigeonhole a share exclusively in a single category. In fact, many shares may fall into two (or even more) categories.

Peter Lynch's Classification: There are different ways of classifying shares. Here is Peter Lynch's classification of companies (and, by derivation shares).

Table 4.8: Peter Lynch's Classification of Shares

Share Types	*Special Characteristics*
Slow Growers	Large and ageing companies that are expected to grow slightly faster than the gross national product.
Stalwarts	Giant companies that are faster than slow growers but are not agile climbers.
Fast Growers	Small, aggressive new enterprises that grow at 10 to 25 per cent a year.
Cyclicals	Companies whose sales and profit rise and fall in a regular, though not completely predictable, fashion.
Turnarounds	Companies which are steeped in accumulated losses but which show signs of recovery. Turnaround companies have the potential to make up lost ground quickly.
Asset Plays	Companies that have valuable assets which have been somewhat overlooked by the stock market.

Source:

Nature of Equity Shares: Benjamin Graham has described the nature of equity shares, referred to as common stocks in the US, very aptly, "Common stocks have one important investment characteristic and one important speculative characteristic. Their investment value and average market price tend to increase irregularly but persistently over the decades, as their net worth builds up through the re-investment of undistributed earnings." However, most of the time common socks are subject in irrational and excessive price fluctuations in both directions, as the consequence of the ingrained tendency of most people to speculate or gamble, i.e., to give way to hope, fear, and greed.

4.10.3 Debenture

According to Companies Act, 1956, "Debenture includes debenture stock, bonds and any other securities of company, whether constituting a charge on the assets of the company or not". Debentures are generally issued by the private sector companies as a long-term promissory note for raising loan capital. The company promises to pay interest and principal as stipulated. Bond is an alternative form of debenture in India. Public sector companies and financial institutions issue bonds.

Characteristic Features of Debentures

Form: It is given in the form of certificate of indebtedness by the company specifying the date of redemption and interest rate.

Interest: The rate of interest is fixed at the time of issue itself which is known as contractual or coupon rate of interest. Interest is paid as a percentage of the par value of the debenture and may be paid annually, semi annually or quarterly. The company has the legal binding to pay the interest rate.

Redemption: As stated earlier the redemption date would be specified in the issue itself. The maturity period may range from five years to 10 years in India. They may be redeemed in installments. Redemption is done through a creation of sinking fund by the company. A trustee in-charge of the fund buys the debentures either from the market or owners. Creation of the sinking fund eliminates the risk of facing financial difficulty at the time of redemption because redemption requires huge sum. Buy back provisions help the company to redeem the debentures at a special price before the maturity date. Usually the special price is higher than the par value of the debenture.

Indenture: Indenture is a trust deed between the company issuing debenture and the debenture trustee who represents the debenture holders. The trustee takes the responsibility of protecting the interest of the debenture holders and ensures that the company fulfills the contractual obligations. Financial institutions, banks, insurance companies or firm atomies act as trustees to the investors. In the indenture the terms of the agreement, description of debentures, rights of the debenture holders, and rights of the issuing company and the responsibilities of the company are specified clearly.

Types of Debentures

Debentures are classified on the basis of the security and convertibility:

1. Secured or unsecured.
2. Fully convertible debenture.
3. Partly convertible debenture.
4. Non-convertible debenture.

Secured or unsecured: A secured debenture is secured by a lien on the company's specific assets. In the case of default die trustee can take hold of the specific asset on behalf of the debenture holders. In the Indian market secured debentures have a charge on the present and future immovable assets of the company.

When the debentures are not protected by any security they are known as unsecured or naked debentures. In the American capital market debenture means unsecured bonds while bonds could be secured or unsecured. Unsecured debentures find it difficult to attract investors because of the risk involved in them. Generally debentures are rated by the credit rating agencies.

Fully Convertible Debenture: This type of debenture is convened into equity shares of the company on the expiry of specific period. The conversion is carried out according to the guidelines issued by SEBI. The FCD carries lower interest rate than other types of debentures because of the attractive feature of convertibility into equity shares.

Partly Convertible Debenture: This debenture consists of two parts namely convertible and non-convertible. The convertible portion can be converted into shares after a specific period. Here, the investor has the advantage of convertible and non-convertible debentures blended into one debenture. Ex. Procter and Gamble had issued PCD of Rs 200 each to its existing shareholders. The investor can get a share for Rs 65 with the face value of Rs 10 after 18 months from allotment.

Non-convertible Debenture: Non-convertible debentures do not confer any option on the holder to convert the debentures into equity shares and are redeemed at the expiry of the specified period.

4.10.4 Bond

Bond is a long term debt instrument that promises to pay a fixed annual sum as interest for specified period of time. The basic features of the bonds are given below:

1. Bonds have face value. The face value is called par value. The bonds may be issued at par or at discount.
2. The interest rate is fixed. Sometimes it may be variable as in the case of floating rate bond. Interest is paid semi-annually or annually. The interest rate is known as coupon rate. The interest rate is specified in the certificate.
3. The maturity date of the bond is usually specified at the issue time except in the case of perpetual bonds.
4. The redemption value is also stated in the bonds. The redemption value may be at par value or at premium.

5. Bonds are traded in the stock market. When they are traded the market value may be at par or at premium or at discount. The market value and redemption value need not be the same.

Secured Bonds and Unsecured Bonds: The secured bond is secured by the real assets of the issuer. In the case of the unsecured bond, the name and fame of issuer may be the only security.

Perpetual Bonds and Redeemable Bonds

Bonds that do not mature or never mature are called perpetual bonds. The interest alone would be paid. In the redeemable bond, the bond is redeemed after a specific period of time. The redemption value is specified by the issuer.

Fixed Interest Rate Bonds and Floating Interest Rate Bonds

In the fixed interest rate bonds, the interest rate is fixed at the time of the issue whereas in the floating interest rate bonds, the interest rates change according to the prefixed norms. For example, in December 1993, State Bank of India issued floating interest rate bonds worth of Rs 500 Cr pegging the interest rate with its own direct and five years fixed deposit rates to provide built in yield flexibility to the investors.

Zero Coupon Bonds

These bonds sell at a discount and the face value is repaid at maturity. The origin of this type of bond can be traced in the US Security Market. The high value of the US Government security prevented the investors from investing their money in the government security. Big brokerage companies like Merril Lynch, Pierce and others purchased the government securities in large quantum and resold them in smaller denomination—at a discounted rate. The difference between the purchase cost and face value of the bond is the gain for the investor.

Since the investor does not receive any interest on the bond, the conversion price is suitably arranged to protect the interest loss to the investor. The discounted value is calculated using the formula:

$$\text{Present value} = \frac{\text{Face value of the bond}}{(1 + R)^n}.$$

$\boldsymbol{R}$ = interest rate, and

$\boldsymbol{n}$ = number of years.

For example, a zero coupon bond that matures in 20 years time with the face of Rs 50,000 would be sold at Rs 5185 to give a return of 12 per cent per annum.

The merit of this bond is that the company does not have the burden of servicing the debt during the execution period of the project. The repayment could be adjusted to fall after the completion of the project. This could result in considerable cost savings for the company.

Deep Discount Bonds

Deep discount bond is another form of zero coupon bond. The bonds are sold at large discount on their nominal value; interest is not paid for them and they mature at par value. The difference between the maturity value, and the issue price serves as an interest return. The deep discount bonds' maturity period may range from three years to 25 years or more. IDBI was the first to issue deep discount bonds in India in 1992 with varying maturity period options. ICICI also issued deep discount bonds with four optional maturity periods in 1997. Early redemption option is provided at the end of the six, 12 and 18 year.

Capital Indexed Bonds

In the capital indexed bond, the principal amount of the bond is adjusted for inflation for every year. For example, an investment of Rs 1,000 in the inflation indexed bonds earns the investor a semi-annual interest income for the five years' period. The reselling of the principal amount is done semi annually based on the WPI movements. The principal amount of the bond is adjusted for inflation for each of the years. On the inflation-adjusted principal, the coupon rate of six per cent is worked.

The benefit of the bond is that it gives the investor an increase in return by taking inflation into account. The investor enjoys the benefit of a return on his principal, which is equal to the average inflation between the issue (purchase) and maturity period of the instrument. To avail the benefit of inflated principal, the investor needs to hold the instrument for the entire five year period.

If the investor wants to exit early, he can do it through the secondary market. The value of the principal repayment will be adjusted by the Index Rate (IR), which will be announced by the RBI two weeks prior to the repayment of the principal. The IR is worked out as follows, IR = Reference WPI as in August 2002/Base WPI (as in August 1997).

In the Indian situation indexed bonds offer more scope since the economy is highly sensitive to the inflation. According to the study conducted by the Development Research Group (DRG) of the RBI, during the period 1972-93, the real rate of interest was negative for most of the years. Average value over the period is minus 1.84 per cent.

This situation warrants an inflation hedge. The inflation protection provided by the bond guarantees real rate of return which means that with the rise in inflation, the return from the inflation protected bond will rise. In 1997, capital indexed bond is introduced.

4.10.5 Warrants

A warrant is a bearer document of title to buy specified number of equity shares at a specified price. Usually warrants can be exercised over a number of years. The life periods of warrants are long. Warrants are generally offered to make the bond or preferred stock offering more attractive. Bonds may bear low interest rate but the warrants offered along with them helps the investor to enjoy the equity appreciation value. Warrants are detachable. The investor can sell the warrants separately and they are traded in the market.

The person who is holding the warrant cannot enjoy the benefits of the equity holder before the conversion of the warrant. The price at which the warrants are converted is called exercise price. The exercise price is always greater than the current market price of the respective equity at the time of issue of warrant. When warrants are issued along with host securities and detachable, they are known as detachable warrants. In some cases the warrants can be sold back to the company before the expiry date, such type is known as puttable warrants. Naked warrants are issued separately and not with any host securities. The investor has the option to convert it into equity or bond.

Advantages of Warrants

1. Warrants make the non-convertible debentures and other debentures more attractive and acceptable.
2. The debentures along with the warrants are able to create their own market and reduce the company's dependence on financial institutions and mutual funds.
3. Since the exercise of the warrants takes place at a future date, the cash flow and the capital structure of the company can be planned accordingly.

4. The cost of debt is reduced if warrants are attached to it. Investors are willing to accept lower interest rate in the anticipation of enjoying the capital appreciation of equity value at a later date.
5. Warrants provide high degree of leverage to the investor. He can sell the warrant in the market or convert it into stocks or allow it to lapse. But if the conversion is compulsory, even if there is a fell in the price of the shares, the investors have to shell out money from his pocket.
6. Warrants are liquid and they are traded in the stock exchanges. Hence, the investor can sell the warrants before exercising there.

Table 4.9: Difference between Share Warrant and Share Certificate

Warrant	*Share Certificate*
1. Issued by public limited company.	Issued by public and private companies.
2. Need for provision in the Articles of Association.	No need to be contained in the Articles of Association.
3. Should be approved by the central government.	Central government approval is not needed.
4. Share warrants are issued to fully paid up shares.	Share certificates are issued to fully and partly paid shares.
5. Transfer of share warrant requires no registration.	Transfer of shares would be complete only if it is registered.
6. It is considered as a negotiable instrument.	Share certificate is not considered like that.

Source:

4.10.6 Government Securities

Genesis

Governments resort to public borrowings to bridge the gap between budgetary receipts and payments, technically known as Gross Fiscal Deficit (GFD). There are three sources of public borrowings such as internal debt, external borrowings, and other liabilities. As the central monetary authority, Reserve Bank of India has the statutory obligation to manage the internal debt (public debt) of the Centre Government. Its obligation to manage the internal debt of State Governments arises from bilateral agreements between the RBI and the respective State Governments.

While formulating policies pertaining to the management of public debt, RBI takes into consideration several factors. The important among these include optimisation of cost of borrowings, achieving dispersion of ownership of government securities down to the retail level, and fostering a deep and vibrant market for government securities. Liquidity conditions in the market are affected by demand for credit from productive sectors and other events such as foreign fund flows and monetary policy actions. With specialised knowledge about the market conditions, Reserve Bank is in a position to advise the governments about the appropriate timing of debt issuance.

It is pertinent to note that government securities dominate the Indian debt market both in terms of outstanding stock as well as turnover. Large statutory pre-emption and borrowings is from the RBI provides the Government with the ability to meet its borrowing requirements to finance large fiscal deficits. While the rates of interest on government debt were administered, Central bank financing was extended at much below the market interest rates.

Government Securities

The marketable debt issued by the government or semi-government bodies, which represents a claim on the government, is known as a Government security or Gilt-edged security or stock. A redeeming feature of government securities is that they are considered to be a totally secure financial instrument as they ensure safety of both capital and income. Centre Government securities are supposed to be the safest amongst all securities.

Government securities are issued for the purposes of refunding the maturing securities, for advance refunding of securities, which have not yet matured, and for cash financing, i.e., raising fresh cash resources.

Government Securities Market—Meaning

A market whereby the government or gilt-edged securities can be bought and sold is called 'Government Securities Market'.

Government Securities—Features

Following are the characteristics of a government securities/market, which plays a significant role in the Indian stock market.

Agencies

Government securities are issued by agencies such as Centre Government, State Governments, semi-government authorities like local Government authorities, e.g., city Governments and municipalities, autonomous institutions such as metropolitan authorities, port trusts, improvement or development trusts, state electricity boards. Public sector enterprises, and other governmental agencies like IDBI, IFCI,

SFCs, NABARD, LDBs, SIDCs, housing boards, etc. These agencies supply government securities. The demand essentially emanates from banks, financial institutions and other investors.

RBI's Special Role

RBI takes a special and an active role in the purchase and sale of these securities as part of its monetary management exercise. There is no underwriting or guaranteeing required in the sale of government securities, as RBI is policy-bound to buy a substantial portion of the loan un-subscribed by the public. Dealings in government securities take place through the mechanism provided by the RBI. The brokers and dealers including banks approved by the RBI are eligible to deal in these securities.

Nature of Securities

Securities offer a safe avenue of investment through guaranteed payment of interest and repayment of principal by the government. They offer relatively a lower fixed rate of interest compared to interest rate on other securities. They are issued in the denominations of Rs 100 and Rs 1,000. They have a fixed maturity spanning a period of time Interest is paid half-yearly. RBI services loans as these are the liabilities of Government of India and the State Governments. This makes the securities safe and risk-free. Further, these securities are eligible as SLR investments. These are also known as 'dated government securities' as the date of maturity is specified in the securities.

Liquidity Profile

The liquidity profile of gilt-edged securities varies. Accordingly liquidity profile of securities issued by Centre Government is high. However, the securities issued by State Governments and local government organisations have limited liquidity.

Tax Rebate

A striking feature of these securities is that they offer wide-ranging tax incentives to investors. This has made these securities very popular. Rebates for investment in these securities are available under the Income Tax and other Acts.

Market

As each sale and purchase has to be negotiated separately, the gilt-edged market is an 'over-the-counter' market, The government securities market in India has two segments namely primary market and secondary market. The issuers such as Centre Government and State Governments constitute the primary market. The secondary market comprises banks, financial institutions, insurance companies, provident funds, trusts, individuals, primary dealers and Reserve Bank of India.

Forms

The securities of Centre and State Governments take such forms as inscribed stock or stock certificate, promissory note and bearer bond. The securities such as bearer bonds and stock certificates are not popular with Indian investors. Stock certificates are considered safe as compared to promissory notes because, the name of the holder of Stock certificate is registered in the books of Public Debt Office (PDO), the certificates are sent to the applicant directly by registered post by the PDO and the half-yearly interest is remitted directly to the holder by an interest warrant drawn at par on any treasury or State Bank of India branch specified by the holder or is remitted by money order. Moreover, the certificates can be sold by signing the transfer form on the reverse of the certificate.

Participants

The participants in government securities market include the Government sector comprising Centre and State Governments whose holdings represent inter-governmental transfer of resources, banking sector comprising RBI, SBI, other commercial and cooperative banks, the institutional sector comprising insurance companies including Life Insurance Corporation and General Insurance Companies, provident funds–both statutory and non-statutory, and other institutions including special financial institutions, joint stock companies, local authorities, trusts, individuals and non-residents.

Trading

Although the secondary market for government security is narrow, small and less active, banks and corporate holders who purchase and sell government securities on the stock exchanges participate in trading. The securities are mainly traded at Bombay Stock Exchange. In terms of size, the primary market for government securities is much bigger than the industrial securities market.

Issue Mechanism

The issue process comprises of the following steps:

Issue Opening: A notification for the issue of the securities is made a few days before the public subscription is open. The opening of the subscription depends on response of the market and varies between two to three days. The issue is made in a number of branches in. This avoids flooding of securities in the market. Further, it facilitates smooth subscription to securities and helps avoid sudden liquidity problems in the system.

Subscription: The offices of RBI and the branches of SBI receive applications for the securities. While making allotment, the government reserves the right to retain over-subscription upto a pre-specified percentage, generally 10 per cent, in excess of the notified amount. Over-subscription as relating to the issue of securities by the State Government will be transferable to other State Governments whose securities are still open for subscription at the option of the subscriber.

Type of Trading

The types of trading practiced by the RBI in dealing with government securities are described below:

Grooming: Gradual acquisition of securities nearing maturity through the stock exchanges by the RBI in order to facilitate redemption is described as 'grooming'. The object is to keep the whole process of issue and redemption of Government securities continuous and thereby facilitate availability of securities on 'tap'.

Switching: The purchase of one security against the sale of another security carried out by the RBI in the secondary market as part of its open market operations is described as 'Switching'. Banks and financial institution are greatly benefited by the switch operations as it helps them improve the yield on their investments in government securities. The RBI fixes an annual quota for the switch transactions of each bank.

Auctioning: A method of trading whereby merchants bid against one another and where the securities are sold to the highest bidder is known as 'auctioning'. This system, for the sale of dated government securities, was introduced in the year 1992. Under the auction sale mechanism operated by the RBI, a number of instruments of wide ranging period, such as 14 day, 91 day, 182 day and 364 day treasury bills and dated securities of Government of India are sold. Bidders furnish written and sealed quotations restricted to notified amounts.

Small variations of the auction sale are the Multiple Price Auction and the Uniform Price Auction. Under the multiple price auction mechanism, every bidder gets allocation according to his bid and the issuer collects a premium from all bidders by quoting a rate lower than the cut-off yield. Under the uniform price auction, competitive bids are accepted on the basis of the minimum discounted price known as the cut-of price. The price is determined at the auction. This minimum price is independent of the bid-prices tendered below; at the cut-of price.

Trading Mechanism

The mechanism of trading in government securities takes place through the following methods:

(a) Direct Sales (DS) method.

(b) Securities General Ledger (SGL) accounts method.

(c) Bank Receipts (BRs) method.

DS method: Under the Direct Sales (DS) method, Public Debt Office effects direct sale of Government securities. This is done by pre-specifying the loan amount and the date of opening of subscription for government loans.

SGL accounts method: Under the Securities General Ledger (SGL) method, RBI records the transactions as book entries only in the ledger, on the date of the transaction, by specifying the value at which the transaction takes place. In respect of each separate dealing, the purchasing banker maintains a separate SGL account with RBI in respect of the purchase and the balance of the Central Government securities. Selling banker effects the transactions by filling out the prescribed SGL form, which is then lodged with RBI.

BR method: Under the Banker receipt (BR) method, the bank selling Government securities, issues a Bank Receipt (BR). This is done in the case of 'repo' or Ready Forward (RF) transactions. These are facilitated by the SGL where it is possible to avoid physical transfer of securities. A 'repo' or Ready Forward (RF) refers to a sale transaction, which buys back the securities at a stipulated future date at a price determined on the date of sale transaction. Under the 'repo' or RF, short operations are conducted by banks which sell Government securities without owning them with a view to neutralising the transaction by buying them at a later date, (though issue of Bankers' Receipt is being discouraged by RBI).

Mode of Issue

Government of India may issue, from time to time, government securities through the following mode:

1. *Issue of Securities Through Auction:* The securities will be issued through auction either on price basis or yield basis. Where the issue is on price basis, the coupon will be pre-determined and the bidders have to quote the price per Rs 100 face value of the security, at which they desire to purchase the security. Where the issue is on yield basis, the coupon of the security is decided in an auction conducted by RBI in the manner hereinafter discussed and further provided by the specific notifications issued from time to time. The security carries the same coupon till maturity.

Yield Basis

The yield per cent per annum or the price, as the case may be, expressed upto and rounded off to two decimal places, should be clearly stated in the application. An applicant may submit more than one bid at different rates of yield or prices, as the case may be, through separate applications for each bid. The aggregate amount of bids submitted by a person should not exceed the aggregate amount of government securities offered for sale. On the basis of the bids received, the RBI determines the maximum rate of yield or the minimum offer price, as the case may be, at which offers for the purchase of government securities will be accepted at the auction. Except in the case of price-based auctions, the maximum rate of yield determined at the auction will be the coupon rate per cent per annum on the securities sold at the auction.

Price Basis

The auctions for issue of securities (on either yield basis or price basis) will be held either on 'Uniform Price' method or 'Multiple Price' method or any other method decided by the Government of India or the RBI in consultation with the Government of India.

Where an auction is held on 'Uniform Price' method, competitive bids offered with rates up to and including the maximum rate of yield or the prices up to and including the minimum offer price, as determined by the RBI, will be accepted at the maximum rate of yield or minimum offer price so determined. Bids quoted higher than the maximum rate of yield or lower than the minimum price as determined by the RBI will be rejected.

Where an auction is held on 'Multiple Price' method, competitive bids offered at the maximum rate of yield or the minimum offer price as determined by the RBI will be accepted. Other bids tendered at lower than the maximum rate of yield or higher than the minimum offer price determined by the RBI, will be accepted at the rate of yield or price quoted in the respective bid. In yield-based auctions, successful bidders, whose quotes are lower than the maximum rate of yield, are required to pay the price differential in the form of a premium. Bids quoted higher than the maximum rate of yield or lower than the minimum price as determined by the RBI will be rejected. Where the auction is held on any other method, the Government of India will decide the method of acceptance of the bids.

Participants

Individuals and institutions as may be specified by the Reserve Bank of India (called 'Retail investors') can participate in the auctions on 'non-competitive' basis, indirectly through a scheduled bank or a primary dealer offering such services or any other agency permitted by RBI for this purpose. RBI will announce eligibility criteria for participation on non-competitive basis and the manner in which such bids should be submitted.

Allocation of the securities to non-competitive bidders will be at the discretion of the RBI and will be at a price not higher than the weighted average price arrived at on the basis of the competitive bids accepted at the auction or any other price announced in the specific notification. The nominal amount of securities that will be al located to retail investors on non-competitive basis will be restricted to a maximum percentage of the aggregate nominal amount of the issue, within or outside the nominal amount, as specified by the Government of India or any other percentage determined by RBI.

The Reserve Bank of India will have the discretion to accept excess subscriptions to the extent as may be specified in the 'Specific Notification' pertaining to the issue of the security and make allotment of the security accordingly. The RBI will have full discretion to accept or reject any or all bids either wholly or partially, without assigning any reason.

2. Issue of Securities with Pre-announced Coupon Rates: The coupon on such securities will be announced before the date of floatation and the securities will be issued at par. In case the total subscription exceeds the aggregate amount offered for sale in respect of a fixed coupon security, the RBI may make partial allotment to all the applicants. The Reserve Bank of India will have the discretion to accept excess subscriptions to the extent as may be specified in the 'Specific Notification' pertaining to the issue of the security and make allotment of the security accordingly. It will have the discretion to accept or reject any or all applications either wholly or partially, without assigning any reason. The Reserve Bank of India will refund the amount of excess subscription or amount of subscription in case of rejection of application to the respective subscribers as soon as possible and no interest will be paid on the amount so refunded.

3. Issue of Securities Through Tap Sale: No aggregate amount is indicated in the notification in respect of the securities sold on tap. Sale of such securities may be extended to more than one day and the sale may be closed at any time during the banking hours on any day.

4. Issue of Securities in Conversion: The holders of treasury bills of certain specified maturities and holders of specified dated securities are provided an option to convert the respective treasury bills/dated security at specified prices into new securities offered for sale. The new securities could be issued on an auction/pre-announced coupon basis.

4.10.6.1 Importance of Government Securities Market

Government securities market is considered important on account of the following reasons:

Vital Segment

Government securities market forms an important segment of the-Indian money market. The market provides an opportunity to banks and other institutions, as part of their SLR requirements, to engage in buying and selling of these securities held in large amounts by RBI. Under the SLR, banks are required to maintain a specified portion of their Net Demand and Time Liabilities (NDTL) as secondary reserve in the form of government securities. The importance of government securities market, from the viewpoint of banks having to meet their changing NDTL requirements, will be clear through the purchase of these securities.

Profitable Avenue

The market provides an opportunity to banks to switch from existing low yielding securities in their portfolio of SLR securities, for securities out of the primary issues of new and better yield securities. This enables banks to keep the yield on securities better aligned with the latest yield rates.

Regulated Speculation

Speculation in Government securities is facilitated in a regulated fashion by the repo transactions. For instance an investment manager undertakes sale of repo where a significant rise in the price of securities in future is expected. This facilitates the sale of securities with an arrangement to buy them back at a future date at the price determined at the time of sale of repo. Securities are bought on the appointed date at the pre-determined price in order to be sold at higher prevailing market price. This earns profit for the investment manager. The reverse is done if investment manager anticipates a fall in the prices of securities.

Ideal Financing

It is possible for the government exchequer to raise long-term finance by means of issue of government securities. It is a convenient and flexible method of raising finance at very moderate interest cost. RBI can also help supplementing execution of its interest rate policy by influencing the behaviour of prices and yields in gilt-edged market.

Monetary Management

The management of government securities market has a considerable impact on the advances and liquidity position of commercial banks. This contributes to an efficient management of the monetary economy of the country.

Role of Central Bank

Central Bank of a country plays a significant role in the government securities market. In fact, the chief supplier of securities is the central bank that uses the gilt-edged securities to carry out qualitative and quantitative operations.

Implementing Fiscal Policy

The government securities market acts as an ideal forum for implementing the fiscal policy of the government. This takes place by requiring financial institutions like commercial banks to maintain their secondary reserve requirements in the form of these securities. The securities come handy for the holders to obtain loans from the RBI and other institutions against the collateral of these securities.

Source of Liquidity

Government securities, in addition to gold and foreign exchange, form the basis for the currency notes issued by the RBI. This way, the securities constitute the ultimate source of liquidity in the economy.

Guaranteed Return

Government security guarantees the certainty of both income and capital. As a 'gilt-edged' security or stock, it is an absolutely secure financial instrument as compared to many alternative instruments like industrial debentures, etc. They have the least market risk, as they are free from default risk or credit risk. The benefits of assured return, Mow risk and high liquidity make this an ideal financial instrument for diversification of investment portfolio.

4.11 Money Market Instruments

Debt instruments which have a maturity of less than one year at the time of issue are called money market instruments. These instruments are highly liquid and have negligible risk. The major money market instruments are commercial papers, certificate of deposits, treasury bills and repos.

The money market is dominated by the government, financial institutions, banks and corporate. Individual investors scarcely participate in the money market directly.

4.11.1 Commercial Papers (CPs)

Meaning

Debt instruments that are issued by corporate houses for raising short-term financial resources from the money market are called Commercial Papers (CPs).

Features

Following are the features of Commercial Papers:

Nature: These are unsecured debts of corporates. They are issued in the form of promissory notes. These are redeemable at par to the holder at maturity. The issuing company should have a minimum tangible net worth to the extent of Rs four crores. Moreover, the working capital (fund-based) limit of the company should not be less than Rs four crores and this allows corporates to issue CPs upto 100 per cent of their-fund based working capital limits. The CPs are issued at a discount to face value in multiples of Rs five lakhs. CPs attract stamp duty. No prior approvals of RBI are needed to issue CPs and no underwriting is mandatory. The issuing company has to bear all expenses (such as dealers' fees, rating agency fee and charges for provision of stand-by facilities) relating to the issue of CP. The issue of CPs serves the purpose of releasing the pressure on bank funds for small and medium sized borrowers, besides allowing highly rated companies to borrow directly from the market.

Market: The market for the CPs comprises of issues made by public sector and private sector enterprises. CPs issued by top rated corporate are considered as sound investments. Conditions attached to the issue are less stringent than those applicable for raising CPs. Beginning from September 1996, Primary Dealers (PDs) were also permitted by RBI to issue CPs for augmenting their resources. This is one of the steps initiated by the RBI to make the CPs market popular.

Rating: As per the guidelines of the RBI, CPs are required to be graded by the organisation issuing them. Accordingly, a rated CP is considered to be a quality and sound instrument. With the liberalisation of interest rate structure, the rate of interest is market-determined. This causes wide variation in the prevailing rates of interest.

Interest Rates: The rate of interest applicable to CPs varies greatly. This variation is influenced by a large number of factors such as credit rating of the instrument, economic phase, the prevailing rate of interest in CPs market, call rates, the position in foreign exchange market, etc. It is however to be noted that there is no benchmark for the interest rate.

Marketability: The marketability of the CPs is influenced by the rates prevailing in the call money market and the foreign exchange market. Accordingly, where attractive interest rates prevail in these markets, the demand for CPs will be affected. This is because, investors will divert their investment into these markets.

Maturity: The minimum maturity of CP has been brought down from three months to 30 days and was further reduced to 15 days with effect from May 25, 1998. This was done with a view to encouraging issuance of CPs.

CPs in Lieu of WC: The nature of credit policy announced by the RBI allows highly rated corporates to have the advantage of banks offering an automatic restoration of working capital limits on the repayment of CP. Accordingly, short-term working capital loans were substituted with cheaper CPs. This was done by the RBI to hasten the growth of the CP market.

Satellite Dealers (SDs): Dealers who are enlisted with the RBI to deal in the Government securities market, are called 'Satellite Dealers'. With effect from June 17, 1998, they are allowed to issue CPs, with prior approval from RBI. The purpose was to enable them to have access to short-term borrowings through CP route. Following are the conditions to be satisfied in this regard.

Rating: In order that the satellite dealers are permitted to trade in CPs, it is essential that the issuing corporates obtain the minimum specified credit rating from a credit rating agency. Such a rating must have been approved by the Reserve Bank for the purpose of issue of commercial paper. The credit rating must not be older than two months.

Maturity: The CPs shall be issued for a maturity period ranging from 15 days to one year from the date of issue.

Target Market: The issue of CPs may be targeted to such persons as individuals, banks, companies, other corporate bodies registered or incorporated in India and unincorporated bodies and non-resident Indian (NRI) on non-repatriationl basis subject to the condition that it shall not be transferable.

Limits of Issue: Each issue of CPs (including renewal) shall be treated as a fresh issue. The CPs issue may take place in multiple: of Rs five lakhs. The investment by any single investor shall be for a minimum amount of Rs 25 lakhs (face value and the secondary market transactions may be dealt in for amounts of Rs five lakhs or multiples thereof. The RBI shall fix the total amount of issue. The issue amount shall be raised within a period of two weeks from the date of approval by the Reserve Bank or may be issued on a single day or in parts on different days as the case may be.

Nature: The CPs shall be in the form of promissory note. It shall be negotiable by endorsement and delivery. It is issued at discount to face value, discount being determined by the SD issuing the CPs. The SDs shall be| the expenses of the issue, including dealer's fee, rating agency fee, etc.

4.11.2 Certificate of Deposit (CD)

Meaning of CD Market

A market for the purchase and sale of certificates of deposit is called 'Certificate of Deposit market'. It is an important constituent of the money market.

Meaning of CDs

A marketable document of title to a time deposit for a specified period may be referred to as a 'Certificate of Deposit' (CD). It takes the form of a receipt given by a bank or any other institution for funds deposited with it by the depositor.

Features

Certificates of Deposit possess the following distinguishing characteristics:

1. ***Negotiable Instruments:*** CDs are negotiable term-deposit certificates issued by commercial banks/financial institutions at discount to face value at market rates. The Negotiable Instruments Act governs CDs.
2. ***Maturity:*** The maturity period of CDs range from 15 days to one year.
3. ***Nature:*** CDs are in the form of usance promissory notes and hence easily negotiable by endorsement and delivery.
4. ***Ideal Source:*** CDs constitute a judicious source of investments as these certificates are the liabilities of commercial banks/financial institutions.

A Certificate of Deposit is different from a Conventional Time Deposit in the following manner.

Table 4.10: Time Deposit *vs.* Certificate of Deposit

Sl. No.	*Feature*	*Conventional Time Deposit*	*Certificate of Deposit*
1.	Negotiability	Not freely negotiable	Freely negotiable
2.	Stamp Duty	Not subject to stamp duty	Requires stamp duty, as it is in the nature of usance note.
3.	Period	Can be for any period	Can be for three to 12 months when issued by banks and for one to three years when issued by specified all-India financial institutions.
4.	Issue at discount	Cannot be issued at dis-count.	Can be issued at discount.
5.	Limits of deposit	No limit on the minimum and maximum amount.	Minimum size of a single CD is Rs 5 lakhs and the minimum size of an issue to a single investor is Rs 25 lakhs.

Source:

Profile: A distinguishing profile of Certificate of Deposit as operating in India is presented below:

The Tambe Working Group: The Tambe Working Group set up in 1982 in India, reported that banks and financial institutions were not willing to support the launch of money market instruments such as CDs, and therefore advised against the introduction of these instruments. The Group cited many reasons for the non-popularity of these instruments including the absence of secondary market, administered interest rate structure on bank deposits and the danger of CDs giving rise to a large number of fictitious transactions.

The Vaghul Working Group: The Vaghul Working Group, setup in 1987, again reviewed the issue and expressed itself against the launch of the instrument by the RBI. The Group reported that the introduction of CDs as a money market instrument would be meaningful only where the short-term deposit rates were aligned with other rates in the financial system. The Group instead recommended, as a prelude, the setting up of a discount house and the alignment of short-term deposit rates.

Based on the recommendations of the Group, the RBI constituted the Discount and Finance House of India Ltd (DFH1) in the year 1988. In the same manner, RBI rationalised the interest rate structure in March, 1989 by abolishing fixed deposits of shortest terms with maturity of 15 to 45 days.

The Launch: The RBI launched the scheme of CDs with effect from March 27, 1989. Following guidelines were laid down in this regard.

Eligible Issuers: The institutions that are eligible to issue CDs are scheduled commercial banks (excluding RRBs) and specified all-India financial institutions, namely, IDBI, IFCI, ICICI, SIDBI, IRBI, and EXIM Bank.

Eligible Subscribers: The parties who are eligible to buy CDs are individuals, associations, companies, corporations, trust funds, etc. NRIs can also subscribe to the CDs. However, this is possible only on a non-repatriation basis; it is not possible for an NRI to endorse CDs to another NRI in the secondary market.

Negotiation: CDs are freely transferable by endorsement and delivery after the initial lock in period of 15 days. The instrument can be purchased by any of the above subscribers and DFHI in the secondary market.

Maturity: The maturity period of CDs issued by banks ranges from three days to 12 months and that issued by specified financial institutions can have a maturity period upto three years. With the announcement of credit policy on April 27, 2000, the maturity period was reduced from three months to 15 days.

Discount: CDs are to be issued at a discount to face value, with the maturity period not having any grace period.

Limits of Issue: The maximum amount of issue by a bank, which was originally fixed at one per cent of its fortnightly aggregate average deposits, was raised to 10 per cent in 1992. This was subsequently abolished totally. The minimum size of issue to a single investor, which was originally fixed at Rs 10 lakhs was reduced to Rs five lakhs with effect from October 21, 1997. Issue of CDs above Rs five lakhs can now be made in multiples of Rs one lakh. CDs can now be issued for a minimum amount of Rs five lakhs, which was originally Rs 25 lakhs. Banks have to maintain SLR and CRR on issue price of CDs for which there is no ceiling.

Stamp Duty: Stamp duty is payable on CDs as applicable to any other negotiable instrument.

Security Paper: CDs are transferable by endorsement and delivery, and shall therefore be issued on a good quality security paper.

Other Requirements: No loans can be granted by banks against CDs:

- Banks cannot have any buyback arrangement of their own CDs before maturity.
- Banks are to submit fortnightly report on their CDs to the RBI under section 42 of the RBI Act, 1935.
- Banks are to show CDs under the head 'liabilities' in the balance sheet.

Yield: CDs are offered at interest rates higher than the time deposits of banks. However, the rate of interest is dependent upon many factors such as urgency of requirement for funds, alternative opportunities for investment of funds mobilised, etc. The rate of discount being deregulated is now determined by the demand and supply of CDs. CDs are issued at a discount to their face value and redeemed at par. CDs are issued at a front-end discount and in such a case, the effective rate of interest is higher than the quoted discount rate.

Effective rate of interest may be calculated as follows:

$$\text{ERR} = [(1 + \text{QDR} \div 100 \times \text{N/M})\ \text{N/M} - 1] \times 100$$

Where,

ERR = Effective rate of interest

QDR = Quoted discount rate

N = Total period in a year. Say 12 months or 365 days, etc

M = Maturity period in months or days as the case may be

Role of DFHI

The Discount and Finance House of India Ltd functions is a market maker in CDs market. It offers bid rate, the rate of discount at which it is prepared to buy CDs, and offer rate at which it would be willing to sell the CDs. The DFHI acts as an ideal conduit for disinvestments of CD holdings, which is done through their banker in Mumbai. DFHI also engages in buying CDs from the bank at its bid discount rate. Settlements are effected through RBI cheque.

Role of Banks

Scheduled commercial banks are the active, players in the realm of CDs market segment. CDs are used as an important money market instrument. CDs provide an ideal avenue of investment for bankers. CDs are considered safe, liquid, and attractive in returns for both scheduled commercial banks and investors.

It is not necessary for banks to encash CDs before maturity under the RBI Act. Banks are under obligation to maintain usual reserve requirements (SLR and CRR) on issue price of CDs. CDs offer the opportunity for banks for the bulk mobilisation of resources as part of effective fund management. Besides, offering an attractive yield helps bankers utilise them as eligible assets for determination of Net Demand and Time Liabilities (NDTL). According to the RBI guidelines, it will not be possible for banks to enter into buyback arrangement with the subscriber of CDs. Similarly, they cannot grant loans against CDs issued by them.

It is possible for investors to sell CDs in secondary market before their maturity. This offers investors the advantage of liquidity through ready marketability. However, the tendency on the part of holders of CDs to hold the instrument till maturity date has not made possible for the creation of an effective secondary market for them, although the primary market for CDs has shown a considerable improvement.

4.11.3 Treasury Bills (TBs)

Meaning

A market for the purchase and sale of treasury bills is known as a 'Treasury Bills Market'. A kind of finance bills, which are in the nature of promissory notes, issued by the government under discount for a fixed period, not exceeding one year, containing a promise to pay the amount stated therein to the bearer of the instrument, are known as 'treasury bills'.

General Features

Treasury bills incorporate the following general features:

- ***Issuer :*** TBs are issued by the government for raising short-term funds from institutions or the public for bridging temporary gaps between receipts (both revenue and capital) and expenditure.
- ***Finance Bills:*** TBs are in the nature of finance bills because they do not arise due to any genuine commercial transaction in goods.
- ***Liquidity:*** TBs are not self-liquidating like genuine trade bills, although they enjoy higher degree of liquidity.
- ***Vital Source:*** Treasury bills are an important source of raising short-term funds by the government.
- ***Monetary Management:*** TBs serve as an important tool of monetary management used by the central bank of the country to infuse liquidity in to the economy.

Features of Indian TBs

History: It was in the year 1877 that Treasury Bills (TBs) came to be issued for the first time in the world. Later, it acquired wide popularity around the world both in developing and developed countries. TBs were first issued in India in October, 1917. The issue aimed at raising resources for financing the First World War efforts of the government and for mopping up excess liquidity in the economy due to heavy war expenditure.

TBs that were initially sold by the government had a maturity period of three months, six months, month months and 12 months. Later on, with the setting up of the RBI in 1935, the issue profile of TBs underwent a lot of changes. Accordingly, RBI came to issue two types of TBs such as Tap Bills that were issued at all times and Intermediate Bills that were sold between auctions, to non-government investors. However, in the year 1965, sale of TBs to public through auction was suspended and issue took place on tap basis at a discount. Thus commercial banks began to invest in them.

Issue: TBs, which were first issued upto 1935 by the Government of India directly, came to be issued by the RBI since its inception in 1935. Thereafter, TBs are issued at a discount by the RBI on behalf of the government of India. Even State Governments were issuing TBs till 1950. The RBI discounts TBs on behalf of the Government of India.

Types: There are two types of treasury bills. They are ordinary treasury bills and ad-hoc treasury Bills. The freely marketable treasury bills that are issued by the Government of India to the public, banks and other institutions for raising resources to meet the short-term financial needs take the form of ordinary TBs.

Ad hoc TBs, on the other hand, are issued in favour of the RBI only. They are used by the RBI as reserve against which the Issue Department issues currency notes. In addition, they are also issued to serve the purpose of replenishing cash balances of the central government. Besides, ad hoc TBs provide an investment avenue to State Governments, semi-government departments, and foreign central banks for parking their temporary surplus and for earning income. Since ad-hoc TBs are not marketable in India, the holders of these bills can always sell them back to the RBI.

Maturity Period: A lot of changes have taken place in the realm of the periodicity of treasury bills, changes having been brought about by the policy announcements made by the RBI from time to time. A brief account of the changes in the period of maturity of TBs is outlined below:

- Maturity period of TBs at the close of the First World War was of three, six, nine and 12 months duration.
- Maturity period of Tap Bills and Intermediate Bills introduced by the RBI immediately after its inception was 91 days which was continued upto November 1986.
- Maturity period of 182 days recommended by Chakraborty Committee was issued upto April, 1992.
- Maturity period of 365 days beginning from April, 1992.
- Maturity period of 14 days introduced in May, 1997 and of 28 days introduced on October 21, 1997.
- Maturity period of 182 days reintroduced with effect from May 26, 1999.

Participants: The participants in the TBs market include the Reserve Bank of India, the State Bank of India, Commercial Banks, State Governments and other approved bodies, Discount and Finance House of India as a market maker in TBs, the Securities Trading Corporation of

India (STCI), other financial institutions, such as LIC, UTI. GIC, NABARD, IDBI, IFCI, ICICI, etc., corporate entities and general public and foreign institutional investors.

Of the above-mentioned participants, RBI and commercial banks are the most popular players. This essentially arises from the nature of relationship between them. TBs are least popular among the corporate entities and the general public.

The Issue Procedure: The procedure followed by the RBI for successful issue of treasury bills is briefly outlined below:

1. ***Notification:*** The RBI issues notifications for the sale of 91 day TBs on tap basis throughout the week and the 14-day, 28-day, 91-day and 364-day TBs through fortnightly auction. The notification mentions the date of auction and the last date for submission of tenders.

2. ***Tendering:*** Immediately after the issue of notification by the RBI, investors are permitted to submit bids through separate tenders. The result of the auction mentioning the price upto which the bids have been accepted is displayed. The successful bidders are expected to collect letter of acceptance from the RBI and deposit the same together with a cheque on RBI.

3. ***SGL:*** SGL is maintained by the RBI for facilitating the purchases and sales of TBs by the investors like Commercial Banks, DFHI, STCI and other financial institutions.

4. ***DFHI:*** Where the SGL facility is not available to certain investors, purchase and sale takes place through OFHI. TBs sold to such investors are held by DFHI on their behalf, which pays the proceeds of the TBs held, to the investor on the date of maturity. DFHI takes an active part in the primary auctions of TBs, besides operating in the secondary market by quoting two-way rates. In addition, the DFHI also gives buyback and sell-back commitments for periods upto 14 days at negotiated interest rates, to commercial banks, financial institutions and public sector undertakings.

Auctioning Methods

Uniform Price Auction: The system of uniform price auction system in respect of 91-day TBs was introduced on experimental basis in October 1997 credit policy. It aimed at eliminating the problem of 'winners' curse so as to broaden market participation. ('Winners' curse is a phenomenon whereby those bidding at lower than the cut-off, end up paying a premium. The introduction of uniform price auction is expected to reduce uncertainty associated with the bidding process. This is peculiar to the underdeveloped nature of Indian money market, which is afflicted by the lack of reliable information, causing wide differences in the yield expectations before the auctions. The amounts of issue are notified in respect of 91-day TBs auctions and the dated securities auction.

Treasury Bills Auction

Auction in TBs takes place both on 'competitive' as well as on 'non-competitive' basis. The State Governments, Provident Funds and the Nepal Rastra Bank are the 'non-competitive' bidders. Commercial banks and other financial institutions comprise 'competitive bidders'. It is to be noted that the merits of enhanced market efficiency and price discovery take place through the competitive bids.

Policy Measures

With a view to improving the depth and liquidity in the government securities market, RBI announced the following policy measures relating to treasury bills with effect from October, 1999:

- Price based auction of government-dated securities
- Auction of 182-day Treasury Bills
- A calendar of Treasury Bills Issuance

TB Rate

The discount rate at which the RBI sells TBs is known as Treasury Bills rate. The effective yield on TBs depends on such factors as the rate of discount, difference between the issue price and the redemption value, and time period of their maturity.

The treasury bills rate is computed as follows:

$$Y - \{[(FV - IP) \div IP] \times [364 \div MP]\} \times 100.$$

Where,

FV = Face Value TBs.

IP = Issue Price of TBs.

MP = Maturity period of TBs in days.

D = Discount.

4.11.3.1 Benefits

TBs being an important money market instruments provide the following benefits.

Liquidity: Treasury bills command high liquidity. A number of institutions such as RBI, the DFHI, STCI, commercial banks, etc take part in the TB market. In addition, the Central bank is always prepared to purchase or discount TBs.

No Default Risk: Since there is a guarantee by the central government, TBs are absolutely free from the risk of default of payment by the issuer. Moreover, the government itself issues the TBs.

Availability: RBI has the policy of making available on a steady basis, the TBs especially through the 'Tap' route since July 12, 1965. This greatly helps banks and other institutions to park their funds temporarily in TBs.

Low Cost: Trading in TBs involves less transaction costs. This is because two-way quotes with a fine margin are offered by the DFHI on a daily basis.

Safe Return: The biggest advantage of TBs is that they offer a steady and safe return to investors. There are not many fluctuations in the discount rate. It is also possible for the investors to earn attractive return by keeping investment in non-earning cash to the minimum and supplementing it with TBs.

No Capital Depreciation: Since TBs command high order of liquidity, safety and yield, there is very little scope for capital depreciation in them.

SLR Eligibility: TBs are of great attraction to commercial banks as it helps them park their funds (Net Demand and Time Liabilities) as per the norms of SLR announced by the RBI from time to time. This reason makes commercial banks dominant dealers in TBs.

Funds Mobilisation: TBs are used as an ideal tool by the government for raising short-term funds required for meeting temporary budget deficit.

Monetary Management: It is also possible for the government to mop up excess liquidity in the economy through the issue of TBs. Since TBs are subscribed by the investors other than the RBI, the issue would neither lead to inflationary pressure nor result in monetisation.

Better Spread: TBs facilitate proper spread of asset mix with different maturity as they are available on tap basis as well as in fortnightly auctions.

Perfect Hedge: TBs can be used as a hedge against volatility of call loan market and interest rate fluctuations.

Fund Management: TBs serve as effective tools of fund management because of the following reasons:

- Ready market availability, both for sale and purchase at market driven prices, thus imparting flexibility.
- Facility of rediscounting TBs on 'tap basis'.
- Facility of refinancing from the RBI.
- Plethora of options available to fund managers to invest in TBs and for raising funds against TBs especially through and with the help of DFHI.
- Ideally suited for investment of temporary surplus.
- Possibility of building up portfolio of TBs with dates of maturities matching the dates of payment of liabilities, such as certificates of deposits and deposits of short-term maturities.
- Possibility of meeting the temporary difficulties of funds by entering into buyback transactions for surplus TBs and reversing the transactions when the financial need is over.
- Possibility of making enhanced profit by indulging in quick raising of money against TBs for investing in call money market when call rates are high and doing the reverse when call rates dip.

4.12 Conclusion

The pattern of disposition of savings is an important factor in determining how the saved amount is utilised for productive purposes. The proportion of professionals' savings in financial assets determines the channelisation of savings for investment in other sectors of the economy. The volume of investment of savings in physical assets determines the productivity and generation of income in that sector itself. This theoretical study is an eye opener to have broader view towards various investment avenues available to investors.

Chapter-V

Analysis and Interpretation

Socio-Economic Profile of the Sample Respondents

Gender: Gender is an important factor used to analyse the attitude towards the investment preferences of professionals and their investment pattern. In practice in a male dominated society though women are working and earning, major decisions are taken by men only. Gender is classified as male and female. Gender-wise distribution of the professionals is presented in Table 5.1.

Table 5.1: Gender-Wise Distribution Of Respondents

Gender	*Professionals*						*Total*	
	Doctor		*Engineer*		*Advocate*			
	No. of Respondents	*per cent*	*No. of Respondents*	*per cent*	*No. of Respondents*	*per cent*	*No. of Respondents*	*per cent*
Male	92	57.5	92	57.5	112	70.0	296	61.7
Female	68	42.5	68	42.5	48	30.0	184	38.3
Total	**160**	**100**	**160**	**100**	**160**	**100**	**480**	**100**

Source: Primary data.

From the above Table 5.1 it is understood that 61.7 per cent of the respondents are male professionals and the rest of the 38.3 per cent respondents are female professionals. It is inferred from the table that majority (37.84 per cent) of the male respondents are advocates and the majority of the female respondents are constituted from Doctors and Engineers equally of 31.8 per cent each.

Age Composition: The success of a profession depends upon the age of the professional. The youngsters are generally interested in learning things and taking risk which are essential for professionals. But middle aged and aged have more knowledge and experience. Therefore, an attempt is made to ascertain the age of the professionals and that is given in Table 5.2.

Table 5.2: Age-wise Distribution of Respondents

Age	*Professionals*						*Total*	
	Doctor		*Engineer*		*Advocate*			
	No. of Respondents	*per cent*	*No. of Respondents*	*per cent*	*No. of Respondents*	*per cent*	*No. of Respondents*	*per cent*
20-30	28	17.5	116	72.5	36	22.5	180	37.5
30-40	80	50.0	36	22.5	80	50.0	196	40.8
40-50	36	22.5	8	5.0	36	22.5	80	16.7
Above 50	16	10.0	0	0	8	5.0	24	5.0
Total	**160**	**100.0**	**160**	**100**	**160**	**100**	**480**	**100.0**

Source: Primary data.

From the above table 5.2 it is seen that 196 (40.8 per cent) respondents fall under the category of 30-40 age group. And the next major age group 180 (37.5 per cent) respondents fall under the category of 20-30. And the rest of the age groups are shared by 40-50 and above 50 and their respective contributions are 80 respondents (16.7 per cent) and 24 respondents (five per cent) each.

Community

Community system was introduced in the ancient India on the basis of occupation. Even though the community behaviour can be molded with the help of education, exposure to multi-media development, it plays its own role in the growth of professionals. Table 5.3 gives the details of the communities to which the professionals belong.

Table 5.3: Community-wise Distribution of Respondents

Community							*Total*	
	Doctor		*Engineer*		*Advocate*			
	No. of Respondents	*per cent*	*No. of Respondents*	*per cent*	*No. of Respondents*	*per cent*	*No. of Respondents*	*per cent*
SC/ST	4	2.5	12	7.5	52	32.5	68	14.2
MBC	32	20	24	15	28	17.5	84	17.5
BC	104	65.0	120	75	76	47.5	300	62.5
FC	20	12.5	4	2.5	4	2.5	28	5.8
Total	**160**	**100**	**160**	**100**	**160**	**100**	**480**	**100**

Source: Primary data.

From the above Table 5.3 it is clear that 300 (62.5 per cent) respondents fall under the category of Backward Community (BC) and the next major group, 84 respondents fall under the category of Most Backward Class (MBC) which constitute 17.5 per cent and 68 respondents (14.2 per cent) belong to Scheduled Caste/Scheduled Tribe (SC/ST) and the least group of 28 respondents belong to Forward Community (FC) which is 5.8 per cent.

Marital Status

The marital status of a person may influence the need for finance. It may also determine the ability of the person to start his career and earn for his family and save some amount for his future. Marital status of professionals is classified into married and unmarried. It is tabulated in Table 5.4.

Table 5.4: Marital Status of Respondents

Marital Status	*Doctor*		*Engineer*		*Advocate*		*Total*	
	No. of Respondents	*per cent*	*No. of Respondents*	*per cent*	*No. of Respondents*	*per cent*	*No. of Respondents*	*per cent*
Married	128	80	92	57.5	144	90	364	75.8
Unmarried	32	20	68	42.5	16	10	116	24.2
Total	**160**	**100**	**160**	**100**	**160**	**100**	**480**	**100**

Source: Primary data.

From the above Table 5.4 it is seen that majority of the respondents have come under the category of 'married' which constitute 75.8 per cent (364 respondents) and the rest of 116 respondents (24.2 per cent) are 'unmarried'. Among the married, majority of the 128 respondents (39 per cent) belong to advocates. Regarding unmarried majority of 68 respondents (58.62 per cent) belong to engineers.

Literacy Level

Education is one of the prime necessities to become an efficient professional. The level of additional higher educational qualifications helps to enrich their knowledge, exposure, personality of the professionals in all aspects.

In this study, literacy level is classified as from basic professional qualification to higher educational level as shown in Table 5.5.

Table 5.5: Literacy Level of Respondents

Literacy Level	*Doctor*		*Engineer*		*Advocate*		*Total*	
	No. of Respondents	*per cent*	*No. of Respondents*	*per cent*	*No. of Respondents*	*per cent*	*No. of Respondents*	*per cent*
BE	—	—	60	37.5	—	—	60	12.5
MBBS	84	52.5	—	—	—	—	84	17.5
BL	—	—	—	—	112	70	112	23.3
ME	—	—	100	62.5	—	—	100	20.8
MD	76	46.5	—	—	—	—	76	15.8
ML	—	—	—	—	48	30	48	10.0
Total	**160**	**100**	**160**	**100**	**160**	**100**	**480**	**100.0**

Source: Primary data.

It is inferred from the above Table 5.5 that majority of the 112 respondents (23.3 per cent) are Bachelors of Lawyers (BL). And the second major group 100 respondents (20.8 per cent) fall under the educational category of Master of Engineering (ME) holders. And the third major group of 84 respondents (17.5 per cent) are MBBS holders and the least 48 respondents (10 per cent) are Master of Law (ML) holders.

Type of Employment

The occupational background provides an idea to start and manage the professional career. The government professionals sometimes are restricted to take some extra effort to build up their career by doing private practices and earn additional income which plays a vital role in taking investment decisions. Private professionals are free to develop their career without any restrictions but they must follow professional ethics. In the present study the type of employment is classified as government and private employment. Table 5.6 shows it in detail the type of employment of the respondents.

It is inferred from the above Table 5.6 that out of 480 respondents majority of 324 respondents (67.5 per cent) belong to Private Sector. And rest of 156 respondents (32.5 per cent) are in government services. Among the private sector major portion is covered by 144 advocates (44.44 per cent) and among the government sector major portion is covered by 120 doctors (76.92 per cent).

Table 5.6: Type of Employment of Respondents

Type of Employment	*Doctor*		*Engineer*		*Advocate*		*Total*	
	No. of Respondents	*per cent*	*No. of Respondents*	*per cent*	*No. of Respondents*	*per cent*	*No. of Respondents*	*per cent*
Govt.	120	75.0	20	12.5	16	10.0	156	32.5
Private	40	25.0	140	87.5	144	90.0	324	67.5
Total	**160**	**100**	**160**	**100**	**160**	**100**	**480**	**100**

Source: Primary data.

Place of Occupation

Place of occupation indicates where the professional is doing his career. It implies the fact that if he is doing his career in an urban place, he has to spend a lot whereas in rural area the cost of living is low and ultimately his savings and investment level also increase, so it plays a vital role. Area is classified into urban, semi-urban and rural and it is described in the following Table 5.7.

Table 5.7: Place of Occupation-wise Distribution of Respondents

Place of occupation	*Doctor*		*Engineer*		*Advocate*		*Total*	
	No. of Respondents	*per cent*	*No. of Respondents*	*per cent*	*No. of Respondents*	*per cent*	*No. of Respondents*	*per cent*
Urban	100	62.5	108	67.5	88	67.5	296	61.7
Semi-urban	44	27.5	32	20.0	32	20.0	108	22.5
Rural	16	10.0	20	12.5	40	25.0	76	15.8
Total	**160**	**100**	**160**	**100**	**160**	**100**	**480**	**100**

Source: Primary data.

From the above Table 5.7 it is inferred that majority of 296 respondents (61.7 per cent) have their occupational place in urban area and the second large group of 108 respondents (22.5 per cent) have their occupational place in the semi-urban and the least number of respondents (15.8 per cent) have their occupational area in the rural area.

Private Practice

Private practice of the professionals is important one in this study. A professional who is a government servant who has additional private practice increases his income and simultaneously it also increases his investment. By having this implied fact, the present study classifies the professionals as having 'private practice' which is clearly described in the following Table 5.8.

Table 5.8: Private Practice-wise Distribution of Respondents

Private Practice	*Doctor*		*Engineers*		*Advocate*		*Total*	
	No. of Respondents	*per cent*	*No. of Respondents*	*per cent*	*No. of Respondents*	*per cent*	*No. of Respondents*	*per cent*
Yes	92	57.5	32	20.0	136	85.0	260	54.2
No	68	42.5	128	80.0	24	15.0	220	45.8
Total	**160**	**100.0**	**160**	**100.0**	**160**	**100.0**	**480**	**100.0**

Source: Primary data.

It is clear from the above Table 5.8 that majority of 260 respondents (54.2 per cent) have private practice and rest of the 220 respondents (45.8 per cent) are not having any private practice, which also indicates that they depend on government service. Individual private practice of the professionals support them to increase their income level which automatically leads them to identify new investment avenues in order to strengthen their investment base.

Spouse Employability

Employment status of the spouse is an important component in making investment decisions. If the spouse is employed, it creates confidence in the minds of the professionals and strengthens their investment scenario which leads to take strong decisions in making more investment in various investment avenues. On the basis of spouse employability, the entire professionals are classified and it is clearly placed in the following Table 5.9.

Table 5.9: Employability of the Respondents' Spouses

Spouse Employment	*Doctor*		*Engineer*		*Advocate*		*Total*	
	No. of Respondents	*per cent*	*No. of Respondents*	*per cent*	*No. of Respondents*	*per cent*	*No. of Respondents*	*per cent*
Yes	100	62.5	64	40.0	96	60.0	260	54.2
No	60	37.5	96	60.0	64	40.0	220	45.8
Total	**160**	**100**	**160**	**100**	**160**	**100**	**480**	**100**

Source: Primary data.

It is seen from the above Table 5.9 that the spouses of the most of the respondents are employed which indicates that it enhances the viability of the professionals to find different investment avenues for their investment. They constitute 54.2 per cent of the total respondents. Rests of the 45.8 per cent respondents' spouses are not employed. In general, their investment aspirations are somewhat lower than the earlier group. Spouse employability always support the respondents in taking investment decisions strongly and at the same time quickly without taking more time for analysing.

Nature of Family

If professionals live in a joint family set up their investment behaviour differs from the professionals who are in a nuclear family system. Since the professionals who are in nuclear family system may take individual investment decisions whereas professionals who are in a joint family system, their decisions are influenced by parents, elders of the family and sometimes, they are controlled by family commitments. So, in order to analyse this, the nature of family is included in this study and it is clearly depicted in the following Table 5.10.

Table 5.10: Nature of Family-wise Distribution of Respondents

Nature of Family	*Doctor*		*Engineer*		*Advocate*		*Total*	
	No. of Respondents	*per cent*	*No. of Respondents*	*per cent*	*No. of Respondents*	*per cent*	*No. of Respondents*	*per cent*
Joint	24	15.0	80	50.0	80	50.0	184	38.3
Nuclear	136	85.0	80	50.0	80	50.0	296	61.7
Total	160	100.0	160	100.0	160	100	480	100

Source: Primary data.

It is inferred from the Table 5.10 that out of 480 respondents 296 respondents, (61.7 per cent) belong to nuclear families and the rest of the 184 respondents (38.3 per cent) belong to joint families. Majority of the respondents belong to nuclear families. In certain cases nuclear family set up reduces the expenditures of the respondents and increase their investment level. Under this nuclear family setup the respondents take the investment decisions individually without the intervention of the parents and elders of the family. In certain cases, joint family setup lessen the expenditures of the respondents which ultimately makes them to concentrate on their investment aspirations.

Size of the Family

The size of the family represents the number of family members living along with the respondents. Since the family is an important demographic variable, it is included in the present study. If the numbers of family members are low it reduces the expenditure and increases the investment level.

Table 5.11: No. of Family Members-wise Distribution of Respondents

Nature of Family Member	*Doctors*		*Engineers*		*Advocates*		*Total*	
	No. of Respondents	*per cent*	*No. of Respondents*	*per cent*	*No. of Respondents*	*per cent*	*No. of Respondents*	*per cent*
2	16	10.0	4	2.5	4	2.5	24	5.0
3	32	20.0	32	20.0	20	12.5	84	17.5
4	56	35.0	36	22.5	52	32.5	144	30.0
5	44	27.5	44	27.5	28	17.5	116	24.2
6	8	5.0	28	17.5	28	17.5	64	13.3
Above 6	4	2.5	16	10.0	28	17.5	48	10.0
Total	**160**	**100.0**	**160**	**100.0**	**160**	**100.0**	**480**	**100**

Source: Primary data.

It is inferred from the above Table 5.11, that majority of 144 respondents (30 per cent) are having four family members and 116 respondents (24.2 per cent) are having five family members and the next 84 respondents (17.5 per cent) are having three family members, and the final 24 respondents (5.0 per cent) are having two family members. In the case of less family members, it induces the investors to increase their investment level.

Number of Earning Members

The earning members of the family reveal the family income and the standard of living of the family members. It is included as an important variable because higher number of earning members will increase the investment level of the professionals. The number of earning members in the present study is classified in the following way in the Table 5.12.

Table 5.12: Number of Earning Members in the Families of the Respondents

Nature of Earning Members	*Doctor*		*Engineer*		*Advocate*		*Total*	
	No. of Respondents	*per cent*	*No. of Respondents*	*per cent*	*No. of Respondents*	*per cent*	*No. of Respondents*	*per cent*
One	36	22.5	12	7.5	32	20.0	80	16.7
Two	112	70.0	104	65.0	80	50.0	296	61.7
Three	12	7.5	32	20.0	16	10.0	60	12.5
Four	—	—	4	2.5	24	15.0	28	5.8
Above 4	—	—	8	5.0	8	5.0	16	3.3
Total	**160**	**100**	**160**	**100**	**160**	**100**	**480**	**100**

Source: Primary data.

It is found out from the above Table 5.12 that out of 480 respondents, 296 respondents (61.7 per cent) are having only two earning members and next 80 respondents (16.7 per cent) are having only one earning member and the least group of 16 respondents (3.3 per cent each) are having more than four earning member in their families. Earning members of the family plays a vital role in taking investment decisions. More number of earning members in the family motivates the respondents to explore new ways for making investments.

Table 5.13: Economic Status of the Professionals

Sl. No.	*Particulars*	*Monthly Average investments*				*F-Statistics*
		Doctors Rs	*Engineers Rs*	*Advocates Rs*	*Overall Mean Rs*	
1.	Monthly professional Income	57475.00	32425.00	26323.75	38741.25	46.321**
2.	Monthly Income of Other Earning Members in the Family	39242.42	26442.10	24781.25	30027.18	25.166**
3.	Monthly Family Income	82000.00	52225.00	51368.75	61864.58	70.036**
4.	Monthly Savings	27700.00	27525.00	22875.00	26033.33	5.155**

Source: Primary Data.

** Significant at one per cent level.

Regarding the economic status of the professionals, the doctors earn higher and the respective overall mean earnings is 51,604.36, whereas among the engineers and advocates the mean earnings are 34,654.28 and 31,337.19 respectively. It reveals that the doctors have high economic status whereas the engineers and advocates are moderate in their income. The doctors have high confidence on their economic status. Regarding the perception on the economic status in all the four variables the F-statistics identifies significant difference among the three groups of professionals at one per cent level.

Table 5.14: Average annual investment of professionals in financial assets

Sl. No.	*Financial Assets*	*Annual Average investments*			*Overall Mean Rs P*	*F-Statistics*
		Doctors Rs P	*Engineers Rs P*	*Advocates Rs P*		
1.	Postal Deposits	25,000.00	26,814.81	23,948.72	25,081.63	1.850[NS]
2.	Bank Deposits	46,810.81	46,948.72	39,360.00	44,284.48	5.367**
3.	Life Insurance	40,000.00	41,358.97	34,777.78	38,815.79	4.459*
4.	Chit Fund	41,150.00	35,600.00	29,863.64	35,402.60	3.141*
5.	Provident Fund	60,375.00	40,210.53	38,193.55	47,317.07	19.288**
6.	Pension Plan	40,095.24	28,250.00	31,393.94	32,769.23	17.374**

Source: Primary Data.

*Significant at five per cent level. **Significant at one per cent level.

Regarding the investments in Financial assets, the doctors invested more on 'Provident fund' since its mean investment is a maximum of Rs 60,375.

Among the engineers, this variable is 'Bank deposits' since its mean value is Rs 46,948.72 whereas among the advocates also this variable is the same 'Bank deposits' since its value is Rs 39,360. The significant difference among the three groups of professionals is identified in the perception on five variables in Financial assets since the respective 'F' statistics are significant at one per cent and five per cent levels. The Average Annual investments of the six variables in Financial assets among doctors, engineers and advocates are 42,238.50, 36,530.50 and 32,922.94 respectively. It indicates that the higher level of perception on the variables in financial assets among the doctors than the engineers and advocates.

Table 5.15: Annual Average Investment of Professionals in Physical Assets

Sl. No.	*Physical Assets*	*Annual Average investments*			*Overall Mean Rs P*	*F- Statistics*
		Doctors Rs P	*Engineers Rs P*	*Advocates Rs P*		
1.	Real Estate	40,771.43	42,852.94	38,705.88	40,776.75	0.724NS
2.	Gold, Silver and other precious metals	39,405.41	47,088.24	35,605.26	40,699.64	4.344*

* Significant at five per cent level.

Regarding the investments in physical assets, the doctors invested more on 'real estate' since its mean value is Rs 40,771.43. Among the engineers, this variable is 'gold, silver and other precious metals' since its mean value is Rs 47,088.24 whereas among the advocates this variable is 'Real estate' since its mean value is Rs 38,705.88. The significant difference among the three groups of professionals is identified in the perception on one variable in Physical assets since the respective 'F' statistics are significant at five per cent level. The Average Annual Investments of both the two variables in Physical assets among doctors, engineers and advocates are 40,088.42, 44,970.29 and 37,1555.57 respectively. It indicates that the higher level of perception on the variables in Physical assets among the engineers than the doctors and advocates.

Table 5.16: Average Annual Investment of Professionals in Marketable Assets

Sl. No.	*Marketable Assets*	*Annual Average investments*			*Overall Mean Rs P*	*F- Statistics*
		Doctor Rs P	*Engineer Rs P*	*Advocates Rs P*		
1.	Mutual Fund	33,542.86	36,342.86	31,375.00	33,753.57	0.514NS
2.	Shares	22,555.56	20,222.22	23,884.62	22,220.80	3.204*
3.	Debentures and Bonds	24,272.73	23,238.10	22,666.67	23,392.50	0.461NS

Source: *Significant at five per cent level.

Regarding the investments in Marketable assets, the doctors invested more on 'Mutual fund' since its mean value is Rs 33,542.86. Among the engineers, this variable is 'mutual fund' since its mean value is Rs 36,342.86, whereas among the advocates also this variable is the same 'mutual fund' since its value is Rs 31,375. The significant difference among the three groups of professionals is identified in the perception on one variable in marketable assets since the respective 'F' statistics are significant at five per cent level. The average annual investments of the three variables in marketable assets among doctors, engineers and advocates are 26,790.38, 26,601.06 and 25,975.43 respectively. It indicates that the higher level of perception on the variables in Marketable assets among the doctors than the engineers and advocates.

Table 5.17: Average Annual Total Investment of Professionals in Financial, Physical and Marketable Assets

Professionals	*No. of Respondents*	*Amount Rs P.*
Doctors	160	3,62,128.20
Engineers	160	3,23,794.87
Advocates	160	2,96,275.00
Total Average	480	3,27,135.59
F-test	2.273^{NS}	

Source: Primary Data.

Regarding average annual total investments by professionals, they are constituted by three important groups of assets such as financial, physical and marketable assets. Among the professionals, doctors become the first and their total average annual investments on the three group of assets is Rs 3,62,128.20 and they are followed by engineers and advocates and their respective average annual total investments are Rs 3,23,794.87 and Rs 2,96,275.00 respectively.

The F-statistics identifies no significant difference among the professionals relating to the total average annual investments by professionals on three groups of assets such as Financial, Physical and Marketable assets.

Table 5.18: Source of Investments of the Professionals

Source of Investments	*Doctor*		*Engineer*		*Advocate*		*Total*	
	No. of Respts.	*per cent*	*No. of Respts.*	*per cent*	*No. of Respts.*	*per cent*	*No. of Respts.*	*per cent*
Savings	124	77.5	112	70	128	80	364	75.83
Pledging or Selling of Jewels	8	5	4	2.5	—	—	12	2.5
Loan	16	10	44	27.5	12	7.5	72	15

Some other Sources	12	12.5	—	—	20	12.5	32	6.7
Total	**160**	**100**	**160**	**100**	**160**	**100**	**480**	**100**

Source: Primary data.

From the above Table 5.18 it is clearly known that among the 480 respondents, 364 (62.5 per cent) respondents are creating resources for making investments from their own savings and they are followed by 72 (15 per cent) respondents who are creating sources through loan. 32 (6.7 per cent) respondents are getting resources for their investment from some other sources. The rest of 12 (2.5 per cent) respondents are pledging or selling their Jewells for their investment purpose.

Table 5.19: Time Horizon for Investments

No. of Years	*Doctor*		*Engineer*		*Advocate*		*Total*	
	No. of Respts.	*per cent*	*No. of Respts.*	*per cent*	*No. of Respts.*	*per cent*	*No. of Respts.*	*per cent*
0 - 5	24	15	52	32.5	24	15.0	100	20.8
5 -10	72	48	60	37.5	96	60.0	228	47.5
10 and above	64	40	48	30.0	40	25.0	152	31.7
Total	160	100	160	100	160	100	480	100

Source: Primary data.

It is found from the above Table 5.19 that out of 480 respondents, 228 (47.5 per cent) respondents are ready to spare five to 10 years for their investments to accumulate and 152 (31.7per cent) respondents are interested to allow 10 and more years for the progress of their investment. Finally 100 (20.8 per cent) respondents are ready to spare to the maximum of 5 years only for the growth of their investments.

Table 5.20: Awareness Level of Professionals on Financial Assets

Sl. No.	*Investment Avenues*	*Mean Scores*				*F-Statistics*
		Doctors	*Engineers*	*Advocates*	*Overall*	
1.	Postal Savings	4.3500	4.0500	4.5250	4.3083	11.593**
2.	Postal Recurring Deposit	4.1750	3.4500	4.2500	3.9583	34.116**
3.	Postal Time Deposit	3.4250	2.8250	3.5000	3.2500	12.345**
4.	Postal NSC	3.4500	2.6500	3.2250	3.1083	16.079**
5.	Bank Savings Account	4.5000	4.6500	4.7000	4.6167	3.724**
6.	Bank Recurring Deposit	4.1500	3.7250	4.1250	4.0000	8.383**

7.	Bank Fixed Deposit	4.4000	4.0250	4.3500	4.2583	7.630**
8.	Chit Funds	3.3000	3.3250	4.0250	3.5500	18.140**
9.	Life Insurance from LIC	4.4000	4.3750	4.5750	4.4500	2.952**
10.	Private Life Insurance	3.1750	3.4000	3.4250	3.3333	2.563**
11.	FD in Companies	1.9500	2.0750	1.8750	1.9667	1.343**
12.	Provident Funds	4.1500	3.7000	4.1500	4.0000	8.224**

Source: Primary Data.

** Significant at one per cent level.

The awareness level towards financial investments is higher among the advocates, since the overall mean score for all the investment avenues is 3.8938, whereas among the doctors and engineers, the mean scores are 3.7854 and 3.5208 respectively. Among variables the highly scored individual variable is 'bank savings account' and the respective score is 4.6167 which implies the fact that all the professional groups are highly attracted towards the avenue.

The highly perceived variable among the three groups of professionals is 'bank savings account'. Apart from this variable, the highly perceived variable among the doctors, engineers and advocates is 'Life Insurance from LIC', since the respective mean scores are 4.4000, 4.3750 and 4.5750. The significant difference among the three groups of professionals is identified in the perception on all the twelve variables related to awareness level, since the respective "F" statistics are significant at one per cent.

Table 5.21: Awareness Level of Professionals on Physical Investment Avenues

Sl. No.	*Investment Avenues*	*Mean scores*				*F-Statistics*
		Doctors	*Engineers*	*Advocates*	*Overall*	
1.	Investment in Valuable Jewellery	4.3250	4.0750	4.6000	4.3333	10.513**
2.	Land and Buildings	4.2750	3.9500	4.4250	4.2157	10.450**
3.	Commercial Vehicles	3.3750	3.1750	3.6250	3.3917	5.895**

Source: Primary Data.

** Significant at one per cent level.

Regarding the awareness level of physical investment avenue, among the professionals the highly scored individual investment avenue is 'investment in valuable jewellery' and the respective overall mean score is 4.3333. Related to the perception of the variables on the awareness level of physical investment avenues among the doctors, engineers and advocates is the same variable 'investment in valuable jewellery' and the respective scores are 4.3250, 4.0750 and 4.6000. The significant difference among the three groups of professionals is identified in the perception on the three variables in awareness level, since the respective 'F' statistics are significant at one per cent. The mean scores of all the three variables in awareness level among doctors, engineers and advocates are 3.9917, 3.7333 and 4.2167 respectively. It indicates the the awareness level of physical investment avenues is higher among the advocates than the doctors and engineers.

Table 5. 22: Professionals' Awareness Level on Marketable Investment Avenues

Sl. No.	*Investment Avenues*	*Mean scores*				*F-Statistics*
		Doctors	*Engineers*	*Advocates*	*Overall*	
1.	Units in UTI	3.5000	3.9500	3.3750	3.6083	8.501**
2.	Pvt. Mutual Funds	3.0750	3.1500	2.7750	3.0000	4.852**
3.	Shares	3.5500	3.8500	3.4750	3.6250	3.495**
4.	Debentures	2.6250	3.1250	2.5000	2.7500	11.874**
5.	Company Bonds	2.4500	2.5750	2.2000	2.4083	3.996**
6.	Government Bonds	3.6250	3.8250	3.2750	3.5750	8.444**
7.	Commodity Markets	1.9000	2.6250	2.4250	2.3167	15.667**
8.	Foreign Currency	2.1250	2.6750	2.0250	2.2750	17.170**

Source: Primary Data.

** Significant at one per cent level.

The advocates' awareness level towards marketable investment avenue in general is lower since the overall mean score on different investment avenues is 2.7563 whereas among the doctors and engineers, the mean scores are 2.8563 and 3.2219 respectively. It reveals that the engineers perceive in a positive way on the marketable investment avenue whereas the doctors are moderate in their perception. The advocates are highly afraid of the ups and downs of the capital market and its impact on marketable investment avenues.

The highly attracted investment avenue among the doctors are 'government Bonds' since the respective high scored mean value is 3.6250. Among the engineers this variable is 'Units in UTI', since its mean value is 3.9500 whereas among the advocates, this variable is 'Shares' since its mean value is 3.4750. The significant difference among the three groups of professionals is identified in the perception on all the eight variables on awareness level of marketable investment avenues, since the respective 'F' statistics are significant at one per cent level.

Table 5. 23: Sources of Awareness on Different Investment Avenues

Sl. No.	*Investment Avenues*	*Mean scores*				*F-Statistics*
		Doctors	*Engineers*	*Advocates*	*Overall*	
1	Govt. Promotional Measures	4.0250	3.8650	3.2750	3.9250	1.527 NS
2	Investment Journals	3.9250	3.5250	3.5750	3.6750	7.646**
3	Financial Newspapers	3.8500	3.6750	3.5000	3.6750	4.119*
4	Advertisements in TV	4.0500	3.8750	3.6750	3.8667	4.507*
5	Advertisements in Radio	2.9000	3.2750	2.8250	3.0000	6.707**
6	Friends and Colleagues	4.1750	3.8250	3.7250	3.9083	11.391**
7	Internet and e-mail	3.5750	3.8000	2.9500	3.4417	22.018**
8	Chartered Accountants	3.0250	3.1250	3.0750	3.0750	.277 NS
9	Investors Association	2.7750	2.7250	2.3000	2.6000	8.703**
10	Brokers and Agents	3.5750	3.2500	3.8750	3.3667	2.899*
11	Cell phone SMS	3.3250	2.9250	2.7500	3.0000	9.469**
12	Companies Annual Reports	2.2000	2.6250	2.2500	2.3583	4.919**

Source: Primary Data.

**Significant one per cent level. *Significant five per cent level.

Regarding the source of awareness on different investment avenues, the overall mean score for doctors is 3.4500 which is higher than engineers and advocates. The overall mean scores for engineers and advocates are 3.3750 and 3.1479 respectively. It reveals that all the source of awareness are highly utilised by doctors than other two professional groups.

The highly perceived factor among the doctors is 'friends and colleagues' and the respective score is 4.1750, whereas among the engineers and advocates these factors are 'advertisements in TV' and 'brokers and agents' and the scores are 3.8750 and 3.8750 respectively. The 'F' statistics identifies significant difference among the professionals regarding the sources of awareness on different investment avenues in ten variables out of twelve variables in total.

Table 5.24: Influencing Personalities of Professional on Investment Decisions

Sl. No.	*Influencing Personalities*	*Mean scores*				*F-Statistics*
		Doctors	*Engineers*	*Advocates*	*Overall*	
1	Self Motivation	4.3750	4.1500	4.5750	4.3667	10.238**
2	Spouse	4.3500	3.9250	4.2250	4.1667	10.245**
3	Parents	3.7250	3.8000	3.8000	3.7750	00.287[NS]
4	Children	2.7000	2.5641	3.0250	2.7647	6.152**
5	Relatives	2.3750	2.8750	2.9500	2.7333	15.325[NS]
6	Friends	3.6000	3.6250	3.9000	3.7083	4.535*
7	Colleagues	3.7750	3.5250	3.8750	3.7250	4.870**

Source: Primary Data

**Significant at one per cent level. *Significant at five per cent level.

Regarding the perception on the variables relating to Influencing Personalities all the three professional groups perceived more on 'Self motivation' irrespective of their profession which means professionals are self motivated in taking investment related decisions, they are less impressed by various external pressures. On 'self-motivation' the mean scores for doctors, engineers and advocates are 4.3750, 4.1500, 4.5750 respectively. Among the seven variables, this variable is highly scored in all the three groups.

The mean scores of all the seven variables regarding Influencing Personalities among doctors, engineers and advocates are 3.5571, 3.4949 and 3.7643 respectively. It indicates that the perception level of advocates is higher than doctors and engineers. Among the seven variables the 'F' statistics identifies significant difference among the professionals on five variables at one per cent and five per cent level.

Table 5. 25: Level of Confidence of Professionals on Expected Returns

Sl. No.	*Different Investment Amvenues*	*Mean scores*				*F-Statistics*
		Doctors	*Engineers*	*Advocates*	*Overall*	
1	Postal Deposits	4.1750	4.0250	4.4250	4.2083	9.004**
2	Bank Deposits	4.1750	3.9000	4.3750	4.1500	17.294**
3	Life Insurance	3.6250	3.7500	3.9500	3.7750	7.2450**
4	Real Estate	3.9000	3.6250	4.2000	3.9083	13.219**
5	Gold, Silver and Other Precious Metals	4.2000	3.9250	4.5750	4.2333	17.671**

6	Mutual Funds	2.9250	3.1250	3.3000	3.1167	6.365**
7	Chit Funds	2.6250	2.7550	3.0250	2.8000	7.694**
8	Shares	2.3500	2.7368	2.3250	2.4661	8.242**
9	Provident Fund	3.7000	3.2250	3.8250	3.5833	17.202**
10	Pension Plan	3.5500	3.7000	3.7500	3.6667	2.113[NS]
11	Debentures and Bonds	3.0250	2.6750	3.0500	2.9167	7.649**

Source: Primary Data.
**Significant at one per cent level.

Regarding the level of confidence on expected returns from the variables of different investment avenues, the doctors perceived more on gold, silver and other precious metals and the mean score is 4.2000. Among the engineers, this variable is 'postal deposits' since its mean value is 4.0250, whereas among the advocates this variable is 'gold, silver and other precious metals' since its mean value is 4.5750. The significant difference among the three groups of professionals is identified in the perception on 10 variables, since the respective 'F' statistics are significant at one per cent.

The mean score of all eleven variables among doctors, engineers and advocates are 3.4773, 3.4038 and 3.7091 respectively. It indicates higher level of confidence prevails among the advocates in getting expected returns than the doctors and engineers.

The Table (Table 5. 26) reveals that the doctors are highly satisfied on the real estate and gold, silver other precious metals investment avenues since their mean satisfaction scores are 4.2564 and 4.2500 respectively. They are having low level satisfaction on shares and debentures and bonds since their respective mean score are 2.4359 and 2.7356 respectively.

The analysis of skewness also reveals that more than average number of respondents are of the same view with regard to postal deposits, bank deposits, life insurance, real estate, gold, silver and other precious metals, provident fund and debentures and bonds. The analysis of co-efficient of variation reveals that there is more consistency in their view with regard to real estate, gold, silver and other precious metals, provident fund and life insurance.

Table 5. 26: Satisfaction of the Doctors on the Returns of their Investment Portfolio

Particulars	*Postal Deposits*	*Bank Deposits*	*Life Insurance*	*Real Estate*	*Gold, Silver and Other metals*	*Mutual Fund*	*Chit Fund*	*Shares*	*Provident Fund*	*Pension Plan*	*Debentures and Bonds*
Mean Score on Satisfaction	3.5250	3.6000	3.8500	4.2564	4.2500	3.1026	2.5897	2.4359	3.3500	3.4750	2.7436
Co-efficient of Variation	30.51	31.03	21.45	18.27	16.48	29.10	41.81	46.44	23.72	20.40	35.83
Skewness per cent	-0.311	-0.693	–0.257	–0.483	–0.389	0.222	0. 383	0.594	–0.105	0.304	–0.290

Source: Primary Data.

Table 5. 27: Satisfaction of the Engineers on the Returns of their Investment Portfolio

Particulars	*Postal Deposits*	*Bank Deposits*	*Life Insurance*	*Real Estate*	*Gold, Silver and Other metals*	*Mutual Fund*	*Chit Fund*	*Shares*	*Provident Fund*	*Pension Plan*	*Debentures and Bonds*
Mean Score on Satisfaction	4.0250	3.9000	3.8750	4.0250	4.1250	3.0250	3.1000	2.8500	3.6000	3.7500	2.9231
Co-efficient of Variation	21.21	21.37	20.21	20.47	19.75	34.37	33.00	30.02	26.29	20.50	30.48
Skewness per cent	–0.294	-0.867	0.224	–0.047	–0.800	0.086	0. 226	0.294	0.519	0.462	–0.070

Source: Primary Data.

Table 5. 28: Satisfaction of the Advocates on the Returns of their Investment Portfolio

Particulars	*Postal Deposits*	*Bank Deposits*	*Life Insurance*	*Real Estate*	*Gold, Silver and Other metals*	*Mutual Fund*	*Chit Fund*	*Shares*	*Provident Fund*	*Pension Plan*	*Debentures and Bonds*
Mean Score on Satisfaction	3.8500	3.8250	4.0500	4.3500	4.4750	3.1750	3.2000	2.8750	3.5500	3.7750	2.9500
Co-efficient of Variation	18.92	21.85	21.41	18.27	17.35	22.21	22.39	35.91	24.43	22.62	25.16
Skewness per cent	–0.551	–0.968	–1.269	–0.714	–2.363	–0.261	0. 100	–0.163	0.078	–0.040	–1.041

Source: Primary Data.

Table 5. 29: Overall Satisfaction of the Professionals on the Returns of their Investment Portfolio

Particulars	*Postal Deposits*	*Bank Deposits*	*Life Insurance*	*Real Estate*	*Gold, Silver and Other metals*	*Mutual Fund*	*Chit Fund*	*Shares*	*Provident Fund*	*Pension Plan*	*Debentures and Bonds*
Mean Score on Satisfaction	3.8000	3.7750	3.9250	4.2101	4.2833	3.1008	2.9664	2.7227	3.5000	3.6667	2.8729
Co-efficient of Variation	24.19	25.03	21.12	19.22	18.15	28.81	33.30	37.81	25.04	21.54	30.62
Skewness per cent	–0.500	–0.909	–0.477	–0.401	–1.182	0. 014	0. 067	0.157	0.262	0.257	-0.426

Source: Primary Data.

The above Table (Table 5.27) reveals that engineers are highly satisfied on gold, silver and other precious metals and real estate investment avenues since their mean satisfaction scores are 4.1250 and 4.0250 respectively. They have low level of satisfaction on debentures and bonds and shares since their respective mean scores are 2.9231 and 2.8500 respectively. The analysis of skewness also reveals that more than average numbers of respondents are of the same view with regard to postal deposits, bank deposits, real estate, gold, silver and other precious metals, and debentures and bonds. The analysis of co-efficient of variation reveals that there is more consistency in their view with regard to gold, silver and other precious metals, postal deposits, bank deposits and real estate.

The above Table (Table 5.28) reveals that the advocates are highly satisfied on the gold, silver other precious metals and real estate investment avenues since their mean satisfaction scores 4.4750 and 4.3500 respectively. They are having low level of satisfaction on shares and debentures and bonds since their respective mean score are 2.8750 and 2.9500. The analysis of skewness also reveals that more than average number of respondents are of the same view with regard to postal deposits, bank deposits, life insurance, real estate, gold, silver and other precious metals, mutual fund, shares, pension plan and debentures and bonds. The analysis of co-efficient of variation reveals that there is more consistency in their view with regard to gold silver and other precious metals, real estate, postal deposits, life insurance, bank deposits, mutual fund and pension plan.

The above Table (Table 5.29) reveals that all the three group of professionals are highly satisfied on the gold, silver and other precious metals and real estate investment avenues since their mean satisfaction scores are 4.2833 and 4.2101 respectively. They have low level of satisfaction on shares and debentures and bonds since their respective mean score are 2.7227 and 2.8729. The analysis of skewness also reveals that more than average number of respondents are of the same view with regard to postal deposits, bank deposits, life insurance, real estate, gold silver and other precious metals and Debentures and Bonds. The analysis of co-efficient of variation reveals that there is more consistency in their view with regard to gold, silver and other precious metals, real estate, life insurance and pension plan.

Table 5. 30: Professionals' Attitude Towards Investment Criteria in General

Sl. No.	Overall Attitude on Different Investment Avenues	Mean scores				F-Statistics
		Doctors	Engineers	Advocates	Overall	
1.	Everyone is willing to save and invest.	4.5000	4.4500	4.4000	4.4500	0.802[NS]
2.	Scope for investments is more among professionals.	3.7500	3.8750	3.7000	3.7750	1.487[NS]
3.	Low risk investments are preferred.	4.1000	3.7500	3.7750	3.8750	8.076**
4.	Assured returns are more preferred.	4.2750	3.8000	3.5500	3.8750	25.806**
5.	Higher preference for Tax saving investments.	4.0500	3.8700	3.6750	3.8667	5.643**

Source: Primary Data.

**Significance at one per cent level.

The doctors perceived as highly on all aspects of investment criteria since the respective mean scores on various factors are higher than scores perceived by engineers and advocates. The highly perceived factors among the doctors are 'everyone is willing to save and invest' and 'assured returns are more preferred' since the respective mean scores are 4.5000 and 4.2750 respectively. Among the engineers these factors are 'everyone is willing to save and invest' and 'scope for investments is more among professionals' since the respective means scores are 4.4500 and 3.8750 respectively. Comparatively the advocates perceived lower in all the criteria especially the factors 'higher preference for Tax saving investments' and 'assured returns are more preferred' since the mean scores are 3.6750 and 3.5500 respectively. The significant differences among the three groups of professionals are identified regarding the perception on the investment criteria especially in three factors since the respective 'F' statistics at one per cent level.

Table 5. 31: Professionals' Attitude Towards Postal Deposits

Sl. No.	Attitude Towards Postal Deposits	Mean scores				F-Statistics
		Doctors	Engineers	Advocates	Overall	
1.	Tax concession schemes are preferred.	4.2750	3.6500	3.9500	3.9583	18.463**

2.	Preferred for its easy redemption.	3.8250	3.6000	4.0000	3.8083	8.780**
3.	Government's backup gives confidence.	4.2500	3.6750	4.3500	4.0917	37.582**
4.	Schemes are available in small denomination.	4.0250	3.7750	4.0500	3.9500	6.317**
5.	Reasonable returns.	4.100	3.6750	3.8250	3.8667	9.031**

Source: Primary Data.
**Significance at one per cent level.

Regarding the attitude of the respondents towards postal deposits, it is inferred from the above Table 5. 31 that doctors perceived as highly on almost all aspects of Postal deposits than the engineers and advocates since the respective mean scores on various factors are higher than the scores of other professional groups. The highly perceived factors among the doctors are 'tax concession schemes are preferred', 'government's backup gives confidence' and 'reasonable returns' since the respective mean scores are 4.2750, 4.2500 and 4.100 respectively. Among the advocates these factors are 'government's backup gives confidence', 'schemes are available in small denomination' and 'preferred for its easy redemption' since the respective mean scores 4.3500, 4.0500 and 4.0000 respectively. Engineers' perception is very low in all the factors, in particular the factors 'tax concession schemes are preferred' and 'preferred for its easy redemption' since the mean scores are 3.6500 and 3.6000 respectively. The significant difference among the three groups of professionals is identified regarding the perception on postal deposits in all the factors since the respective 'F' statistics are significant at one per cent level. The analysis infers that engineers are not showing much interest on postal deposit schemes compared to doctors and advocates.

Table 5.32: Professionals' Attitude Towards Bank Savings and Deposits

Sl. No.	*Attitude Towards Bank Savings and Deposits*	*Mean scores*				*F-Statistics*
		Doctors	*Engineers*	*Advocates*	*Overall*	
1.	Preferred due to its necessity.	4.4000	4.5250	4.1500	4.3583	12.723**
2.	It is very secured.	4.4750	4.3750	4.0000	4.2833	17.765**
3.	Preferred for its easy liquidity.	4.2500	4.1750	3.7500	4.0583	16.760**
4.	Steady returns is possible.	4.2000	3.8000	3.7300	3.9167	10.717**

5.	Easy loan for customers	3.9750	3.7500	3.7000	3.8083	3.279*
6.	Enjoy special privileges	4.1250	4.0000	3.7750	3.9667	5.808**

Source: Primary Data.

*Significance at five per cent level. **Significance at one per cent level.

It is inferred from the above Table 5.32 that doctors perceived as highly on all aspects of bank savings and deposits more than the engineers and advocates since the respective mean scores on various factors are greater the scores of other professional groups. The highly perceived factors among the doctors are 'it is very secured', 'preferred due to its necessity' and 'preferred for its easy liquidity' since the respective mean scores are 4.4750, 4.4000 and 4.2500 respectively. Among the engineers these factors are 'preferred due to its necessity', 'it is very secured' and 'preferred for its easy liquidity' since the respective mean scores are 4.5250, 4.3750 and 4.1750. The advocates perceived as very low in all the factors like 'easy loan for customers' and 'steady returns is possible' since the mean scores are 3.7000 and 3.7300 respectively. The significant difference among the three groups of professionals is identified in almost all the factors since the respective 'F' statistics are significant at one per cent and five per cent level. The analysis infers that the advocates are not showing much interest in investing their money in bank savings and deposits compared to doctors and engineers.

Table 5.33: Professionals' Attitude Towards Life Insurance

Sl. No.	*Attitude Towards Life Insurance*	*Mean scores*				*F-Statistics*
		Doctors	*Engineers*	*Advocates*	*Overall*	
1	Preferred for its risk coverage.	4.5750	4.0000	4.3500	4.3083	18.024**
2	Preferred for tax concession.	4.4750	3.9500	4.1750	4.2000	17.973**
3	Maturity value is added with profits.	3.8750	3.8000	3.9500	3.8750	1.712 NS
4	Money back facilities during the policy term.	3.9250	3.6500	3.9250	3.8167	7.060**
5	Preferred as a security for loan.	3.8000	3.6000	3.6250	3.6917	1.347 NS
6	Policies are available for all age groups.	4.2250	3.7500	3.9400	3.9750	12.564**

Source: Primary Data. **Significant at one per cent level.

It is inferred from the Table 5.33 that the doctors perceived as highly on all aspects of attitude towards life insurance investment more than the advocates and engineers since the respective mean scores on various factors related to life insurance are greater than others. The highly perceived factors among the doctors are 'preferred for its risk coverage', 'preferred for tax concession' and 'policies are available for all age groups' since the mean scores are 4.5750, 4.4750 and 4.2250 respectively. Among the advocates these factors are 'preferred for its risk coverage', 'preferred for tax concession' and 'maturity value is added with profits' since the mean scores are 4.3500, 4.1750 and 3.9500 respectively. The engineers perceived as slightly low in all the factors compared with doctors and advocates especially the factors like 'money back facilities during the policy term' and 'preferred as a security for loan' since the mean scores are 3.6500 and 3.6000 respectively. The significant difference among the three groups of professionals is identified regarding the perception on the aspects related to life insurance investments especially in 'preferred for its risk coverage', 'preferred for tax concession', 'money back facilities during the policy term', 'policies are available for all age groups' since the respective 'F' statistics are significant at one per cent level. The analysis infers that the engineers are not showing much interest in having the life insurance as their investment avenue compared to doctors and engineers.

Table 5. 34: Professionals' Attitude Towards Real Estate

Sl. No.	*Attitude towards Real Estate*	*Mean scores*				*F-Statistics*
		Doctors	*Engineers*	*Advocates*	*Overall*	
1.	Investment in house property is a necessity.	4.6750	4.5000	4.2750	4.4833	14.012**
2.	Owning a house is an ambition for many.	4.6500	4.2750	4.1250	4.3500	23.469**
3.	Returns in the form of rent is low but regular.	3.6000	3.6500	3.5250	3.5917	0.695^{NS}
4.	Easy availability of housing loan.	3.7000	3.5250	3.4000	3.5417	4.088*
5.	Comparatively higher investment appreciation.	4.4250	4.4000	3.6250	4.1500	50.123**
6.	Availability of tax concession for housing loan.	4.3500	4.0500	3.3900	3.9333	53.188**

Source: Primary Data.

*Significance at five per cent level. **Significance at one per cent level.

It is inferred from the above Table 5.34 that the advocates' attitude towards the investment of real estate is not so favourable since the overall mean score on the consequences is 3.7458 whereas among the doctors and engineers, the mean scores are 4.2333 and 4.0458 respectively. It reveals that the doctors perceived in a positive way whereas the engineers are moderate in their perception. The highly perceived factors among the doctors are 'investment in house property is a necessity', 'owning a house is an ambition for many' and 'comparatively higher investment appreciation' since the scores are 4.6750, 4.6500 and 4.4250 respectively. Among engineers these factors are 'investment in house property is a necessity', 'comparatively higher investment appreciation' and 'owning a house is an ambition for many' since the scores are 4.5000, 4.4000 and 4.2750 respectively. The advocates perceived as slightly low in all the factors compared with doctors and engineers especially the factors such as 'availability of tax concession for housing loan' and 'easy availability of housing loan' and the scores are 3.3900 and 3.4000 respectively. The analysis infers that the attitude towards real estate investments is better among the doctors and engineers whereas it is slightly unfavourable among the advocates. The 'F' statistics identifies significant difference among the three groups of professionals regarding the perception on the real estate investment avenue in five variables out of six.

Table 5.35: Professionals' Attitude Towards Gold, Silver and Other Precious Metals

Sl. No.	*Attitude Gold, Silver and Other Precious Metals*	*Mean scores*				*F-Statistics*
		Doctors	*Engineers*	*Advocates*	*Overall*	
1.	Its' necessity like two and four wheelers.	4.1250	4.6000	3.9250	4.2167	25.274**
2.	Symbol of status and prestige.	4.0000	4.1750	3.8500	4.0083	7.549**
3.	Purchased due to Indian customs.	4.1750	3.8500	4.0500	4.0250	8.437**
4.	It can be pledged for getting loans.	4.3000	4.1000	4.3250	4.2417	4.346*
5.	Capital appreciation.	4.3500	3.9000	4.4250	4.2083	23.299**
6.	Investments are made because of the loan facilities/ instalment payments	3.7000	3.7250	3.6250	3.6833	0.498^{NS}

Source: Primary Data.

*Significance at five per cent level. **Significance at one per cent level.

Regarding the perception on the variables about the professionals' attitude towards gold, silver and other precious metals the doctors perceived more on 'capital appreciation' since the respective highest mean score is 4.3500. Among the engineers this variable is 'its' necessity like two and four wheelers' since its mean score value is 4.6000 whereas among the advocates this variable is 'it can be pledged for getting loans' since its mean value is 4.2417. The significant difference among the three group of professionals is identified in the perception on five variables since the respective 'F' statistics are significant at one per cent and five per cent level. The overall mean score of all the six variables on attitude towards gold, silver and other precious metals among the doctors, engineers and advocates are 4.1000, 4.0583 and 4.0333 respectively. It indicates that the higher level of perception on the variables is found among the doctors than the engineers and advocates.

Table 5.36 Professionals' Attitude Towards Mutual Funds

Sl. No.	*Attitude Towards Mutual Fund*	*Mean scores*				*F-Statistics*
		Doctors	*Engineers*	*Advocates*	*Overall*	
1	Tax concession funds are preferred.	4.0500	3.7000	3.8500	3.8667	5.098**
2	Pledged as a security for availing loan.	3.5500	3.3250	3.8750	3.2500	27.138**
3	Gives higher returns paralleled with share market.	3.1500	3.3000	3.4250	3.2917	3.372*
4	Preferred to directly investing in shares.	3.3000	3.3000	3.4750	3.3583	1.895^{NS}
5	Preferred for easy liquidity.	3.9500	3.9000	3.7750	3.8750	1.793^{NS}

Source: Primary Data.

*Significance at five per cent level. **Significance at one per cent level.

Regarding the perception on the variables about the professionals' attitude towards Mutual Fund the doctors perceived more on 'Tax concession funds are preferred' since the respective highest mean score is 4.0500. Among the engineers this variable is 'preferred for easy liquidity' since its mean score value is 3.9000 whereas among the advocates this variable is 'pledged as a security for availing loan' since its mean value is 3.8750. The significant difference among the three group of professionals is identified in the perception on five variables since the respective 'F' statistics are significant at one per cent and five per cent level. The overall mean score of all the five variables on attitude towards

Mutual fund among the doctors, engineers and advocates are 3.6000, 3.5050 and 3.6800 respectively. It indicates that the higher level of perception on the variables is found among the advocates than the doctors and engineers.

Table 5. 37: Professionals' Attitude Towards Chit Funds

Sl. No.	*Attitude Towards Chit Funds*	*Mean scores*				*F-Statistics*
		Doctors	*Engineers*	*Advocates*	*Overall*	
1.	Preferred for its convenience.	3.7000	3.6250	4.2000	3.8417	15.259**
2.	It is like a loan without interest.	3.5500	3.5500	3.6000	3.5667	0.160**
3.	Formalities are very minimum.	3.6500	3.6750	4.1750	3.8333	16.463**
4.	Suitable for emergency expenses.	3.6000	3.6500	3.9500	3.7333	6.182**
5.	Scheme finished in a short duration.	3.4250	3.6000	3.9500	3.6583	10.712**

Source: Primary Date. **Significance at one per cent level.

The advocates perceived highly on all aspects of the factors relating to investments on chit funds than the doctors and engineers since the respective mean scores on various variables regarding chit fund investments are greater than others. The overall mean scores for doctors, engineers and advocates are 3.5850, 3.6200 and 3.9750 respectively.

The highly perceived factors among the advocates are 'convenience', 'minimum formalities' and 'suitable for emergency' since the respective mean scores are 3.8417, 3.8333 and 3.7333. Among the engineers, these factors are 'minimum formalities' and 'suitable for emergency expenses' since the mean scores are 3.6750 and 3.6500 respectively. The overall mean score for doctors are lower than engineers and advocates since they have negative attitude towards investment on chit funds. The doctors perceived as very low for the factors like 'scheme finished in a short duration' and 'a loan without interest' since the mean scores are 3.4250 and 3.5500 respectively.

Significant difference among the three groups of professionals is identified regarding their perception on chit fund investments in almost all the factors, since the respective F-statistics are significant at one per cent level. The analysis infers that the attitude towards chit fund investments are favourable among the advocates whereas the doctors do not show much interest on chit fund investments compared to engineers and advocates.

Table 5. 38: Professionals' Attitude Towards Investment in Shares

Sl. No.	*Attitude Towards Investment in Shares*	*Mean scores*				*F-Statistics*
		Doctors	*Engineers*	*Advocates*	*Overall*	
1.	Preferred for its easy liquidity and transferability.	3.6000	3.7000	3.8750	3.7250	2.880**
2.	Trading in higher volume by depositing margin money.	3.4000	3.5500	3.4750	3.4750	1.317**
3.	Price appreciation provides high reward in the long run.	3.3750	3.2750	3.6250	3.4250	5.312**
4.	Scope for incomparable profits if proper shares are chosen.	3.2750	3.0250	3.6750	3.3250	15.571**
5.	Ambition to gain knowledge of share market.	3.5500	3.4500	4.0750	3.6917	14.874**

Source: Primary Data.**Significance at one per cent level.

Regarding the attitude of the professionals towards investment in shares, as a whole they are favourable much towards the factor 'easy liquidity and transferability' since the respective overall mean score is 3.7250 which is the highest among them. The advocates' attitude towards investments on shares is highly favourable, since the overall mean score on five factors is 3.7450 whereas among the doctors and engineers the mean scores are 3.4400 and 3.4000 respectively.

The highly perceived factors among the advocates are 'ambition to gain knowledge', 'its easy liquidity and transferability' and 'scope for incomparable profits' since the mean scores are 4.0750, 3.8750 and 3.6750 respectively. Among the doctors, these factors are 'its easy liquidity and transferability and 'trading in higher volume by depositing margin money' since the respective mean scores are 3.7000 and 3.5500. The overall mean score for engineers are lower than advocates and doctors since they have negative attitude towards investment on shares. The engineers perception is very low for the factors like 'scope for incomparable profits, and 'price appreciation in the long run' since the mean scores are 3.0250 and 3.2750 respectively.

The significant difference among the three group of professionals is identified regarding their perception on share investments in all the factors, since the respective 'F' statistics are significant at one per cent level. The analysis infers that the attitude towards share investments is highly favourable among the advocates whereas it is unfavourable among the engineers.

Table 5. 39: Professionals' Attitude Towards Provident Fund

Sl. No.	*Attitude Provident Fund*	*Mean scores*				*F-Statistics*
		Doctors	*Engineers*	*Advocates*	*Overall*	
1.	Preferred due to its tax concession.	4.5250	3.9500	3.6750	4.0500	36.385**
2.	Preferred for its loan facility.	3.9500	3.6750	3.5000	3.7083	9.562**
3.	Low risk investment.	4.2250	3.6500	3.9000	3.9250	22.128**
4.	Convenient method of deposits.	4.3250	3.6250	4.1250	4.0250	30.803**
5.	Preferred for its reasonable returns.	3.7750	3.3750	3.5000	3.5500	6.639**

Source: Primary Data. ** Significance at one per cent level.

The attitude of the doctors towards Provident fund, in general, is higher since the overall mean score of all the variables is 4.1600 whereas among the engineers and advocates the mean scores are 3.6550 and 3.7400 respectively. It reveals that doctors perceived in a positive way on the investment in provident fund whereas the advocates are moderate in their perception. The engineers are not much favourable to this investment avenue. The highly scored individual variable is 'preferred due to its tax concession' its respective overall mean score is 4.0500 which reveals that majority of the professionals want to reduce their tax burden.

The highly perceived factors among the doctors are 'tax concession, convenient method of deposits and low risk' since the respective mean scores are 4.5250, 4.3250 and 4.2250. Among the advocates these factors are 'convenient method of deposits, low risk and tax concession' since the respective mean scores are 4.1250, 3.9000 and 3.6750. Engineers are not much in favour of this investment. They perceived as very low in the factors like 'convenient method of deposits and reasonable returns' since the mean scores are 3.6250 and 3.3750 respectively.

The significant difference among the three group of professionals is identified regarding the attitude towards provident fund investments in all the variables since the respective 'F' statistics are significant at one per cent level. The analysis infers that the doctors are much interested towards provident fund investments where as advocates are moderate and engineers are not much favourable to this investment.

Table 5. 40: Professionals' Attitude Towards Pension Plan

Sl. No.	*Attitude Towards Pension Plan*	*Mean scores*				*F-Statistics*
		Doctors	*Engineers*	*Advocates*	*Overall*	
1.	Preferred for security after retirement.	4.3500	4.2250	4.1500	4.2417	2.662^{NS}
2.	Contributions are tax deductable.	4.2250	4.1500	3.9750	4.1167	4.827**
3.	In case of death, surviving spouse or legal heir is benefited.	4.3000	4.2500	4.5750	4.3750	9.792**
4.	Risk level is very low.	4.1750	3.9000	3.8250	3.9667	10.954**
5.	Steady growth is possible.	3.9500	3.8000	3.5000	3.7500	9.792**

Source: Primary Data. ** Significance at one per cent level.

Regarding the perception on the variables towards pension plan, the highly scored individual variable is, 'In case of death, surviving spouse or legal heir is benefited' and the respective overall mean score is 4.3750. Relating to the individual groups, the doctors perceived high on the variable, 'preferred for security after retirement' and its mean score is 4.3500. Among the engineers this variable is, 'In case of death, surviving spouse or legal heir is benefited' and the relevant mean score is 4.2500 whereas among the advocates, this variable is similar to engineers, 'In case of death, surviving spouse or legal heir is benefited' and its mean value is 4.5750.

The significant difference among the three groups of professionals is identified in the perception on four variables relating to pension plan since the respective 'F' statistics are significant at one per cent level. The mean scores of all the five variables among the doctors, engineers and advocates are 4.2000, 4.0650 and 4.0050 respectively. It indicates that the doctors perceived high and their favourability towards investments in pension plan is higher than engineers and advocates.

Table 5. 41: Professionals' Attitude Towards Debentures and Bonds

Sl. No.	*Attitude Towards Debentures and Bonds*	*Mean scores*				*F-Statistics*
		Doctors	*Engineers*	*Advocates*	*Overall*	
1.	It is very secured while comparing shares.	3.6250	3.5250	3.9500	3.7000	8.784**
2.	Preferred for its fixed interest rates.	3.5750	3.7750	3.4250	3.5917	8.342**
3.	Convenience of converting into shares.	3.1750	3.7750	3.2000	3.3833	25.223**
4.	Assured returns are possible.	3.3250	3.5750	3.1250	3.3417	10.667**
5.	Steady capital appreciation is possible.	3.1500	3.5128	3.1250	3.2605	7.351**

Source: Primary Data. ** Significance at one per cent level.

The advocates' attitude towards debentures and bonds in general is not so favourable since the overall mean score on all the variables is 3.3650 whereas among the doctors and engineers the mean scores are 3.3700 and 3.6326 respectively. It reveals that the engineers have perceived a positive approach towards the investments on debentures and bonds and the doctors are moderate in their perception. The highly scored individual variable is 'It is very secured while comparing shares' and the respective score is 3.7000 which indicates that the professionals are security conscious rather than risk takers.

The highly agreed variables among the engineers are 'fixed interest rates, converting into shares and assured returns are possible' whereas among the doctors these variables are 'secured while comparing shares and fixed interest rates' and highly disagreed factors among advocates are 'assured returns are possible and steady capital appreciation'. The analysis infers that the attitude towards investments on debentures and bonds are favourable among the engineers whereas it is unfavourable among the advocates. The significant difference among the three groups of professionals is identified on all the five variables since the respective 'F' statistics are significant at one per cent level.

Factors Motivating in Making Investment Decision

A motive is a driving force that causes a person to take action to satisfy specific needs. Motivation marketers can analyse the major forces influencing the investors to select or not to select certain investment avenues. Asian investors, in particular are strongly motivated by status and appearance. Asians are always conscious of their place in a group, institution or society as a whole. The importance of gaining social recognition forms Asians into some of the most image-conscious investors in the world. While choosing a particular investment avenue, the factors that motivate the investors to the study area are classified into regular returns, safety and security, capital appreciation, minimum formalities, tax relief, risk involved, liquidity. Among these various motivating factors the dominant factors were analysed with the help of Factor analysis.

Factor Analysis

Mathematically, factor analysis is somewhat similar to multiple regression analysis. Each variable is expressed as a linear combination of underlying factors. The amount of variance a variable shares with all other variables included in the analysis is referred to communality. The co-variation among the variables is described in terms of a small number of common factors plus a unique factor for each variable. These factors are not over observed. If the variables are standardised, the factor model may be represented as:

$$Xi = A_{ij} F_i + A_i 2F_2 + A_i 3F_3 + \ldots\ldots\ldots\ldots + A_{im} F_m + V_i U_i .$$

Where,

X_i = ith standardised variable.

A_{ij} = Standardised multiple regression coefficient of variable *i* on common factor *j*.

F = Common factor.

V_i = Standardised regression coefficient of variable *i* on unique factor *i*.

U_i = The unique factor for variable *i*.

m = Number of common factors.

The unique factors are uncorrelated with each other and with the common factors. The common factors themselves can be expressed as linear combinations of the observed variables.

$$F_i = W_{i1} X_1 + W_{i2} X_2 + W_{i3} X_3 + \ldots\ldots\ldots W_{ik} X_k.$$

Where,

F_i = Estimate of ith factor.

W_i = Weight or factor score coefficient.

K = Number of variables.

It is possible to select weights or factor score coefficient, so that the first factor explains the largest portion of the total variance. Then a second set of weight can be selected, so that the second factor accounts for most of the residual variance, subject to being uncorrelated with the first factor. This same principle could be applied for selecting additional weights for the additional factors. Thus, the factors can be estimated so that their factor scores, unlike the value of the original variables, are not correlated. Furthermore, the first factor accounts for the highest variance in the data, the second factor the second highest and so on.

Rotated Factor Matrix for the Attributes of Investors' Motives Towards Different Investment Avenues

The rotated factor matrix for the attributes relating to the investors' motives towards different investment avenues is given in table 5.42.

Table 5.42: Rotated Factor Matrix for the Attributes of Investors' Motives Towards Different Investment Avenues

Sl. No.	*Variables*	*Components*					
		Factor	*Factor*	*Factor*	*Factor*	*Factor*	*Factor*
1.	Assurance of Safety	0.827	0.173	0.069	0.122	0.011	0.080
2.	Investments are not Disturbed	0.770	0.217	0.083	-0.045	0.006	-0.070
3.	Assured Growth	0.666	0.067	0.127	0.143	0.124	0.003
4.	Free from Fear of Loss of Capital	0.605	-0.005	-0.028	0.359	-0.193	0.348
5.	Capital Appreciation is Assured	0.086	0.692	0.306	0.083	0.287	-0.048
6.	Steady Growth is Achieved	0.080	0.681	0.165	-0.243	-0.028	0.292
7.	Improve the Confidence Level	0.364	0.636	-0.123	0.298	-0.103	0.223
8.	Increase the Purchasing Power	0.398	0.635	-0.002	0.314	0.021	0.052
9.	New Investment Avenues are Explored	0.321	0.627	-0.020	0.270	0.195	0.052
10.	Minimum Formalities are Required	0.051	-0.068	0.762	0.093	0.140	0.248
11.	Scope for Recurring Investment	-0.013	0.241	0.754	0.065	-0.075	0.057
12.	Unplanned Tax Payments are Avoided	0.131	0.159	0.045	0.795	-0.037	0.160
13.	Fear of Tax Burden is Minimised	-0.130	0.162	0.311	0.681	0.158	0.256
14.	Tax Relief Motives to Invest Further	0.109	0.017	0.487	0.517	0.274	-0.052
15.	Minimum Fluctuations in Getting Return	-0.119	-0.018	-0.026	0.065	0.799	0.262
16.	No Risk in Getting Back the Capital	0.060	0.169	0.088	-0.019	0.759	0.077

17. Shifting Risk Level is Possible	0.137	0.094	0.484	0.250	0.522	0.005
18. A Portion can be Converted into Cash	-0.001	0.123	0.104	0.041	0.082	0.738
19. Help in Emergencies	0.050	0.074	0.069	0.289	0.206	0.670
20. Loan can be Availed by Pledging	0.233	0.026	0.358	0.074	0.415	0.509

Source:

The above table exhibits the rotated factor loadings for the twenty statements (Attributes) of different investment avenues. It is clear from the table that all the twenty statements have been extracted into six factors.

The Rotated Factor Matrix, for the investment decision factors or attributes of different investment avenues towards making investment is given below:

Factor 1: Safety and Security

Sl. No.	*Variables*	*Factor Loading*	*Communality (H^2)*	*Cronbach's Alpha*
1.	Assurance of Safety	0.827	0.740	
2.	Investments are not Disturbed	0.770	0.653	0.782
3.	Assured Growth	0.666	0.501	
4.	Free from Fear of Loss of Capital	0.605	0.654	

Source:

Among the attributes of motives of investors' on different investment avenues, the attributes such as 'assurance of safety', 'investments are not disturbed', 'assured growth' and 'free from fear of loss of capital' constituted the Factor-1 with higher factor loadings. The above said four attributes with higher factor loading on Factor-1 are characterised as 'Safety and Security'. All the four attributes have high communality indicating that the attributes with the Factor-1, have very high association among them.

Factor 2 : Capital Appreciation

Sl. No.	*Variables*	*Factor Loading*	*Communality (H^2)*	*Cronbach's Alpha*
1.	Capital Appreciation is Assured	0.692	0.671	
2.	Steady Growth is Achieved	0.681	0.643	
3.	Improve the Confidence Level	0.636	0.701	0.682
4.	Increase the Purchasing Power	0.635	0.664	
5.	New Investment Avenues are Explored	0.627	0.612	

Source:

The attributes such as 'assured capital appreciation', 'steady growth', 'improve the confidence level', 'increase the purchasing power' and 'new investment avenues are explored' with high factor loading constituted Factor-2. The above said attributes with high factor loading on factor-2 are characterised as 'Capital Appreciation' The higher factor loading on its attributes helps in identifying attributes associated with factor-2. All the attributes have high communality indicating that the variables within factor-2 have very high association.

Factor 3: Minimum Formalities

Sl. No.	*Variables*	*Factor Loading*	*Communality (H^2)*	*Cronbach's Alpha*
1.	Minimum Formalities are Required	0.762	0.678	0.617
2.	Scope for Recurring Investment	0.754	0.640	

Source:

It is observed from the above table that the attributes of different investment avenues such as 'minimum formalities are required' and 'scope for recurring investment' constituted Factor-3 with higher factor loading. The above said two attributes with high factor loading on Factor-3 are characterised as 'Minimum Formalities'.

The higher factor loading of the attributes indicate that the Factor 3 underlies that variable. The higher value of communality for the two attributes indicates that higher amount of variance is explained by the extracted factors.

Factor 4: Tax Relief

Sl. No.	*Variables*	*Factor Loading*	*Communality (H^2)*	*Cronbach's Alpha*
1.	Unplanned Tax Payments are Avoided	0.795	0.704	0.719
2.	Fear of Tax Burden is Minimised	0.685	0.694	
3.	Tax Relief Motives Invest Further	0.517	0.594	

Source:

Among the attributes of different investment avenues, the attributes, 'unplanned tax payments are avoided', 'fear of tax burden is minimised' and 'tax relief motives invest further' constituted Factor-4 with higher factor loading. The above said three attributes with higher factor loading on Factor-4 are characterised as 'Tax Relief'. The higher factor loadings of the attributes indicate that the Factor-4 underlies the above three variables. The high communality value of the attributes indicates that the attributes within the Factor-4 have very high association among them.

Factor 5 : Risk Involved

Sl. No.	*Variables*	*Factor Loading*	*Communality (H^2)*	*Cronbach's Alpha*
1.	Minimum Fluctuations in Getting Returns	0.799	0.727	0.751
2.	No Risk in Getting Back the Capital	0.759	0.622	
3.	Shifting Risk Level is Possible	0.522	0.596	

Source:

Among the attributes of different investment avenues, the attributes, 'minimum fluctuations in getting returns', 'no risk in getting back the capital' and 'shifting risk level is possible' constituted Factor-5 with higher factor loading. The above said three attributes with higher factor loading on Factor-5 are characterised as 'Risk Involved'. The higher factor loading of the attributes indicates that the Factor-5 underlies the above three variables. The high communality value of the attributes indicates that the attributes within the Factor-5 have very high association among them.

Factor 6 : Liquidity

Sl. No.	*Variables*	*Factor Loading*	*Communality (H^2)*	*Cronbach's Alpha*
1.	A Portion can be Converted into Cash	0.738	0.579	0.653
2.	Help in Emergencies	0.670	0.587	
3.	Loan can be Availed by Pledging	0.509	0.620	

Source:

The attributes, 'a portion can be converted into cash', 'help in emergencies', and 'loan can be availed by pledging' characterised as 'Liquidity', are constituted as Factor-6 with higher factor loadings. These three factors are very important because liquidity provided by the investment avenues play a vital role in making investment decision. The high communality value of the attributes indicates that the attributes within the Factor-5 have very high association among them.

Table 5.43: Investment Motive Factors for Different Investment Avenues

Sl. No.	*Variables*	*Factor Loading*	*Communality (H^2)*	*Cronbach's Alpha*
1.	Safety and Security	5.080	25.399	25.399
2.	Capital Appreciation	2.670	13.348	38.75
3.	Minimum Formalities	1.458	7.289	38.75
4.	Tax Relief	1.363	6.816	52.85
5.	Risk Involved	1.243	6.217	59.07
6.	Liquidity	1.068	5.338	64.41

Source: Primary data.

Kaiser-Meyer-Olkin measure of Sampling Adequacy	:	0.766
Bartlett's Test of Sphericity Chi-square	:	3317.138
Degrees of freedom	:	190
Significance	:	0.000

It is observed from Table 5.43 that the six factors such as safety and security, capital appreciation, minimum formalities, tax relief, risk involved, liquidity were extracted out of seven attributes. These factors account for about 64.61 per cent of variance in the data, Eigen value for the first factor 'safety and security' is 5.080, which indicates that the factor contains very high information than the other factors. The first factor 'safety and security' provides the maximum insights of investment decision of different investment avenues in the study area. It is a very important factor, because the respondents prefer to make investments on different investment avenues which have safety and security for their invested seed money. To improve this situation, the service providers and marketers of different investment avenues will give more importance on the attributes concerning 'safety and security'. The second important factor called 'capital appreciation' account for 13.348 per cent variance. The Eigen value of this factor is 2.670. It explains that people choose to make investments if they possess the attribute of capital appreciation. The third and the fourth factors, 'minimum formalities' and 'tax relief' account for 7.289 per cent and 6.816 per cent variance with the Eigen value of 1.458 and 1.363 respectively. It shows that the professionals are encouraged to make investments if the avenues possess the attributes of minimum formalities and at the same time they give tax relief also. The fifth and sixth factors 'Risk involved' and 'liquidity' account for 6.217 per cent and 5.338 per cent variance with the Eigen value of 1.243 and

1.068 respectively. These factors are also important in making a investment decision.

High value of Kaiser-Mayer-Olkin (KMO) test of sampling adequacy (0.766) indicates the correlation between the pairs of variables explained by other variables and thus factor analysis is considered to be appropriate in this model.

Impact of Motivating Factors on Investment Decisions

The impact study is essential for some policy implications to enrich the motivating factors' involvement among the professionals. The scores of independent (motivating variables) and dependent variables (Professionals' involvement index) are included for the analysis. The multiple regression analysis is used to find out the impact of motivating variables on professionals' involvement. The fitted regression model is:

$$Y = a \,.\, X_1^{b1}\, X_2^{b2}\, X_3^{b3}\, X_4^{b4}\, X_5^{b5}\, X_6^{b6}\, e^{a}.$$

Which is converted into log form,

$$\text{Log } Y = b_0 + b_1 \log X_1 + b_2 \log X_2 + b_3 \log X_3 + b_4 \log X_4 + b_5 \log X_5 + b_6 \log X_6 + \mu.$$

Where,

Y	– Investment index of the respondents.
X_1	– Safety and security.
X_2	– Capital appreciation.
X_3	– Minimum formalities.
X_4	– Tax relief.
X_5	– Risk involved.
X_6	– Liquidity.
$b_0 - \log_a$	– intercept or constant term.
μ	– error terms.

$b_0\, b_1 \ldots b_6$ regression co-efficient of the independent variables.

The regression analysis is carried out for doctors, engineers and advocates and the total professionals. The resultant regression co-efficients of motivating variables on professionals' decision are shown in Table 5.44.

Table 5.44: Impact of Motivating Factors on Investment Decisions

Sl. No.	*Variables*	*Notation*	*Regremssion Co-efficient*			
			Doctor	*Engineer*	*Advocate*	*Overall*
1.	Constant	b_0	2.277**	0.782**	2.237**	1.579**
2.	Safety and Security	X_1	0.652**	0.729**	0.658**	0.725**
3.	Capital Appreciation	X_2	0.151*	0.209*	0.327**	0.119*
4.	Minimum Formalities	X_3	0.040*	0.104^{NS}	0.351*	0.088**
5.	Tax Relief	X_4	0.624**	0.073*	0.103*	0.210**
6.	Risk Involved	X_5	0.114*	0.150*	0.219*	0.022*
7.	Liquidity	X_6	0.085^{NS}	0.077^{NS}	-0.168^{NS}	0.095^{NS}
	R^2		0.809	0.767	0.695	0.786
	F-test		108.236**	36.357**	57.987**	127.53**

Source: Primary Data. * Significant at five per cent level N.S – Not Significant. **Significant at one per cent level.

From the above Table it is seen that the motivating variables have significant influence among the doctors on safety and security, capital appreciation, minimum formalities, tax relief and risk involved with the regression co-efficients of 0.652, 0.151, 0.040, 0.624 and 0.114 respectively. Among the engineers the influencing variables are safety and security, capital appreciation, tax relief and risk involved with the regression co-efficients of 0.729, 0.209, 0.073 and 0.150 respectively. Among the advocates these influencing variables are safety and security, capital appreciation, minimum formalities, tax relief and risk involved with the regression co-efficients of 0.658, 0.327, 0.351, 0.103 and 0.219 respectively. The regression analysis for the overall professionals revealed that the significantly influencing variables are safety and security, capital appreciation, minimum formalities, tax relief and risk involved. The co-efficient of determination conveys the idea that the change in overall attitude towards different investment avenues is explained by the change in included variables to the extent of 78.60 per cent.

Impact of Personal Profile on Investment Decision-Making

In this section, an attempt has been made to analyse the impact of profile variables on perception of motivating factors in preferring different investment avenues with the help of multiple regression analysis.

$$Y = a \, . \, X_1^{b1} X_2^{b2} X_3^{b3} X_4^{b4} X_5^{b5} e^a \ldots$$

Which is converted into log form,

$$\text{Log } Y = b_0 + b_1 \log X_1 + b_2 \log X_2 + b_3 \log X_3 + b_4 \log X_4 + b_5 \log X_5 + \mu$$

Where,

Y – Investment index of the respondents.

X_1 – Gender.

X_2 – Age.

X_3 – Community.

X_4 – Literacy level.

X_5 – Place of occupation level.

b_0 – $\log_a$ – intercept or constant term.

μ – error terms.

$b_0 b_1 \ldots b_6$ regression co-efficient of the independent variables.

The regression analysis is carried out for doctors, engineers and advocates and the total professionals. The resultant regression co-efficients of motivating variables on professionals' decision are shown in Table 5.45.

Table 5.45: Impact of Personal Profile on Investment Decision-Making

Sl. No.	*Personal Profile Variables*	*Notation*	*Regremssion Co-efficient*			
			Doctor	*Engineer*	*Advocate*	*Overall*
1.	Constant	b_0	4.194**	2.593**	2.978**	3.494**
2.	Gender	X_1	0.408**	0.042^{NS}	-0.150^{NS}	0.208*
3.	Age	X_2	0.047^{NS}	0.241*	0..188*	0.043*
4.	Community	X_3	0.267**	0.366**	0.081^{NS}	0.198**
5.	Literacy Level	X_4	0.063*	0.067*	0.0229**	0.139**
6.	Place of Occupation	X_5	-0.195*	0.011^{NS}	-0.127^{NS}	-0.058^{NS}
	R^2		0.736	0.642	0.784	0.716
	F- test		20.541**	16.921**	18.112**	20.569**

Source: Primary Data. * Significant at five per cent level N.S – Not Significant.
**Significant at one per cent level.

It is revealed from the above Table 5.45 that among the doctors the significantly influencing profile variables towards the attitude on different investment avenues are gender, community, literacy level and place of occupation with the regression coefficients of 0.408, 0.267, 0.063 and 0.195 respectively. Among the engineers the significantly influencing profile variables are found to be age, community and literacy level with the regression coefficients of 0.241, 0.366 and 0.067 respectively. And among the advocates these variables are gender, age, community and literacy level with the regression coefficients of 0.208, 0.043, 0.198 and 0.139 respectively. The analysis on overall data reveals that a unit increase in gender, age, community and literacy level variables results in 0.208, 0.043, 0.198 and 0.139 units respectively. The change in the included five profile variables explains the change to the extent of 71.60 per cent. The significant 'F' statistics reveals the viability of the fitted regression models.

Impact of Family Domain Variables on Investment Decision

In this section an attempt has been made to analyse the impact of family domain variables on perception of motivating factors in preferring different investment avenues with the help of multiple regression analysis.

$$Y = a \,.\, X_1^{b1} X_2^{b2} X_3^{b3} X_4^{b4} X_5^{b5} X_6^{b6} e^{a} \ldots$$

Which is converted into log form,

$$\text{Log } Y = b_0 + b_1 \log X_1 + b_2 \log X_2 + b_3 \log X_3 + b_4 \log X_4 + b_5 \log X_5 + b_6 \log X_6 + \mu.$$

Where,

Y – Investment index of the respondents.

X_1 – Private practise.

X_2 – Spouse employed.

X_3 – Nature of family.

X_4 – No. of Children.

X_5 – Monthly income.

X_6 – Marital status.

b_0 – $\log_a$ – intercept or constant term.

μ – error terms.

$b_0 b_1 \ldots . b_6$ regression co-efficient of the independent variables.

The regression analysis is carried out for doctors, engineers and advocates and the total professionals. The resultant regression co-efficients of motivating variables on professionals' decision are shown in Table 5.46.

Table 5.46: Impact of Family Domain Variables on Investment Decision

Sl. No.	*Family domain Variables*	*Notation*	*Regremssion Co-efficient*			
			Doctor	*Engineer*	*Advocate*	*Overall*
1.	Constant	b_0	5.715**	2.270**	4.524*	4.611**
2.	Private Practice	X_1	0.664**	–0.081 NS	0.067 NS	0.381**
3.	Spouse Employed	X_2	0.111*	0.690**	0.135*	0.147*
4.	Nature of Family	X_3	0.045 NS	0.112 NS	–0.110 NS	–0.103NS
5.	No. of Children	X_4	–0.304**	–0.215 NS	–0.110 NS	–0.214*
6.	Monthly Income	X_5	0.579**	0.617**	0.763**	0.673**
7.	Marital Status	X_6	–0.340 NS	0.723**	0.167 NS	–0.046NS
	R^2		0.617	0.674	0.702	0.614
	F-test		14.907**	15.801**	16.723**	12.279

Source: Primary Data. * Significant at five per cent level N.S. – Not Significant.
**Significant at one per cent level.

It has been revealed from the above Table 5.46 that among the doctors the significantly influencing variables of family domain are private practice, spouse employed, number of children and monthly income with the regression coefficient of 0.664, 0.111, –0.304 and 0.579 respectively. Among the engineers the significantly influencing family domain variables are spouse employed, monthly income and marital status with regression coefficient of 0.690, 0.617 and 0.723 respectively. And among the advocates these variables are spouse employed and monthly income with the regression coefficient of 0.135 and 0.763 respectively. The regression analysis for the overall professionals revealed that the significantly influencing variables are private practice, spouse employed, number of children and monthly income.

The change in included family domain variables explains the change in professionals' perception to the extent of 61.40 per cent. The remaining change in professionals' perception is explained by some unknown variables.

Association Between Profile Variable and the Investment Motivating Factors

Since the profile of the professionals may be associated with their investment motivating factors such as safety and security, capital appreciation, minimum formalities, tax relief, risk involved, liquidity. The present study has made an attempt to analyse it with the help of One way Analysis of Variance. The included profile are gender, age, community, literacy level, profession, type of employment and place of occupation. The result of one-way analysis is summarised in the following table.

Table 5.47: Association Between Profile Variable and the Investment Motivating Factors

		'F' statistics					
Sl. No.	*Profile Variables*	*Safety & Security*	*Capital Appreciation*	*Minimum Formalities*	*Tax Relief*	*Risk Involved*	*Liquidity*
1.	Gender	8.403**	4.176**	5.439**	3.461**	8.838**	3.968**
2.	Age	7.916**	3.916**	4.871**	4.975**	4.386**	3.898**
3.	Community	4.947**	7.029**	2.613*	5.580**	4.536**	2.532**
4.	Literacy Level	3.928**	4.018**	1.393^{NS}	6.330**	5.046**	3.884**
5.	Profession	9.397**	7.564**	3.260**	4.255**	5.463**	4.287**
6.	Type of Employment	8.137**	13.521**	6.515**	7.450**	6.240**	7.189**
7.	Place of Occupation	5.763**	8.677**	5.091**	7.051**	4.161**	11.954**

Source: Primary Data.

* Significant at five per cent level N.S. – Not Significant. **Significant at one per cent level

Regarding the perception on safety and security, all the profile variables are significantly associated with it and their respective 'F' statistics is significant at one per cent level. Except the motivating factor 'minimum formalities' all the other motivating factors such as capital appreciation, tax relief, risk involved and liquidity are significantly associated with the profile variables at five per cent level. Regarding 'minimum formalities', it is significantly associated with gender, age, profession, type of employment and place of occupation and their respective 'F' statistics is significant at five per cent level, in connection with' community' its association is significant at one per cent level and it does not have significant relationship with 'literacy level'.

Association Between Family Domain Variable and the Investment Motivating Factors

The family domain variables may have their own influence on the professionals' perception on motivating factors such as safety and security, capital appreciation, minimum formalities, tax relief, risk involved, and liquidity. Hence the present study has made an attempt to analyse the association with the help of One-way Analysis of Variance. The included family domain variables are marital status, private practise, spouse employed, nature of family, number of children, number of family members, number of earning members, monthly professional income, monthly earnings of family members, monthly family income, monthly other income, monthly Professional expenses, monthly family expenditure, monthly savings. The results are given by a table in a form of summarised one-way analysis in the next page.

Table 5.48: Association Between Family Domain Variable and the Investment Motivating Factors

		'F' statistics					
Sl. No.	*Profile Variables*	*Safety & Security*	*Capital Appreciation*	*Minimum Formalities*	*Tax Relief*	*Risk Involved*	*Liquidity*
1.	Marital Status	5.593**	5.556**	8.919**	5.893**	4.253**	6.238**
2.	Private Practise	5.657**	6.322**	7.413**	3.295**	5.636**	6.669**
3.	Spouse Employed	2.569**	3.272**	8.335**	4.137**	6.873**	1.150^{NS}
4.	Nature of Family	6.925**	13.282**	3.558**	6.557**	10.797**	6.354**
5.	No. of Children	4.036**	9.752**	3.548**	12.532**	1.949*	7.503**
6.	No. of Family Members	7.430**	7.317**	4.158**	3.186**	5.108**	3.162**
7.	No. of Earning Members	7.246**	4.716**	4.860**	2.092*	5.267**	4.956**
8.	Monthly Professional Income	4.035**	11.764**	13.848**	4.533**	3.183**	1.964*
9.	Monthly Earnings of Family Members	3.633**	4.776**	4.851**	3.567**	2.858**	3.195**
10.	Monthly Family Income	2.610**	7.889**	4.151**	3.929**	2.736**	5.300**
11.	Monthly Other Income	1.979*	3.462**	16.873**	3.255**	2.263*	2.840**
12.	Monthly Profess-ional Expenses	8.246**	45.270**	5.034**	17.189**	6.189**	6.076**
13.	Monthly Family Expenditure	2.108*	6.158**	4.153**	4.797**	11.346**	7.535**
14.	Monthly Savings	12.107**	9.924**	4.923**	4.951**	2.732**	1.773 ^{NS}

Source: Primary Data

* Significant at five per cent level NS – Not Significant. **Significant at one per cent level

Regarding the perception on safety and security, except 'monthly other income' and 'monthly family expenditure' all the family domain variables are significantly associated with it and their respective 'F' statistics is significant at 1 per cent level. In connection with 'monthly other income' and 'monthly family expenditure' both of these have association with the motivating variable 'safety and security' and their respective 'F' statistics is significant at five per cent level. Regarding capital appreciation and minimum formalities both of these motivating factors are having association with all the family domain variables and their respective 'F' statistics is significant at one per cent level. Regarding the perception on the investment motivating variable 'tax relief', except 'number of earning members' all the other family domain variables having association with 'tax relief' and their respective 'F' statistics is significant at one per cent level and the family domain 'number of earning members' is having association with 'tax relief' and its respective 'F' statistics is significant at five per cent level. Regarding the fifth motivating variable 'risk involved', except two family domain variables, it has association with all the other family domain variables and their respective 'F' statistics is significant at one per cent level. And the two family domain variables such as 'mumber of children' and 'monthly other income' are having association with the motivating variable 'risk involved' and the respective 'F' statistics is significant at five per cent level. And the sixth and final motivating variable is 'liquidity', except two, it has significantly association with all the other family domain variables. It does not have any association with two family domain variables such as 'spouse employed' and 'monthly savings'.

Garrett Ranking Technique

It analyses the influencing factors that created motivation in the minds of the investors in selecting a series of investment avenues for their children's education, children's marriage, acquisition of properties, Future secured life and so on. And at the same time the respondents were also asked to rank the group of investment avenues such as postal deposits, bank deposits, life insurance and real estate, etc. Relating to this each respondent was asked to rank two group of factors such as 'factors relating to purpose of investment' and 'factors relating to different investment avenues'. The order of significance assigned by the respondents with mentioning their ranks was converted into scores by using Garrett ranking technique. Garrett suggested this method for converting ranks into scores when a number of items ranked are different from respondent to respondent. The present position of each rank is found by using the formula.

$$\text{Present position} = \frac{100\,(R_{ij} - 0.5)}{N_j}.$$

Where,

R_{ij} = Rank given to ith factor by the *j*th individual.

N_j = Number of factors ranked by *j*th individual.

By referring to the table given by Garrett, the present position was estimated and converted into scores. Then for each factor, the scores of various respondents are added and divided by the number of respondents. The scores thus obtained for each factor are arranged in descending order. The factor with the highest mean value is considered the most important.

Purpose of Making Investments in Different Investment Avenues

An investment is an important and useful factor in the context of present day conditions. Some factors that have made investment decisions increasingly important are: longer life expectancy or planning for future secured life, future needs, contingencies, precautionary purposes or growth in future wealth, leading to rise in the standard of living, etc. The amounts not consumed are saved and invested. These investments are useful for present and future consumption in the case of consumer durables, cars, gold, etc. So the professionals were asked to rank the purpose of their investments according to their priorities.

Table 5.49: Investment Purposes and Reasons of the Professionals

Sl. No.	*Purpose of Investment*	*Garrett Mean Score*	*Rank*
1.	Children's Education	65.61	I
2.	Children's Marriage	53.57	III
3.	Acquisition of Property	52.56	IV
4.	Future Secured Life	61.88	II
5.	Purchase of Consumer Durables	46.65	VII
6.	Provision for Additional Income	44.97	VIII
7.	Repayment of Old Debts	43.82	IX
8.	Managing Emergencies	50.63	V
9.	Provision for Festivals	33.79	X
10.	Construction of House	47.11	VI

Source:

The analysis reveals that 'children's education' has the highest mean score of 65.61. Professionals take hard efforts in generating income for the welfare of their children when they are properly educated and which is followed by 'future secured life' with 61.88 mean score which denotes that after giving due recognition to their children's education, the professionals think about their own future secured life. Among the investment purposes the one which scored lowest is 'provision for festivals' and its respective score is 33.79.

Dominating Investment Avenues

There are large number of investment avenues for savers in India. Some of them are marketable and liquid while others are risky and less safe. Risk and returns are the major characteristics which an investor has to face and handle.

There are different methods of classifying the invest avenues. A major classifications is physical investments and financial investment. Some physical assets like ploughs, tractors are useful for agricultural production. A few physical assets like lorries, cars, jeeps, etc are useful for business. Many items of physical assets are not useful for further production of goods or to create income as in the case of consumer durables, gold, silver, etc. But most of the financial assets, barring cash are used for production or consumption.

Among different types of investments some are marketable and transferable and others are not. Examples of marketable assets are shares and debentures of listed companies, bonds of Public sector undertakings, government securities, etc. Non-marketable investments are bank deposits, provident and pension funds, insurance certificates, post office deposits, national savings certificates and company deposits. The professionals have to choose proper avenues from the above said avenues depending on their preferences, needs and abilities to minimum the and maximise the returns. The preferences of the professionals from his study area are presented in the following table.

Table 5.50: The Investment Avenues Dominating in the Investment Pattern of the Professionals

Sl. No.	*Purpose of Investment*	*Garrett Mean Score*	*Rank*
1.	Postal Deposits	60.80	IV
2.	Bank Deposits	65.83	I
3.	Life Insurance	58.78	V

4.	Real Estate	62.06	III
5.	Gold silver and other precious metals	62.20	II
6.	Mutual funds	43.65	VIII
7.	Chit funds	42.48	IX
8.	Shares	33.06	X
9.	Provident fund	50.49	VI
10.	Pension plan	44.13	VII
11.	Debentures and Bonds	26.54	XI

Source:

It is evident from the above Table 5.50 that among the listed investment avenues the topmost is 'bank deposits' which reveals the fact that the bank accounts and the bank deposits are much essential for all of us and the professionals are not exempted. So they ranked it as the first and it is followed by 'gold, silver and other precious metals' with the mean score of 62.2 which exhibits that besides the various disparities Indians are giving much importance to hold and to wear these precious metals to show their social status and security and the least scored investment avenue is 'debentures and bonds' with the mean score of 26.54 which denotes the fact that the respondents have fear towards this avenue.

Table 5.51: Problems Faced by Professionals in the Process of Developing their Investment Patterns

Sl. No.	*Problems Faced During Investment Process Made*	*Mean Scores*				*F-Statistics*
		Doctors	*Engineers*	*Advocates*	*Overall*	
1.	Low Returns	3.6250	3.8250	3.8250	3.7583	1.973 NS
2.	Fear of Market Risks	3.6000	3.5750	3.6000	3.5917	0.032NS
3.	Minimum Transparency	3.3750	3.3000	3.6500	3.4417	6.688**
4.	Poor after Sales Service	3.5000	3.1750	3.9250	3.5333	18.417**
5.	Complicated Hidden Charges	3.3250	3.4250	3.0000	3.2500	6.517**
6.	Lack of Proper Communication	3.3250	3.1500	3.7500	3.4083	12.670**
7.	Poor Investor Education	3.7500	3.3250	4.1750	3.7500	21.267**
8.	Slow in Grievance Handling	3.4500	3.5750	3.8500	3.6250	6.842**
9.	Fear of Frauds	3.2750	3.4000	2.8250	3.1667	10.683**
10.	Lack of product Innovation	3.4000	3.3590	3.7000	3.4874	5.217**

11. Improper Portfolio Management.	3.6000	3.1750	3.4000	3.3917	7.130**
12. Misguiding Advices of Agents	3.7250	3.1000	3.5500	3.4583	13.095**
13. Inconvenience in Operation	3.5250	3.1000	3.6750	3.4333	13.021**
14. Ambiguous Terms and Conditions	3.3250	3.4750	3.2500	3.3500	1.786 NS
15. Long Term Maturity	3.6750	3.5500	3.5500	3.5917	0.669 NS

Source: Primary Data. **Significant at one per cent level N.S. – Not Significant.

Regarding the perception of the problems faced by the professionals in the process king their investment pattern, the doctors perceived more on 'Poor investor education' since its mean score is maximum of 3.725. Among the engineers, this variable is 'low returns' since its mean value is 3.8250 whereas among the advocates, this variable is 'poor investor education' since its mean value is 4.1750. The overall mean scores of the fifteen variables in problems related to investment making process among doctors, engineers and advocates are 3.4983, 3.3673 and 3.5817 respectively. It indicates that the advocates perceived higher on the variables related to problems in the investment making process than doctors and engineers. The significant difference among the three groups of professionals is identified in the perception on the eleven variables since the respective 'F' statistics are significant at one per cent level.

Table 5.52: Rotated Factor Matrix for the Problems Faced by the

Sl. No.	*Variables*	*Components*			
		Factor 1	*Factor 2*	*Factor 3*	*Factor 4*
1.	Lack of Proper Communication	0.820	0.154	-0.045	0.031
2.	Inconvenience in Operation	0.788	0.113	0.024	0.076
3.	Poor Investor Education	0.748	0.118	0.044	0.223
4.	Lack of Product Innovation	0.690	0.190	0.111	-0.050
5.	Poor after Sales Service	0.668	0.354	0.092	0.112
6.	Slow in Grievance Handling	0.628	0.306	-0.184	-0.121
7.	Fear of Frauds	0.087	0.854	-0.077	-0.017
8.	Complicated Hidden Charges	0.294	0.766	0.090	-0.097
9.	Long Term Maturity	0.170	0.748	0.105	0.062
10.	Ambiguous Terms and Conditions	0.317	0.671	0.065	0.103
11.	Fear of Market Risks	0.413	0.481	0.285	-0.174
12.	Low Returns	-0.052	-0.007	0.832	0.117

13.	Minimum Transparency	-0.041	0.013	0.141	0.824
14.	Improper Portfolio Management.	-0.033	0.114	-0.053	0.702
15.	Misguiding Advices of Agents	0.182	-0.012	-0.052	0.763

Source:

Professionals in the Investment Making Process

The above Table exhibits the rotated factor loading for the 15 problems (attributes) related to different investment avenues. It is clear from the table that all the fifteen problems have been extracted into four factors.

Factor 1: Institutional Failures

Sl. No.	*Variables*	*Factor Loading*	*Communality (H^2)*
1.	Lack of Proper Communication	0.820	0.699
2.	Inconvenience in Operation	0.788	0.640
3.	Poor Investors' Education	0.748	0.624
4.	Lack of Product Innovation	0.690	0.527
5.	Poor after Sales Service	0.668	0.593
6.	Slow in Grievance Handling	0.628	0.536

Source:

Among the various problems of investment avenues, the attributes such as 'lack of proper communication', 'inconvenience in operation', 'poor investors' education', 'lack of product innovation', 'poor after sales service' and 'slow in grievance handling' constituted the Factor-1 with higher factor loadings. The above said six attributes with higher factor loadings on Factor 1 are characterised as 'Institutional Failures'. All the six attributes have high communality indicating that the attributes within the Factor-1 have very high association among them.

Factor 2: Complication

Sl. No.	*Variables*	*Factor Loading*	*Communality (H^2)*
1.	Fear of Frauds	0.854	0.743
2.	Complicated Hidden Charges	0.766	0.691
3.	Long Term Maturity	0.748	0.604
4.	Ambiguous Terms and Conditions	0.671	0.565

Source:

The attributes such as 'fear of frauds', 'complicated hidden charges', 'long term maturity'and 'ambiguous terms and conditions' with high factor loading constituted Factor-2. The above said attributes with high factor loading on factor-2 are characterised as 'Complication'.

The higher factor loading on its attributes helps in indentifying attributes associated with Factor-2. All the attributes have high communality indicating that the variables within Factor-2 have very high association.

Factor 3: Doubtfulness

Sl. No.	*Variables Loading*	*Factor (H^2)*	*Communality*
1.	Fear of Market Risks	0.285	0.514
2.	Low Returns	0.832	0.709
3.	Minimum Transparency	0.141	0.700

Source:

It is observed from the above table that the attributes related to problems prevailing in the investment making process such as 'fear of market risks', 'low returns' and 'minimum transparency' constituted Factor-3 with higher factor loading. The above said three attributes with high factor loading on Factor 3 are characterised as 'Doubtfulness'.

The higher factor loading of the attributes indicate that the Factor-3 underlies that variable. The higher value of communality for the three attributes indicates that higher amount of variance is explained by the extracted factors.

Factor 4: Mishandling

Sl. No.	*Variables Loading*	*Factor (H^2)*	*Communality*
1.	Improper Portfolio Management	0.702	0.527
2.	Misguiding Advices of Agents	0.763	0.640

Source:

Among the attributes related to problems in making investment process, the attributes such as 'improper portfolio management' and 'misguiding advices of agents' constituted Factor-4 with higher factor loading. The above said two attributes with higher factor loading on Factor 4 are characterised as 'Mishandling'.

The higher factor loadings of the attributes indicate that the Factor-4 underlies the above two variables. The high communality value of the attributes indicates that the attributes within the Factor-4 have very high association among them.

Table 5.53: Problem Factors of Professionals' Investment Patterns

Sl. No.	*Factors*	*Eigen Value*	*Percentage of Variance*	*Cumulative Percentage of Variance*
1.	Institutional Failures	3.601	22.508	22.508
2.	Complication	2.879	17.992	40.408
3.	Doubtfulness	2.132	13.327	53.825
4.	Mishandling	1.421	8.879	62.704

* Kaiser-Meyer-Olkin Measure of Sampling Adequacy = 0.801.
* Bartlett's Test of Sphericity Chi-square = 2875.145.
Degrees of freedom = 120.
Significance = 0.000.

It is observed from Table 5-53 that the four factors such as institutional failures, complication, doubtfulness and mishandling are extracted out of fifteen attributes. These factors account for about 71.587 per cent of variance in the data. Eigen value for the first factor 'Institutional failures' is 3.601, which indicates that the factor is the major obstacle among the respondents. The first factor, 'institutional failures' causes maximum hurdles in the growth of investments and in reaping higher returns in certain investment avenues such as Mutual funds and Unit Linked Insurance Plans (ULIPs).

The second important factor called 'complication' accounts for 17.992 per cent variance. The Eigen value of this factor is 2.879. It explains that professionals face lot of complications in in making investments in certain investment avenues. The third factor 'doubtfulness' account for 13.327 per cent variance with Eigen value of 2.132. It shows that the investors are discouraged in making investments in certain avenues which arouse lot of doubts in the minds of investors regarding the progress of investment and their returns.

The fourth factor 'mishandling' account for 8.879 per cent variance with the Eigen value of 1.421. This factor is also an important discouraging factor while making investment decisions. High value of Kaiser-Meyer-Olkin (KMO) test of sampling adequacy (0.801) indicates the correlation between the pairs of variables explained by other variables and thus factor analysis is considered to be appropriate in this model.

Chapter-VI

Summary of Findings, Suggestions and Conclusion

6.1 Introduction

Savings form an important part of the economy of any nation. With the savings invested in various options available to the people, the money acts as the driver for growth of the country. Indian financial scene too presents a plethora of avenues to the investors. Though certainly not the best or deepest of markets in the world, it has reasonable options for an ordinary man to invest his savings. This chapter contains the summary of findings, suggestions and conclusion. This study is conducted with the objectives to find out the level the different investment avenues available to the investors, to analyse the investors' attitudes towards a specific investment pattern, to understand the problems faced by them in the process of building their investment pattern and to examine the level of satisfaction of the investors towards their preferred investment pattern. The approach to the study is both descriptive and analytical. The findings of the study are briefly presented in this part.

6.2 Summary of Findings

- It is understood that 61.7 per cent of the respondents are male professionals and the rest of the 38.3 per cent respondents are female professionals. It is inferred that majority of the male respondents are advocates and the majority of the female respondents are constituted from doctors and engineers equally of 31.8 per cent each.
- It is found out that 40.8 per cent of respondents fall under the category of 30-40 age group. And the next major age group of 37.5 per cent respondents fall under the category of 20-30 age group. And the rest of the age groups are shared by 40-50 and above 50. Their respective

contributions are 80 respondents (16.7 per cent) and 24 respondents (5 per cent) each.

- It is clearly understood that 62.5 per cent of respondents fall under the category of Backward Community (BC). The next major group of 17.5 per cent respondents fall under the category of Most Backward Class (MBC) and 14.2 per cent respondents belong to Scheduled Caste/ Scheduled Tribe (SC/ST) and the least group of 5.8 per cent respondents belong to Forward Community (FC).
- It is known from the study that majority of 75.8 per cent respondents have come under the category of 'married' and the rest of 24.2 per cent respondents are 'unmarried'. Among the married, majority of 39 per cent respondents belong to advocates. Regarding unmarried the majority of 58.62 per cent respondents belong to engineers.
- Regarding educational qualifications, a majority of 23.3 per cent respondents are Bachelor of Law (BL). And the second major group of 20.8 per cent respondents fall under the educational category of Master of Engineering (ME) holders. And the third major group of 17.5 per cent respondents are MBBS holders and the least 10 per cent respondents are Master of Law (ML) holders.
- It is known that among the total respondents majority of 67.5 per cent respondents belong to private sector. And the rest of 32.5 per cent respondents are in government services. Among the private sector major portion of 44.44 per cent is covered by advocates and among the government sector major portion of 76.92 per cent is covered by doctors.
- It is inferred that a major portion of 61.7 per cent respondents have their occupational place in urban area and the second large group of 22.5 per cent respondents have their occupational place in the Semi-Urban and the least number of 15.8 per cent respondents have their occupational area in the rural area.
- It is clear that majority of 54.2 per cent respondents have private practice and the rest of the 45.8 per cent respondents are not having any private practice, which also indicates that they depends on government service.
- It is known that the spouses of the most of the 54.2 per cent respondents are employed which indicates that it enhances the viability of the professionals to find different investment avenues for their investment. The rest of the 45.8 per cent respondents' spouses are not employed.

- It is inferred that out of the total respondents 61.7 per cent respondents, belong to nuclear families and the rest of the 38.3 per cent respondents belong to joint families. Majority of the respondents belong to nuclear families.
- It is understood that majority of 30 per cent respondents are having four family members and 24.2 per cent of respondents are having five family members and the next 17.5 per cent of respondents are having three family members, and the final 24 respondents (five per cent) are having two family members. In the case of less family members, it induces the investors to increase their investment level more.
- It is found out that out of the total respondents, 61.7 per cent respondents are having only two earning members. The next 16.7 per cent respondents are having only one earning member and the least group of 3.3 per cent respondents are having more than four earning members in their families. Earning members in the family plays a vital role in taking investment decisions. More number of earning members in the family, motivates the respondents to pursue in finding new ways for making investments.
- Regarding the economic status of the professionals, the doctors earned higher and the respective overall mean earnings is Rs 51,604.36 whereas among the engineers and advocates the mean earnings are Rs 34,654.28 and Rs 31,337.19 respectively. It reveals that the doctors are having high economical status whereas the engineers and advocates are moderate in their income. Significant differences are identified among the professionals in all the variables, namely, monthly professional income, monthly income of other earning members in the family, monthly family income, monthly savings.
- Regarding the investments in financial assets, the doctors invested more on 'provident fund' since its mean investment is a maximum of Rs 60,375. Among the engineers, this variable is 'bank deposits' since its mean value is Rs 46,948.72 whereas among the advocates also this variable is the same 'bank deposits' since its value is Rs 39,360. Significant differences are identified among the professionals in all the variables except one namely pension plan, life insurance, chit fund, provident fund, bank deposits. The highest scored variable among the doctors are provident fund which reveals the fact that the doctors feel this financial investment is more profitable than the others and engineers, advocates this variable is bank deposits respectively each. In addition to that, a higher level of concentration in financial assets is identified among the doctors than the engineers and advocates.

- Regarding the average annual investment of professionals in physical assets, significant differences are identified among the professionals in one variable, namely, 'real estate'. The highly concentrated physical asset among the doctors is 'real estate' and the engineers pay more attention on gold, silver and other precious metals and the advocates also feel comfort like doctors in investing 'real estate'. Moreover the Average annual investments of both the two variables in physical assets among doctors, engineers and advocates are Rs 40,088.42, Rs 44,970.29 and Rs 3,71,555.57 respectively. It indicates that regarding physical assets a higher level of investing attitude is identified among the engineers than the doctors and advocates.
- Regarding the average annual investment of professionals in marketable assets, significant differences are identified among the professionals in one variable, i.e., shares. The highest scored variable among the all the three professional groups is 'mutual fund'. The average annual investments in marketable assets among doctors, engineers and advocates are Rs 26,790.38, Rs 26,601.06 and Rs 25,975.43 respectively. It indicates that regarding marketable assets a higher level of investing attitude is identified among the doctors than the engineers and advocates.
- Regarding average annual total investments of professionals, they are constituted by three important groups of assets such as financial, physical and marketable assets. Among the professionals, doctors become the first and their total average annual investments on the three group of assets is Rs 3,62,128.20 and they are followed by engineers and advocates and their respective average annual total investments are Rs 3,23,794.87 and Rs 2,96,275.00 respectively. No significant difference is identified among the professionals relating to average annual total investments of professionals on three group of assets.
- It is clearly understood that among the total respondents, 62.5 per cent respondents are creating resources for making investments from their own savings and they are followed by 15 per cent respondents who are creating sources from getting loan. Next to them, 6.7 per cent respondents are getting resources for their investment from some other sources. The rest of two and a half per cent respondents are pledging or selling their Jewells for their investment purpose.
- It is found that out of total respondents, 47.5 per cent respondents are ready to spare five to 10 years for their investments to grow and 31.7per cent respondents are interested to allow 10 and more years for the progress of their investment. Finally, 20.8 per cent respondents are

ready to spare to the maximum of five years only for the growth of their investments.

- The awareness level towards financial investments is higher among the advocates, since the overall mean score for all the investment avenues is 3.8938, whereas among the doctors and engineers, the mean scores are 3.7854 and 3.5208 respectively. Further, significant differences are identified among the professionals in all the investment avenues. The highly known financial investment avenue among the three groups of professionals is Bank Savings Account.
- Regarding the awareness level of physical investment avenues among the doctors, engineers and advocates, the highly scored variable among the three professional groups is 'investment in valuable jewellery' and the respective scores are 4.3250, 4.0750 and 4.6000. Significant differences are identified among the professionals in all the physical investment avenues. The overall mean scores of all the three physical investment avenues among doctors, engineers and advocates are 3.9917, 3.7333 and 4.2167 respectively. It indicates the awareness level of physical investment avenues is higher among the advocates than the doctors and engineers.
- The advocates' awareness level towards marketable investment avenue in general is lower since the overall mean score on different investment avenues is 2.7563, whereas among the doctors and engineers, the mean scores are 2.8563 and 3.2219 respectively. It reveals that the engineers and doctors are having a positive approach towards marketable investment avenues whereas the advocates are highly afraid of the ups and downs of the capital market and they have a negative opinion. Significant differences are identified among the professionals in all the variables. The highly known marketable investment avenue among the doctors are government bonds and this variable among the engineers are units in UTI and among the advocates, they a have well awareness towards shares.
- Regarding the source of awareness on different investment avenues, the overall mean score for doctors is 3.4500 which is higher than engineers and advocates. The overall mean scores for engineers and advocates are 3.3750 and 3.1479 respectively. It reveals that all the source of awareness are highly utilised by doctors than other two professional groups. In addition to that, significant differences are identified among the professionals in all the variables except two. The highest scored variable among the doctors is 'friends and colleagues' which reveals the fact that the doctors become familiar with different investment avenues through friends and colleagues and engineers their most informing source of awareness are government promotional

measures and brokers and agents, for advocates the most attractive source of awareness are Brokers and agents.

- Regarding the influencing personalities of professional on investment decisions significant differences are identified among the professionals in few variables, namely, self-motivation, spouse, children, friends, colleagues. Among these, the highest scored variable among the all the three professional groups is 'self-motivation' the mean scores for doctors, engineers and advocates are 4.3750, 4.1500, 4.5750 respectively which reveals a fact that regarding investment decisions, what kind of external forces making a impact on a investor but the real motivation comes from one's inner urge and desire which is called self-motivation and this is the important factor in making investment decisions. The mean scores of all the seven variables regarding influencing personalities among doctors, engineers and advocates are 3.5571, 3.4949 and 3.7643 respectively. It indicates that the perception level of advocates is higher than doctors and engineers.

- Regarding the level of confidence in getting expected returns from different investment avenues, significant difference among the three groups of professionals is identified in the perception on ten variables. 'gold, silver and other precious metals' is the highly scored variable among the doctors and advocates and they are having similar opinion and the respective scores are 4.2000 and 4.5750. Regarding engineers the highly scored variable is 'postal deposits' and the respective scores is 4.5750. The mean score of all eleven variables among doctors, engineers and advocates are 3.4773, 3.4038 and 3.7091 respectively. It indicates that higher level of confidence prevails among the advocates in getting expected returns than the doctors and engineers.

- Regarding satisfaction of the doctors on the returns of their investment portfolio, they are highly satisfied on the real estate and gold, silver other precious metals since their mean satisfaction scores are 4.2564 and 4.2500 respectively. The analysis of skewness also reveals that more than average number of respondents are of the same view with regard to postal deposits, bank deposits, life insurance, real estate, gold silver and other precious metals, provident fund and debentures and bonds. The analysis of co-efficient of variation reveals that there is more consistency in their view with regard to real estate, gold silver and other precious metals, provident fund and life insurance.

- Regarding satisfaction of the engineers on the returns of their investment portfolio they are highly satisfied on gold, silver and other precious metals and real estate investment avenues since their mean satisfaction scores are 4.1250 and 4.0250 respectively. The analysis of skewness also reveals that more than average numbers of respondents are of the same view with regard to postal deposits, bank deposits, real estate, gold, silver and other precious metals and debentures and bonds. The analysis of co-efficient of variation reveals that there is more consistency in their view with regard to gold, silver and other precious metals, postal deposits, bank deposits and real estate.

- Regarding satisfaction of the advocates on the returns of their investment portfolio they are highly satisfied on the gold, silver and other precious metals and Real estate investment avenues since their mean satisfaction scores are 4.4750 and 4.3500 respectively. The analysis of skewness also reveals that more than average numbers of respondents are of the same view with regard to postal deposits, bank deposits, life insurance, real estate, gold, silver and other precious metals, mutual fund, shares, pension plan and debentures and bonds. The analysis of co-efficient of variation reveals that there is more consistency in their view with regard to gold, silver and other precious metals, real estate, postal deposits, life insurance, bank deposits, mutual fund and pension plan.
- Regarding overall satisfaction of the professionals on the returns of their investment portfolio all the three group of professionals are highly satisfied on gold, silver and other precious metals and real estate investment avenues since their mean satisfaction scores are 4.2833 and 4.2101 respectively. The analysis of skewness also reveals that more than average number of respondents are of the same view with regard to postal deposits, bank deposits, life Insurance, real estate, gold silver and other precious metals and debentures and bonds. The analysis of co-efficient of variation reveals that there is more consistency in their view with regard to gold, silver and other precious metals, Real estate, life insurance and pension plan.
- Regarding the attitude towards investment criteria of professionals in general, significant differences are identified among the professionals in few variables namely low risk investments are preferred, assured returns are more preferred, higher preference for tax-saving investments. The highly scored variable among the three group of professionals are 'everyone is willing to save and invest' which reveals the fact that all the professional groups are having a habit of save and invest.
- Regarding the attitude of the professionals towards postal deposits, significant differences are identified among the professionals in all the variables. The highly scored variable among the doctors is 'tax concession schemes are preferred', which informs us that doctors preferring postal schemes which provide tax concession and the

engineers are having the opinion in preferring postal deposits by emphasing the variable, schemes are available in small denomination and the advocates this variable is 'government's backup gives confidence'.

- Regarding the attitude of the professionals towards bank savings and deposits, significant differences are identified among the professionals in all the variables. The highly scored variable among the doctors is It is very secured, which informs us that doctors preferring bank deposits which is very secured in nature and the engineers and advocates are having the same opinion in preferring bank deposits by giving importance to the variable that preferred due to its necessity.
- Regarding the attitude towards life insurance, significant differences are identified among the professionals in few variables namely preferred for its risk coverage, policies are available for all age groups, money back facilities during the policy term, preferred for tax concession. The highly scored variable among the three group of professionals is preferred for its risk coverage. Since all the three group of professionals are ready to invest in life insurance to get life risk coverage.
- Regarding the attitude towards real estate, significant differences are identified among the professionals in all the variables except one The highly scored variable among the three group of professionals is investment in house property is a necessity. The analysis infers that the attitude towards real estate investments is better among the doctors and engineers whereas it is slightly unfavourable among the advocates.
- Regarding the attitude towards gold, silver and other precious metals, significant differences are identified among the professionals in all the variables except one. The highly scored variable among the doctors is 'capital appreciation', which informs us that doctors identify this avenue is a better folio to park their money which gives good amount of returns and the engineers and advocate are having the similar opinion in preferring this investment avenue by emphasising the variable, 'its necessity like two wheelers and four wheelers', by this, one can understand that what kind of importance both the professional groups are giving for precious metals.
- In connection with the attitude of the professionals towards mutual funds, significant differences are identified among the professionals in three variables, such as tax concession funds are preferred, pledged as a security for availing loan, preferred for easy liquidity. The highly scored variable among the doctors is tax concession funds are preferred, which informs us that doctors are conscious about schemes

which provide tax concession and the engineers are having concentration in preferring this investment avenue by emphasising the variable, 'preferred for easy liquidity' and the advocates this variable is 'pledged as a security for availing loan'.

- Relating to the attitude of the professionals towards chit funds, significant differences are identified among the professionals in all the variables. The analysis infers that the attitude towards chit fund investments are favourable among the advocates, whereas the doctors are not showing much interest on chit fund investments compared to engineers and advocates.
- Regarding the attitude of the professionals towards shares, significant differences are identified among the professionals in all the variables. The doctors and engineers are preferring this avenue because of easy liquidity and transferability, whereas advocates are preferring this avenue in order to gain knowledge about share market. The overall mean score for engineers are lower than advocates and doctors since they have negative attitude towards investment on shares.
- Relating to the attitude of the professionals towards provident fund, significant differences are identified among the professionals in all the variables. The doctors and engineers are preferring this avenue because of its tax concession, whereas advocates are impressed by the variable, convenient method of deposits. The analysis infers that doctors are much interest towards provident fund investments where as advocates are moderate and engineers are not much favourable to this investment avenue.
- Pertaining to pension plan, significant differences are identified among the professionals in all the variables except one. The highly scored variable among the doctors is 'preferred for security after retirement' since the doctors are more cautious about their future security, whereas engineers and advocates are similar in their opinion since the highly scored variable among them is In case of death, surviving spouse or legal heir is benefited. Engineers and advocates feel their insecurity of life and they want to secure their dependants with a regular income by a pension plan. The analysis finds out that the doctors perceived high and their favourability towards investments in pension plan is higher than engineers and advocates.
- In connection with debentures and bonds, significant differences are identified in all the variables. Doctors and advocates feel this investment avenue is very secured while comparing shares which implies a fact that they are not ready to face challenges and ups and downs of the capital market, whereas engineers are preferring this avenue due to its

fixed interest rate and they need a regular steady income without any disturbance. The analysis infers that the attitude towards investments on debentures and bonds are favourable among the doctors and engineers whereas it is unfavourable among the advocates.

- The rotated factor matrix analysis reveals the motives of the professionals towards different investment avenues through twenty statements and all these are classified into six heads of factors, namely, safety and security, capital appreciation, minimum formalities, tax relief, risk involved and liquidity. Among these twenty statements the important motives for making investments in different avenues are 'assurance of safety', 'minimum fluctuations in getting returns' and 'unplanned tax payments are avoided' as their factor loading values are high.
- The factor analysis reveals the motives of the professionals towards different investment avenues by six factors, namely, safety and security, capital appreciation, minimum formalities, tax relief, risk involved and liquidity. Among these factors which are having high Eigen values are the important factors that motive the professionals for making investments in different avenues and they are 'safety and security factor', 'capital appreciation factor', 'minimum formalities'.
- The multiple regression analysis is used to find out the impact of motivating variables on investment decisions of the professionals. The regression analysis for the overall professional respondents revealed that the significantly influencing variables are Safety and security, capital appreciation, minimum formalities, tax relief and risk involved. The analysis on overall data reveals that a unit increase in the above said variables results in decrease involvement of the professionals in taking investment decisions. The change in the included variables to the extent of 78.60 per cent.
- The regression analysis for the overall professional respondents revealed that the significantly influencing variables are gender, age, community and literacy level. The analysis on overall data reveals that a unit increase in the above said variables results in decrease involvement of the professionals in taking investment decisions. The change in the included five profile variables explains the change to the extent of 71.60 per cent.
- The regression analysis for the overall professionals revealed that the significantly influencing variables are private practice, spouse employed, number of children and monthly income. The analysis on overall data reveals that a unit increase in the above said variables results in decrease involvement of the professionals in taking

investment decisions. The change in included family domain variables explains the change in professionals' perception to the extent of 61.40 per cent.

- Regarding the association between profile variables of the professionals and the investment motivating factors significant differences are identified among the professionals in all the variables except one pair that is 'association between literacy level and minimum formalities'. The above said analysis reveals a fact that professionals are having difference of opinion in preferring the investment avenues in considering their motivating factors, namely, safety and security, capital appreciation, minimum formalities, tax relief, risk involved and liquidity according to their profile variable such as gender, age, literacy level, etc.

- Regarding the association between family domain variables of the professionals and the investment motivating factors significant differences are identified among the professionals in all the variables except one pair that is 'association between monthly savings and liquidity'. The above said analysis reveals a fact that professionals are having difference of opinion in preferring the investment avenues in considering their motivating factors, namely, safety and security, capital appreciation, minimum formalities, tax relief, risk involved and liquidity according to their family domain variables such as marital status, private practice, number of children, etc.

- Regarding the purpose of the professionals in making investments in different investment avenues the Garrett ranking analysis reveals that 'children's education' has the highest mean score of 65.61 because professionals taking hard efforts in generating income for the welfare of their children that becomes true when they are properly educated and then which is followed by 'future secured life' with 61.88 mean score which denotes that after giving due recognition to their children's education the professionals think about their own future secured life. Among the investment purposes the one which scored lowest is 'provision for festivals' and the respective score is 33.79.

- The investment avenues dominating in the investment pattern of the professionals that among the listed investment avenues the Garrett ranking analysis reveals that the toppest one is "bank deposits" which reveals the fact that the bank accounts and the bank deposits are much essential for all the walk of life of us and the professionals are not exempted. So they ranked it as the first and it is followed by 'gold, silver and other precious metals" with the mean score of 62.2 which exhibits the among the various disparities the Indians are giving much importance to hold and wear this precious metals to show their social status and security and the least scored investment avenue is 'debentures and bonds' with the mean score of 26.54 which denotes the fact that the respondents are having fear over this avenue.

- The significant differences are identified among the three groups of professionals regarding the problems faced by them in the process of developing their investment patterns in eleven variables. 'Poor investor education' is the highly scored variable among the doctors and advocates. Regarding engineers, the highly scored variable is 'Low returns', which gives more difficult in the process of developing their investment portfolio. The analysis indicates that the advocates perceived higher on the variables related to problems in the investment making process than doctors and engineers.
- The rotated factor matrix analysis reveals the problems faced by the professionals during the investment making process through fifteen statements and all these are classified into four heads of factors, namely, institutional failures, complication, doubtfulness and mishandling. Among these fifteen statements the important problems faced by the professionals for making investments in different avenues are 'fear of frauds', 'low returns' and 'lack of proper communication' as their factor loading values are high.
- The factor analysis reveals the problems faced by the professionals during the investment making process in different investment avenues by four factors, namely, institutional failures, complication, doubtfulness and mishandling. Among these factors those have high Eigen values are the important problems that disturb the professionals for making investments in different avenues are 'institutional failures factor', 'complication factor', and 'doubtfulness factor'.

6.3 Suggestions

- The investor has to choose proper avenues depending on his preferences, needs and abilities to minimise his risk and maximise his returns.
- The investor should be very careful in selecting their areas and patterns of investment.
- Regarding the risk in the investment making process, in addition to the theoretical knowledge the investors should use their self experiences and knowledge and the experiences of their friends and relatives.
- Never put all eggs in one basket, however attractive the returns may be. Always go for diversity in investments. If the investors are investing in shares, it is suggested to deal in at least ten different

shares from different industry sectors. If the investors are investing in mutual funds, they are advised to invest in five–six different mutual fund houses.

- Even though the professionals may have sufficient capital, they always avail home loan for purchasing of house properties. It will give them dual tax benefits—deduction of housing loan interest while computing income tax and also deduction of interest while computing capital gains.
- Investors are always interested in deriving maximum tax benefits. This can be achieved by the following:
    - Investing up to Rs one Lakh per year in eligible avenues.
    - Investing in mutual funds where dividend is tax-free.
    - Investing in authorised provident funds where the investment, interest and terminal benefits all are tax-free.
    - Investing in health insurance policies.
    - Sale of securities after holding them for one year.
    - Sale of other assets after holding them for three years.
    - Systematic Investment Plans of various mutual funds which are effective against market fluctuations.
- Investors must try to make withdrawals when the securities market is booming and make investments when it is low. A number of investors have benefited by making investments in securities and mutual funds in the month of August, 2007 when the securities market in India crashed owing to the news of security risks in home loans in the USA.
- Highly known financial investment avenue among the three groups of professionals is Bank savings account. Never let money lie idle in the savings account of a bank. The least one can do is to open fixed deposit accounts from time to time.
- Investors are suggested to view any business channel on TV and read *Economic Times* regularly and pay much attention on the experts' advice regarding investment. It is not necessary to believe each individual 'expert', the experts may be biased or incorrect. It is better to understand the reasoning behind the comments of the expert analysts before taking their advice.
- Regarding mutual funds, investors are expected to note the following suggestions:
    - Invest in a scheme depending upon their investment objectives and risk appetite.

- Investors must note that Net Asset Value of a scheme is subject to change depending upon market conditions.
- Investors should insist for a copy of the offer document/key information memorandum before investing.
- They must note that the past performance of a scheme is not indicative of future performance.
- Investors must remember that past performance of a scheme may or may not be sustained in future. Investors are suggested to keep track of the Net Asset Value of a scheme, where they have invested, on a regular basis. Investors must ensure that they receive an account statement for the money that they have invested. They should update themselves on the performance of the scheme on a regular basis.
- Investors must peruse the annual reports and half yearly financial results of mutual funds. These are published in national newspapers and on websites of mutual funds.
- Investors must find out about entry load and exit load in case of open-ended schemes and check for initial expenses and exit load in case of close-ended schemes. Actual expenses for each scheme are disclosed in half-yearly results.
- Investors must find out about the investment profile provided in portfolio disclosures which is available on half-yearly basis.
- With assistance from sources of information like Scheme Offer documents, key information memorandum, statement of accounts, annual and half-yearly reports, portfolio disclosures etc, they are recommended to take informed investment decisions, not based on hearsay.
- Waiver of Entry Load is provided for direct applications. Investors wanting to make applications for mutual fund schemes without a distributor/broker, should cut across the section on 'distributor information' in application form, mark it as 'direct application' and countersign. The waiver of entry load for direct applications is available for new applications and for switch-ins from one scheme to another.
- If an investor is seeking the help of a distributor, they must find out the value added services that are provided by distributor in respect of investments in mutual fund schemes.
- Investors should verify that no entry/exit load is charged to them for bonus units issued, if any, and in lieu of units allotted on reinvestment of dividend.

- The offer documents for mutual Fund Schemes are now bifurcated as 'Scheme Information Document (SID)' and 'Statement of Additional Information (SAI)'. Each scheme has a SID, whereas SAI is common for all schemes. While making investment decisions, they, as investors, are expected to peruse the SID and SAI besides the existing Key Information Memorandum (KIM).

- Professionals are not much interested in investing in stock market. A common problem associated with equity investing is the method of selection. The investor must understand the prospects of the company, the factors that affect the same; he must have an understanding of the economy, interest rates, political and legal environment, and a host of other factors. Clearly, equity investing is like a full-time job that is best left to experts. Despite equities not offering assured returns or safety of capital, they have the potential to add value to the portfolio. Over longer time frames, equities have historically delivered higher returns as compared to other avenues like fixed income instruments, gold and real estate. However, instead of directly investing in equities, it is recommended that professionals invest in the same via the mutual funds route or even, very selectively, the unit linked insurance plan route.

- There is an explosion in the growth of middle class families due to double income and increase in number of working women. Hence, effort should be made to attract women investors by providing right information and knowledge about the market through advertisement.

- The savings are to be pooled and channelised into productive investments. Thereby enhancing the return to the investors which may result in the further investment in corporate securities also.

- Professionals pay less attention while evaluating the pros and cons of investing in different securities. The need and benefits of the systematic and analytical evaluation of different alternatives and competitive avenues need to be explained to them. Then only it is possible to park their surplus funds in economical viable condition.

- Before entering into the stock market, the investors have to gain a complete knowledge about the stock market.

- The investors have to invest their money in less risky securities like mutual funds, debentures, government bonds, because the above securities have a minimum risk when compared to equity shares.

- The gold investors can opt for the gold bars or gold coins because it has no wastages.

- The real estate investors can purchase urban land because it will have increase in value day by day.
- Post office may offer more savings schemes compared with banks, so that the investors can properly invest their money in postal schemes. Especially one of the best routes everyone suggests is post office monthly scheme. It gives safety apart from steady monthly returns.
- If the investors preferred to cover their risk of life and to get tax benefits they can opt for the insurance schemes.
- SEBI and its associates must promote investor's education and training. Rumors and misleading opinions are to be controlled. A prospective investor must not care to those gossips; he must rely only on the facts available to him.
- Due to liberalisation and globalisation foreign banks came in with new technology and latest services, so investors must use these services to improve their standard of life.
- Due to privatisation, the number of life assurance companies has increased to 23. Investors must analyse the various insurance products before selecting and investing in particular scheme. Insurance agents must educate, explain the policies in insurance that matches their requirement.
- For aggressive investors, there is an opportunity to look at dividend yielding stocks. Dividend income is exempt from income tax in the hands of investors and that make equity investment an attractive option. The investors should select companies which are strong, giving consistent dividend and finally where yield is good. These ways investors can get better return compared to bank rates. Investors should do some homework before venturing into investment.
- Finally, investors need to reduce their portfolio to minimum to keep a close watch. Investments should be spread like PPF, post office deposit, LIC, equity, etc. Investors have to be careful and watchful before committing their funds. If the principle of safety and liquidity is adhered to by investors, certainly investments made will be fruitful.
- The respondents of the study have expressed their view points towards the financial companies. They suggested certain measures.
    - Detailed Information regarding all the contents of the instrument like return and risk must be given in layman's language.
    - Seminars must be conducted in various parts of the country within the approach of the perspective investor.
    - Demonstrations with the help of duly developed slides describing all the contents should be given on home to home basis.

- Pamphlets in the daily newspapers can be given regarding the financial instruments.
- Older customers may be informed of the new schemes by the letters/SMSs.

6.4 Conclusion

The study on investment pattern and preferences of professionals in different Investment avenues has been undertaken with the objective to analyse the investment choice in Tirunelveli district. After analysis and interpretation of data it is concluded that respondents are moderately aware of various investment avenues but they are not aware of stock market, equity, bond and debentures. The study is conducted by taking a limited sample size which is stated earlier. And this study reflects the perceptions of those respondents who are residing in Tirunelveli district. There might be a chance that the perceptions of the respondents of different areas are varied due to diversity in social life, living pattern, income level, etc. All the age groups give more importance to invest in bank deposit, gold and other precious metals, real estate, insurance, etc. Income level of a respondent is an important factor which affects the portfolio of the respondent. In Tirunelveli district respondents are more aware about various investment avenues like bank deposits, small savings like post office savings, gold investments, insurance, provident fund, etc.

It can be concluded that the modern investor is a mature and adequately groomed person. In spite of the phenomenal growth in the security market and quality Initial Public Offerings (IPOs) in the market, the individual investors prefer investments according to their risk preference. For example, risk averse people choose life insurance policies, fixed deposits with banks and post office, provident fund and national saving certificate. Occasions of blind investments are scarce, as a majority of investors are found to be using some source and reference groups for taking decisions. Though they are in the trap of some kind of cognitive illusions such as overconfidence and narrow framing, they consider multiple factors and seek diversified information before executing some kind of investment transaction.

'No pain no gain' it is the golden principle of investment management. In this fast moving world, we can earn more and more money. More risk leads to more profit. Investors cannot avoid risk but they can minimise the risk by investing their money in various forms of investments so that they can get a moderate profit. Most of the investors prefer bank deposits followed by gold investment in the study area.

It is very interesting to know that even with good, guaranteed rate of returns from mutual fund and share market, investors hesitate to invest in them, similarly, bank deposit remain the preferred avenue, in addition to that gold and other precious metals and real estate are also preferred by investors. It is understood from the study that awareness programme has to be conducted by stock brokering firms because most of the respondents are unaware about this new service and about stock market.

In general, saving today increases a nation's capacity to produce more goods and services and generate high income in the future. Saving entails a tradeoff because it requires consuming less now in exchange for consuming more later. While those who sacrifice to save now can themselves enjoy higher consumption in the future, some of the resulting increase in the nation's stock and the related income will also benefit future generations. Thus, current saving and investment decision have profound implication for the level of wellbeing in the future and current generations are in a sense stewards of the economy on behalf of future generations.

Index

R